THE COMPLETE BOOK OF FRUITS AND VEGETABLES

F. BIANCHINI and F. CORBETTA

THE
COMPLETE
BOOK OF
FRUITS AND
VEGETABLES

Illustrations by MARILENA PISTOIA

Translated from the Italian by Italia and Alberto Mancinelli

Introduction by MAURICE MESSÉGUÉ

CROWN PUBLISHERS, INC. · NEW YORK

ACKNOWLEDGMENTS

The publishers are indebted to Dr. Harvey Barké,
Professor and Chairman, Department of Biological
Sciences, State University of New York College,
Farmingdale, New York, and to Virginia Pease Barké,
and to Mr. James Lovely of the Department of Botany,
Imperial College of Science and Technology, London, for
their close review of the text and numerous valuable
suggestions and additions, and to the editor, Marie Dejey,
who added much of the culinary, historical and
mythological information.

Contents

HERBS AND SPICES

STIMULANTS

STARCH- AND OIL-YIELDING PLANTS

Introduction

What a splendid book this is. Page after page, it lets us rediscover the "fruits of the earth," charming the eye by the delicacy and accuracy of its illustrations, and enchanting the mind with the secrets it unveils of the origins, virtues, and properties of the plants.

A work of great quality, this book recaptures the traditions of the herbals kept by our grandmothers, adding to them the knowledge acquired through the centuries.

I, a countryman, son of a farmer whose interests I have inherited, and nourished by a love of nature, wholeheartedly subscribe to this idea and applaud the result.

It was with pleasure, but also with a certain nostalgia, that I accepted the invitation to write an introduction to this book. It recalls my youth, when I pushed my schoolbooks to the back of my desk and transformed it into a veritable herbarium, wanting at all costs to preserve what, to my mind, was far more important than study; all those plants which linked me to my father who knew and loved them, and used them to cure and heal.

I hope that this book will reach out beyond the circle of nature lovers and influence the hesitant, the skeptics, the oblivious, and those who, despite the stresses of modern living, are willing to appreciate the true reality of things.

I am sure that no one can remain indifferent to this subject, even if they only glance through the pages, and that it will do much to reconcile man with Nature. Those who read it will be unable to resist the temptation to extract from Nature all she has to offer for our health and happiness.

However, even after we have won over the majority, there still remain those to whom material gain is of more importance than the well-being of humanity, and who poison the earth for the sake of better "fruits." The fruits of the earth, even when they are as beautiful as those depicted here, become mortal poisons when subjected to the chemistry of those to whom "the quality of life" is a meaningless phrase, and whose ultimate end is profit, irrespective of the harm to man and nature.

If, with these few lines, I have been able to warn man against those of his own kind who are intent on destruction, then this introduction will not have been completely useless.

Glossary

ACHENE   A dry, one-seeded fruit that does not open when mature.

ALTERNATE   Arranged not opposite each other on the central stem, but singly at regular intervals at different levels.

AMENT (also **amentum**)   A dry scaly spike of small, closely clustered flowers, usually unisexual, such as the inflorescences of willows, birches, poplars. Commonly known as a catkin.

ANTHER   The pollen-bearing part of a stamen.

ARISTA   Having a beard (*v.* **awn**), e.g., oats.

ARISTATE (awned)   With stiff bristle-shaped appendages.

AWN   Bristle-shaped appendage (*v.* **arista**), e.g., seen on the glumes of many grasses.

AXIL   The angle formed between two organs, e.g., between a branch or leaf and the axis from which it arises.

BERRY   A fleshy fruit which does not open, containing seeds. It usually has a fleshy or pulpy pericarp, e.g., grapes, gooseberries, tomatoes, etc.

BLADE (also **lamina**)   The expanded green portion of a leaf.

BRACT   A modified leaf just below the flower cluster, e.g., poinsettia.

BULB   An organ of storage and vegetative reproduction, consisting of a flattened, short underground stem, bearing fleshy leaves above and growing adventitious roots below.

BULLATE   Blistered or puckered, usually applied to foliage.

CALCAREOUS   Growing on limy soil.

CALYX   The outer covering of a flower, its separate leaves called sepals.

CAMPANULATE   Bell-shaped.

CAPSULE   A dry fruit that opens to release seeds when mature.

CARPEL   A simple pistil, or a division of a pistil, regarded as a modified leaf, forming and bearing ovules.

CARYOPSIS   A grain, the typical seedlike fruit of all grasses, including cereals, with pericarp and seed coat firmly united.

CATKIN   An ament.

CLADOPHYLL   A leaflike branch.

COMPOUND   Divided into separate leaflets, or formed of several ripened ovaries, e.g., blackberries.

CORIACEOUS   Having a leathery texture.

CORM   The short, fleshy subterranean part of a stem resembling a bulb, but solid. In it are stored reserve materials.

COROLLA   The inner wall of petals of the floral envelope.

CORYMB   A flat-topped or round-topped inflorescence of stalked flowers sprouting from different levels.

COSTATUS   Ribbed, as in leaves.

CULM   The hollow stem of grasses and sedges.

CULTIVAR   A variety obtained through cultivation; a horticultural selection.

CYME   A branched inflorescence in which the stem terminates in a flower, and other flowers are developed at the end of lateral branches.

DECURRENT   Extending downward from the point of insertion.

DEHISCENT   Opening or splitting at maturity to discharge seeds (used of a seed pod), or opening to discharge pollen (used of an anther).

DENTATE   Toothed, e.g., the edges of leaves.

DICLINOUS   Unisexual, of flowers having stamens in one flower and pistils in another.

DIOECIOUS   Plants having male flowers on one plant and female on another.

DRUPE   Fruit with a hard kernel and a fleshy pericarp, as in cherry, peach, apricot, etc. The stony endocarp is commonly known as a stone.

ENDOCARP (also **apicarp**)   The inner layer of the pericarp, i.e., fruit wall, often different in texture.

EPICARP (or **exocarp**)   The outer layer of the pericarp, often different in texture from the rest e.g., marrow.

EPIGYNOUS   Having sepals, petals, and stamens growing above the ovary (used of a flower). In this flower the ovary is called inferior.

EPIPHYTE   A plant that grows upon another without deriving any nourishment from it, e.g., ferns, mosses, and some orchids.

EXFOLIATING   Peeling off in thin layers, as the bark of a birch or plane tree.

EXOCARP   *v.* **epicarp**.

FILAMENT   The stalk of a stamen connecting the anther with the corolla.

FRUIT The seed-bearing product of a plant, usually derived from the transformation of the ovary. The result is usually called a true fruit. When any other parts are also involved, e.g., receptacle, sepals, petals, bracts, the result is known botanically as a false fruit or pseudocarp, e.g. the strawberry.

GIBBOUS Swollen on one side.
GLABROUS Smooth, especially not hairy or pubescent.
GLUCOSIDE A glycoside that yields glucose on hydrolysis.
GLUMES Chafflike bracts; specifically one of a pair of dry bracts enclosing the flowers of grasses and sedges.
GYNOECIUM The carpels taken collectively; the female organs.

HABITAT The kind of locality in which a plant grows; its native country.
HEAD A group of flowers placed closely together; a dense cluster of sessile or nearly sessile flowers on a short receptacle, e.g., sunflower.
HERB A plant of which the stem dies to the ground at the end of the season. Also a plant used in cooking for its savory or aromatic qualities, or in medicine.
HESPERIDIUM A fruit structured like an orange, pulpy within and with a leathery, separable rind.
HIRSUTE Hairy.
HISPID Bristly; with bristles.
HYMENIUM The fertile, spore-producing structure of certain fungi.
HYPERTROPHY A condition of excessive enlargement of a plant organ as when some part of a plant is invaded by a fungus parasite, e.g., witches'-broom on cherries (swollen branches), crown gall in apples (swollen roots), etc.
HYPOCOTYL The part of the axis of a plant embryo or seedling below the cotyledon (first leaves).
HYPOGENOUS Growing upon the underside of anything; developing underground.

IMPARIPINNATE (odd pinnate) Of compound pinnate leaves with an odd terminal leaflet.

INCISED Cut sharply or irregularly more or less deeply.
INDEHISCENT Not opening in a definite manner when ripe to release seeds.
INFLORESCENCE A cluster of flowers borne on the same stalk; raceme spike, corymb, head, umbel, compound umbel, panicle, dichasium, monochasium, cyme.
INFRUCTESCENCE The fruiting stage of an inflorescence.
INTERNODE The space on a stem between two nodes or knots from which the leaves arise.
INVOLUCRE A ring of bracts surrounding several flowers, e.g., the green parts around a dandelion.

LEMMA The lower of two bracts enclosing the flower of the grasses.
LENTICEL A pore on the young bark of the stem to allow air to reach the underlying tissue, especially during the winter. Often the color contrasts with the bark.
LIPID Any of a group of substances soluble in a fat solvent, but only sparingly soluble in water, that with proteins and carbohydrates constitute the principle structural components of living cells. Fats are lipids.

MARBLED Having irregular streaks of color.
MESOCARP The middle layer of the fruit wall (v. endocarp).
MONOECIOUS Bearing reproductive structures of both sexes on the same plant, but not in the same flower, e.g., chestnut, corn, cucumber.
MUST The juice of grapes or other fruit before and during fermentation.
MYCELIUM The thallus or vegetative part of a fungus, made of threadlike filaments called hyphae.
MYCORRHIZA The symbiotic association between a fungus and the roots of a plant, by which both are likely to benefit. Is common in epiphytes.

NECTARY The part or organ of a flower where nectar is secreted.
NODE Joint. The part of a branch or stem from which a leaf arises. Roots form more readily at a node when taking cuttings.

NODULES Small, hard lumps or swellings.

NUT A hard, indehiscent fruit usually containing one seed only, e.g. acorn, hazelnut, etc.

OVARY The part of the pistil enclosing the ovules.

PALEA The inner bract which, together with the lemma, encloses the stamen and pistil in the flower of grasses (also palet). There are two palea to each flower (*v.* **glume**).

PALMATE In a leaf, of main veins radiating from a point at the base of the leaf blade.

PANICLE A loose, compound inflorescence with pedicellate flowers, usually of the racemose type, as in oats.

PARALLEL-VEINED With the main veins running parallel in the leaves from origin to end.

PARENCHYMA A soft tissue made of relatively undifferentiated cells.

PARIPINNATE (*v.* **pinnate**) Pinnate with an even number of leaflets as in a rose leaf.

PARTED (partite) Cleft clearly, but not quite to the base.

PARTHENOCARPY Process of development of seedless fruit without fertilization.

PECTIN One of the substances found in the cell walls of plants.

PEDICEL The stalk of a single flower, especially the small stalks which bear the flowers in a branched inflorescence (*v.* **peduncle**).

PEDUNCLE The main or primary stalk of a plant.

PELLICULE A thin, papery skin or layer.

PEPO A many-seeded, fleshy fruit with a hard rind, e.g., watermelon, squash, cucumber.

PERIANTH The floral envelope, composed of the calyx and the corolla.

PERICARP The rind or shell of fruits derived from the wall of the matured ovary.

PETAL One of the parts forming the corolla of a flower; often colorful.

PETIOLE The stalk of a leaf.

PINNATE Having leaflets arranged on each side of a common stalk, as in a rose leaf (*v.* **paripinnate**).

PINNATELY VEINED Leaf with an evident central midvein and primary branches departing laterally along its length.

PISTIL The female organ of the flower consisting of the ovary, style, and stigma, made of one or more carpels.

POLLEN The fine, yellowish powder formed within the anthers in flowering plants; the male fecundating elements in seed plants.

POLYMORPHIC Having many forms; variable.

POME A fleshy fruit with a papery endocarp forming a core with several seeds, e.g., apples, pears, quinces. Also, to form a compact head as in a lettuce or cabbage.

PRUINOSE Covered with a waxy, powdery secretion as though frosted.

PUBESCENT Covered with soft hair; downy.

RACEME An inflorescence in which the flowers are arranged on short stalks (*v.* **pedicel**) at equal intervals along an elongated stem.

RACHIS The axis or main stem of an inflorescence or of a compound leaf.

RECEPTACLE The enlarged upper part of a stalk bearing a flower or an inflorescence.

RHIZOME A creeping, underground stem, usually horizontally elongated, sending up leafy shoots or flowering stems.

ROSETTE A cluster of leaves or other organs on an axis with very short internodes.

RUNCINATE Sharply incised or saw-toothed leaves with the segments directed backward (*v.* **dentate**).

SAMARA An indehiscent, dry, winged fruit, e.g., ash, elm, maple.

SAPROPHYTE A plant living and feeding on dead organic matter. Many fungi live in this manner.

SCAPE A flower-stalk, leafless or nearly so, arising directly from the base of a plant, bearing one or many flowers, or an inflorescence.

SCLEROTIUM A mass of hardened mycelium stored with reserve food material in various fungi.

SEPAL One of the elements of the calyx, usually protective.

SEPTUM A wall of tissue dividing the ovary, anther, fruit, etc., into cells.

SERRATE Of leaf margins having sharp teeth pointing forward.

SESSILE Without a stalk.

SHEATH A tubular envelope often formed by the leaf base.

SILIQUE An elongated, podlike seed vessel.

SPADIX An inflorescence with a thick, fleshy spike thickly set with flowers embedded in pits.

SPIKE A raceme of sessile flowers.

SPORE An asexual reproductive structure.

STAMEN Pollen-bearing organ of the flower, consisting of filament and anthers.

STIGMA The upper part of a pistil which receives the pollen when mature, situated either directly on the ovary, or at the summit of the style.

STIPE The stalk of a mushroom.

STIPULES Outgrowths from the base of a leaf stalk.

STYLE The narrow prolongation of the ovary connected to the stigma.

SYCONIUM A multiple fruit in which the ovaries are borne within an enlarged fleshy receptacle, as in the figure.

SYMBIOSIS A close association between two organisms, usually with benefit to both.

TAPROOT A long, usually central root directed vertically downward, bearing smaller lateral roots.

THALLUS An indifferentiated plant body without true stems, leaves, or roots.

TOMENTOSE Hairy.

TUBER A thickened, underground branch from which new plants are produced.

TUBERCLES *v.* **nodules**.

TURION A scaly, solitary shoot springing out of the ground, often fleshy as in the asparagus.

UMBEL An inflorescence in which the pedicels of the flowers arise at the same point.

VELUM In mushrooms a membranous structure or covering extending from the margin of the cap to the stipes, whose torn parts often form a ring on the stipes, also known as a partial veil.

VOLVA The membraneous covering which completely envelopes some mushrooms during the early stage of growth, becoming ruptured as the mushroom grows, and sometimes remaining as a cup around the base of the stipes.

Edible plants

Wheat

Wheat is undoubtedly the most important of the cereals. To the complex of species generally known as wheat is owed the production of the greatest amount of foods of plant origin. Wheat originated in the Eurasian continent and has probably been cultivated since prehistoric times, and man has spread it throughout the world. Today wheat is cultivated practically everywhere, with the exception of the coldest regions and the hot tropical zones. The areas of higher production are localized in the temperate plains between latitude $30°$ and $60°$ north and between latitude $30°$ and $40°$ south. Nations producing the largest wheat crops are Russia (about 60–70 million tons), the United States (about 30–35 million tons), China (about 30 million tons), France (about 15 million tons), India (about 2–3 million tons), and Italy (about one million tons). Wheat, like most of the plants commonly known as "cereals," belongs to the *Gramineae*. All the various species of wheat are members of the genus *Triticum*. Commercially "durum" or hard wheats (cultivars of *T. durum*) are distinguished from "soft" wheats (cultivars of *T. vulgare*) on the basis of the characteristics of the caryopsis, the dry fruit typical of the *Gramineae*. The caryopsis is a fruit containing only one seed which adheres closely to the pericarp, so that the two parts, seed and fruit, form a single unit. Within the caryopsis are the embryo, from which the mature plant develops, a starchy storage tissue, known as the albumen, and the pericarp, which forms the bran. Depending on the consistency of the grain are distinguished "hard" or macaroni wheats with a horny texture, from "soft," that is, common bread wheats with a floury texture. This distinction is very important for wheat's commercial uses. The hard wheats are more suitable for the manufacture of spaghetti and pasta in general. The soft wheats are used exclusively for making bread. The wheat grains, in spite of differences among cultivars, have the following average composition: water, 14%; nitrogen compounds, 12%; carbohydrates, 70%; lipids, $1–2\%$; cellulose and ash, $1–2\%$. The endosperm (constituting the central and floury part of the wheat grain) consists of two portions: the outermost or "aleurone" layer, rich in proteins and mineral salts (phosphates of calcium and magnesium; potassium salts), and the center floury mass, the endosperm, full of starch and containing a protein known as gluten. It is the gluten that imparts the elastic and tenacious consistency to dough and allows leavening naturally through the action of yeast, a process which is indispensable for making bread. It is because of these latter characteristics that wheat is the best cereal for breadmaking, even though in some areas rye, barley, corn (maize), and occasionally, in periods of shortage, even rice, are used. Although the main use of wheat is for bread, it is also important in the manufacture of spaghetti, pastry, cakes, and cookies. Pawnee, Thatcher, and Marquis are standard wheat varieties. Red Fife is a well-known Canadian variety, and in Britain, Yeoman, Holdfast and Redman are used in breadmaking.

durum wheats

soft wheats

Rye
Oats

Rye and **Oats** should be considered today as less important cereals. In the past they were cultivated more extensively because poverty forced people to make use even of land high in the mountains and, in the case of oats, because of the larger number of horses used for work and in the armed forces.

Rye (*Secale cereale*) is native to Central Asia where it can still be found as a wild species. It is a large, herbaceous annual plant whose stalks can grow to more than a meter (approximately 1 yard) high. Because of this characteristic rye straw is greatly used to manufacture such things as handbags and straw hats and to protect ornamental plants during moving or in the cold winter season. For centuries rye has been cultivated in Asia and central Europe; later it spread to southern Europe and the Mediterranean regions. The various cultivated varieties of rye do not show as many differences as those of wheat. From the cultural viewpoint they can be divided into autumn and spring cultivars. The countries with the largest outputs of rye are Russia (15 million tons), Poland (8 million), and Germany (5 million). Chemically, grains of rye contain 10–15% protein, 1–2% lipids, and 70% carbohydrates. Rye flour is used in human foodstuffs, and is mixed with wheat to make bread, which is characteristically dark, much appreciated for its flavor and recommended for certain diets. It is used mostly in central and northern Europe, some Alpine regions and in the United States. Sometimes rye flour can be contaminated by the parasitic fungus *Claviceps purpurea* or black sclerotia. In the past, many cases of poisoning were caused by this parasite and one case was recorded in France in 1951. The presence of this fungus in the flour causes a pathological condition known as ergotism; the symptoms of the acute form are hallucinations and other nervous disturbances; those of the chronic form are constriction of the blood vessels and gangrene, especially of the lower limbs. In the United States whisky is distilled from rye and maize, although in Britain it is made from malted barley.

Oats have a lesser role as food for human consumption, although they are used as a base for the famous Scottish breakfast food, porridge (oatmeal), which is eaten with milk and salt, although elsewhere, in the United States and even in England, it is more commonly eaten with sugar. Cultivated oats (several different botanical varieties are known) belong to the species *Avena sativa*, widely scattered in grassy and uncultivated fields of the northern hemisphere and naturalized in many other regions. Oats are an annual grass and can grow to heights of from 2–5 feet. From a cultural standpoint the various cultivars are differentiated on the basis of the structure of the panicle which can be one-sided (banner oats), with the spikelets growing on the same side, or spreading toward all sides, contracted, sparse, or drooping. Oats are used primarily as animal feed, though not for pigs, or cut as hay or grits. The flour can also be used to make bread, biscuits and cookies. Alamo, Barnett, Clinton, Cherokee, Fulghum and Mankton are commonly planted cultivars.

rye

oats

grains of oats

grains of rye

Barley

Barley (*Hordeum vulgare*) is another of the cereals belonging to the family of the *Gramineae*. It is an annual grass of moderate size, approximately $3\frac{1}{2}$ feet, which is believed to have originated from a wild form, var. *spontaneum* of western Asia and northern Africa. The taxonomy of the cultivated forms of barley is complex and there is disagreement among different authorities. Basically, barley can be divided into three types: two-rowed, with kernels on two lines; four-rowed (kernels on four lines); and six-rowed (kernels on six lines). Agronomically, winter barley which is sown in autumn, can be distinguished from spring or summer barley, sown in spring, and early or late barleys identified by the duration of the life cycle.

Barley may also be divided into three types based on the nature of the hulls. Some have none; some have loosely attached hulls and others have tightly attached ones. This characteristic permits recognition of two different centers of origin for the cultivation of this cereal, which goes back to prehistoric times. The hull-less species originated in the mountains of China, while hulled barley is thought to have its origin in southwestern Asia. Today barley is grown over large areas, in a variety of different climates from Norway to the equator. Among cereals barley thrives at the highest latitudes (if the early varieties are used), and in a given latitude it can grow, as rye does, at higher altitudes than other cereals. Russia is the largest producer of barley (25 million tons), followed by Great Britain, France, the United States (around 10 million each), then Canada and other countries. Barley has a great variety of uses such as the manufacture of beer and whiskey; the grains can be milled into flour for breadmaking or the preparation of some soups; also for livestock feeding. These are only the uses made directly by man. For malting purposes (the first step of the brewing process to make beer) the preferred varieties are those of two-rowed barley of various cultivars such as Chevalier, Hanna, Probstein, Franken and others. The barley used in the preparation of soups can be either simply "cleaned" barley, which has the grains freed from the hulls, or "pearl barley" in which the grains have been freed of hull and pericarp by a special polishing process. Barley bread is found only in northern Europe and some Alpine valleys. The food value of barley is similar to that of wheat (further information will be found under that heading). A special use of barley is as a coffee substitute after the kernels have been toasted and ground. Plumage-Archer and Sprat-Archer are grown in Great Britain for food barley.

six-rowed barley

two-rowed barley

four-rowed barley

Corn or Maize

Corn, Indian corn or **Maize** (*Zea mays*) is a sturdy, annual plant of North American origin, belonging to the *Gramineae*, sub-family *Maydeae*. The male and female flowers are borne in separate inflorescences on the same plant. The male flowers are in a panicle, commonly known as a "tassel," at the top of the stalk. The female inflorescences are borne in spikes, commonly called "ears," which number from 2 to 4, and arise at the axils of the leaves, about halfway up the stalk. The ears are enclosed by thick bracts forming the husk, which were once used to make cheap mattresses. They also show long, silky strands called "silks" that some botanists consider as styles, others as stigmas. The kernels develop in the ears and are arranged in rows on the tough axis of the inflorescence, the "cob." Corn is therefore mono-ecious, with unisexual flowers bearing reproductive structure of both sexes (stamens and pistils) on the same plant but not in the same flower.

Despite the occasional doubt, there is almost irrefutable proof that corn originated in America. Although no native plant that could be traced back to a wild form of corn has ever been found there, it is thought that it developed through cultivation from *Euchlaena mexicana*, known as *teosinte*, which grows wild in the Mexican highlands and some areas of South America. Most scholars agree with the theory that corn was introduced into Europe after the discovery of America by Christopher Columbus. Both the botanical name, *mays*, and the common name, *maize*, come from the term *mahiz* which is an Arawak-Carib name.

The use of this cereal for brewing was also known to Columbus. Even today, in some parts of the world, alcohol is made from the fermentation of corn kernels. Peruvian beer, *chica* or *chica morada*, is brewed from varieties of corn with red kernels, and spiced with cloves. The theory that corn was introduced into Europe not by Columbus, but by Scandinavian adventurers who sailed from the north along the coasts of Greenland and Canada down to America, is unlikely. But, even assuming that from a historical and geographical point of view this were true, it would mean that those navigators had to sail far enough to the south to see cultivated corn. It must be remembered that corn requires a warm climate and cannot be cultivated at high latitudes. Apart from the doubts that have been cast on the so-called "classic" theories and assumptions, further complications have been added by the use of a variety of different names for corn. "Maize" is acceptable. "Polenta" is understandable as one of those instances where the name of the product has replaced that of the original plant. But "Turkish grain" is doubtful. The reason appears to lie in an error made by some sixteenth-century botanists who confused corn with buckwheat, the latter being granted, with no thought for its origins, the appellation of *turcicum*. Another explanation may be that in those times "Turkish" generally meant foreign or exotic, and both buckwheat and corn were plants of foreign extraction.

The use of corn as a crop is steadily increasing. Not only is there tremendous use of flint (*Z. indurata*) or field corn for fodder and silage, but uses for human food are increasing, especially in the United States. Apart from sweet corn (*Z. saccharata*) cooked as a vegetable, and popcorn (*Z. evorata*), it primarily provides the flour which is used in the manufacture of polenta in its various forms, and for breadmaking. Corn is also valuable as an oil-producing plant. The young embryo in the caryopsis contains from 35 to 50% oil, and many brands of oil and margarine on the market today are made partly or completely of corn oil.

Polenta, a coarse meal left after the oil is squeezed out of the kernels, and formerly used mainly by the poor, has become a more sophisticated food. Modern packaged mixes make the preparation of this dish easy even for inexperienced cooks. It is a pity that, because of the trend toward weight-consciousness and the "slim look," the use of polenta has decreased. It is an easily digested food with a high calorific value, $3\frac{1}{2}$ ounces (100 grams) contain 8–9% protein, 4–5% lipids, and 70% carbohydrates. Despite old memories of pellagra that was prevalent among the poor who fed only

corn (maize)

on cereals, deficient in nicotinic acid, or vitamin PP (i.e., "pellagra preventing"), it should not be forgotten that corn, although lacking in nicotinic acid, is rich in other vitamins such as vitamin A, thiamine (vitamin B_1 or aneurine) and riboflavin. Some vitamins, however, are lost during the grinding and sifting process.

Sweet corn varieties popular in the United States are Sugar and Gold, Buttercorn, Butter and Sugar, Gold Mine, Sunchief, Golden Cross Bantam, White Jewel, and Silver Queen. Eastern Sunburst and White Cloud are two standards for popcorn use. Standard flint or field corn varieties vary from state to state. Pioneer 306, Cornell M4, De Kalb 29, Funk's G6, and Seneca XX155 are proven ones.

When boiling sweet corn a teaspoon of sugar should be added to the water to bring out the flavour. Salt should not be used during cooking as it toughens the kernels. Oven-roasting in the leaves is an excellent way of cooking corn.

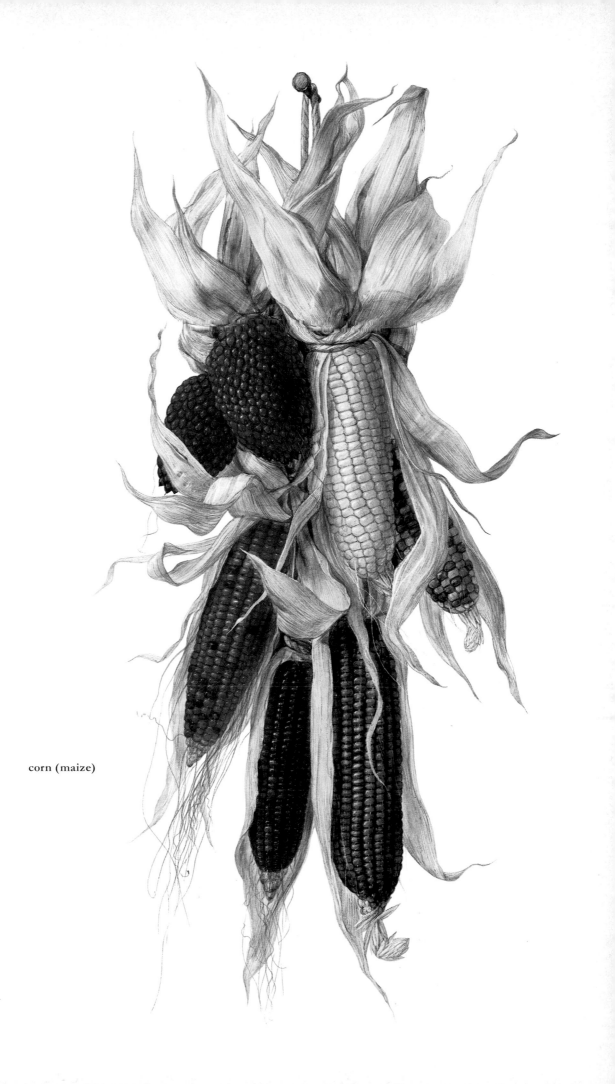

corn (maize)

Rice
Sorghum

Rice is widely cultivated throughout the world, in areas with warm climates and abundant water. If the general rule is observed that each continent has its specific cereal (Europe and north-central Asia being the wheat continents, America the corn continent, and Africa more or less the durra or sorghum continent), rice is, without doubt, the typical cereal of Southeastern Asia. It is also largely cultivated in Africa, some parts of America, and is intensely, though not widely, cultivated in some parts of southern Europe. Rice, of the *Gramineae*, genus *Oryza*, subfamily *Orizeae*, is an annual grass of variable size, with rough and coarse tissues because of the presence of the element silicon. From the standpoint of cultivation "upland rice" with a low water requirement, can be distinguished from ordinary rice, growing up to 3–6 feet high, and "floating (lowland) rice," which can reach a considerable height. The rice grains after threshing are still covered by the hulls consisting of glumes and glumellae. At this stage it is known as "paddy rice." Before reaching the market the rice grains are put through a succession of operations, consisting first of the removal of the hulls, then removal of the bran layer and most of the embryo, bleaching, cleaning, and pearling (a polishing operation with talc), and eventually, oiling and coating. These various processes, of which only the first is necessary to make the grains edible, while making rice more appetizing to the consumer, deprive it of most of its nutritional qualities. During milling much of the vitamin B_1 (thiamine) is lost. Vitamin B deficiency can cause beri-beri. Fats decrease from 1.6% to 0.25%; protein from 6.9% to 5.8%; carbohydrates increase from 90% to 93%. The calorific content of rice is approximately 350 calories per $3\frac{1}{2}$ ounces (100 grams). Dietetically rice is extremely digestible and nourishing, recommended for infants, the elderly, convalescents, and those who suffer from gastroenteritic disorders. However, rice is good not only for special diets. It can be used in the preparation of many excellent dishes, including soups, risottos, pilafs and desserts. Rice flour is used for making bread only in emergencies, but semolina rice is very good.

By contrast, the dietary interest in **Sorghum** or **Millet** (*Sorghum vulgare*) is very limited. In most countries it is cultivated almost exclusively for fodder and cut when still green. Even when the plants are allowed to reach full maturity the grains are used only for livestock feeding. Another use of sorghum (*S. vulgare technicum*) is in the manufacture of brooms for which the male panicles, freed of the grains, are employed.

The variety *cernium* is cultivated in the warm highlands of Africa where it is known as durra. The grains are ground into a flour used to make bread.

Japanese or Sanwa millet, Barnyard, Proso, Pearl and Ragi millets are some of the varieties currently in use.

sorghum

rice

Buckwheat

Buckwheat (*Fagopyrum sagittatum* or *F. esculentum*), commercially, is considered to be a cereal, although it does not belong to the *Gramineae*, as do true cereals, but to the *Polygonaceae* or buckwheat family. It is a plant for which, unlike so many others, the exact native area is known: a wide region extending from Lake Baikal in Siberia to Manchuria. From there the plant spread in very early times, through China, Japan, India, and later, in medieval times, to Europe. Scholars have proposed several different hypotheses concerning the routes followed by buckwheat in its penetration into Europe. According to Giacomini, a contemporary Italian botanist who has made a thorough study of the history of buckwheat, there are three possible ways: one, going from Asia through southern Russia, Poland, and Germany, reached Belgium and France, where buckwheat appeared in the fifteenth century; a second possible route through the Balkan peninsula, from Asia Minor to Greece, Hungary and southern Russia, and finally, a third one through the well-known maritime commercial channels, from Asia Minor to Venice and thence to the rest of Italy and to France. The last two alternatives would explain the adjective "Saracen" associated with the cereal throughout Europe. Saracen was the term used in Europe for the Moslems, especially as opposed to the Crusaders, and therefore also for Turks. But it is true too, that in those times most things foreign were usually granted the name of Saracen. It is interesting that in western Europe (England, France, Italy) the use of the term Saracen or its derivatives still prevails, while in central Europe (Germany, Czechoslovakia) or eastern Europe (Poland) the term Tartaric or others similar to it is more common. The scientific name *Fagopyrum* is derived from "fagus," beech tree, and "pyrum," cereal, because of the resemblance between the buckwheat fruits and those of the beech tree. The plant first appeared in Germany in 1436 and in France in 1460. In Italy the reliable dates are those cited by Aldrovandi (1552) and Pier Andrea Mattioli (1561). However, it is known that buckwheat made its first appearance in Italy at the beginning of the sixteenth century, in the region of Verona, and then spread especially in Valtellina which is still today the largest producing area in Italy. A typical dish from this region is *polenta taragna* in which the meal is cooked in milk with butter and melted cheese. Buckwheat plantations give a characteristic air to the countryside: "The fields of buckwheat look like a garden of white and pink flowers, or speckled with green, red, and white, all clustered at the top of the stems." This is a quotation from a nineteenth-century French history of European plants.

buckwheat

Bean
String bean
Shell bean

The **Kidney bean** (*Phaseolus vulgaris*) is without doubt the best known, most useful and appreciated species within the genus. A great number of varieties or cultivars which have been obtained either by selection or cross-breeding belong to this species. From a taxonomic viewpoint the genus *Phaseolus* belongs to the *Leguminosae* and to the subfamily *Papilionoideae* or, according to some authorities, to the family *Papilionaceae*. It is noteworthy that while in 1860 only seven species of beans for a total of 180 cultivars were reported, at the beginning of the twentieth century the number of varieties, cultivars, or races mentioned had increased remarkably to 472. Today it would be almost impossible to draw a complete list of them all as fashion continually eliminates some old cultivars while imposing new ones. There is also a tendency to give different, more personal names to products which are in effect almost the same. Commercially, beans can be divided primarily into shell beans and pod beans. The latter are marketed and consumed when still unripe and are known as green or string beans. Shell beans, looked at culturally and commercially, are divided into two principal categories: dwarf beans, low, not needing supports, and climbing (pole) beans which require supports in the form of thin poles. For a long time botanists and agronomists mistakenly considered the bean as native to India, but by the end of the nineteenth century, exhaustive studies by the botanists Asa Gray, Trumbull, and Bonnet, proved that the common bean originated in America. Although some Latin authors, including Virgil and Columella, have written about *Phaseolus* and *Phaselus*, this does not prove that beans were known in ancient times. It is now believed that those terms indicated other leguminous plants ascribed now to the genus *Dolichos* (Hyacinth bean). Paleoethnological and ethnographical researches have ascertained the existence of the bean in the American continent before its discovery by Europeans. The bean, another gift from the New World, thus appeared in Europe at the beginning of the sixteenth century. It was first described and illustrated in 1542 by the botanists, Tragus and Fuchs. The French term *haricot* became part of the language in 1640, but a few decades earlier (1572) in England, the bean was already called *French bean*, thus emphasizing its introduction from France. Linnaeus recognized two different species, the common bean, which is a climber (*P. vulgaris*), and the dwarf bean (*P. nanus*). At the beginning of the nineteenth century, the Italian botanist Pietro Savi subdivided the Linnaean classification into eight species, for the most part the same as those identified by the great botanist, De Candolle (1806–1893). More recently, in the early twenties, Fiore recognized within the great Linnaean species five varieties of climbing beans and one dwarf (without distinguishing between their commercial characteristics, that is, whether they were shell or green beans). It seems difficult to attribute the forms cultivated now to these varieties, especially in consideration of the continuous changes. For cooking purposes, shell beans can be used both fresh and dried. For better results the drying process should take place on the plant, instead of the fresh beans being picked and dried in the sun. Before cooking, dry beans should be immersed in salted, tepid water. Early in the season 2–3 hours is long enough to soak haricots. Later on 3–5 hours may be necessary. It is commonly believed that beans should be soaked all night, but this is not only unnecessary, it can also be dangerous as they may start to ferment and become slightly poisonous. If, for any reason, the beans have to be left for a longer period, the water should be changed about halfway through the soaking process. Beans can be prepared in many different ways, from soups (with rice, pasta, and other vegetables) to stewed or baked beans such as France's famous cassoulet cooked with pieces of goose,

kidney bean

Scotch bean

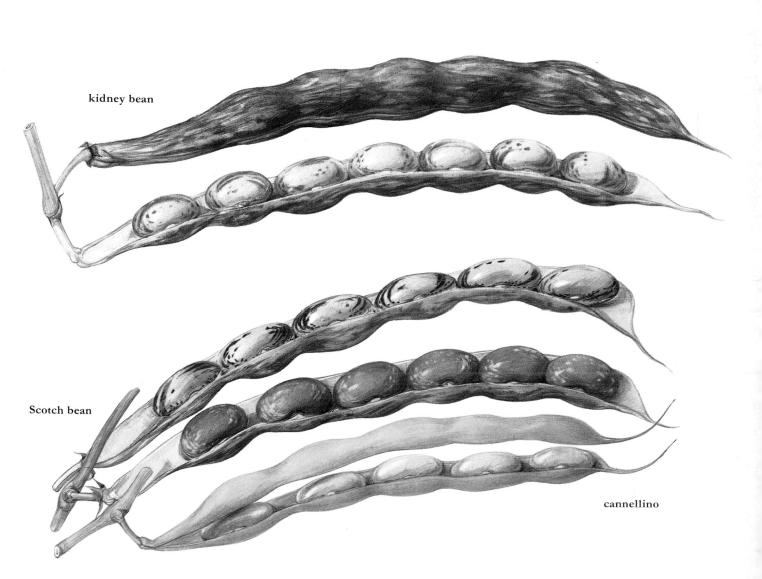

cannellino

pork and lamb, to salads. Dietetically, shell beans have a high nutritive value, as proved by the following data: upon analysis, dry beans of various cultivars show 23–24% protein, 48% carbohydrates, 2–3% lipids, 3–4% ash. They also have a high calorific content, about 300 calories per $3\frac{1}{2}$ ounces (100 grams), which has earned them the name "poor man's meat." The high carbohydrate content, however, makes them almost useless for people with weight problems. One of the disturbances caused by their consumption is a troublesome form of flatulence, possibly because of over-soaking. The cellulose content of the bean coat shows that the consumption of beans is indicated in cases of atonic constipation, while it is contraindicated in cases of spastic constipation. But for those whose work requires intense muscular activities and for those who do not have a weight problem, beans are a highly nutritious and tasty food.

There is no botanical difference between green beans and shell beans. They differ only in the way they are used. The fresh vegetables known and consumed as green beans are simply the unripe pods of a normal bean plant. Green beans, like dry beans, are produced by both tall, climbing plants and low, dwarf plants. The color of the unripe pods can basically be either yellow or green. Many of the differences among the many cultivars are almost impossible to define, and concern characteristics like some of those found in ripe seeds, and which are not noticeable at the time of consumption. Among the yellow dwarf varieties: Brittle Wax, Goldencrop Wax, Surecrop Stringless Wax, Pencil Pod Wax, and Rustproof Golden Wax, and among the green dwarf varieties: Tenderpod, Bountiful, Topcrop, Tendergreen, Contender, King of Belgium, and Bush Romano make a long list because the number of cultivars named in various catalogs is very large indeed. Among the climbing yellow varieties particular mention should be made of Golden Pole, Kentucky Wonder Wax, and Burpee Golden, with ripe seeds of various colors and large, flat, fleshy pods. Another yellow climber is the peculiar "ring" or "hook bean" with curved hooklike pods. Among the climbing or pole beans with green pods, Kentucky Wonder, McCaslan and Romano Italian Pole, with fleshy, flat pods, have qualities similar to those of the yellow forms. There are also many cultivars of beans with cylindrical pods. One of the most desired qualities in green beans is the absence of strings, the tough and inedible fibrous formations along the sutures of the pods. Green beans can be used in soups, but their principal use is as a vegetable, boiled and served with butter, or in a salad dressed with garlic and tomato purée, or with oil and vinegar. When they are very young they can also be pickled. Chemically, the solid residue of green beans is much less than in shell beans; they are actually unripe pods. It is 7–8% instead of the 44–45% of fresh shell beans and the 87% of dry beans. The protein content is 2%, carbohydrates 2–3%, and the calorific value is 18 calories per $3\frac{1}{2}$ ounces (100 grams).

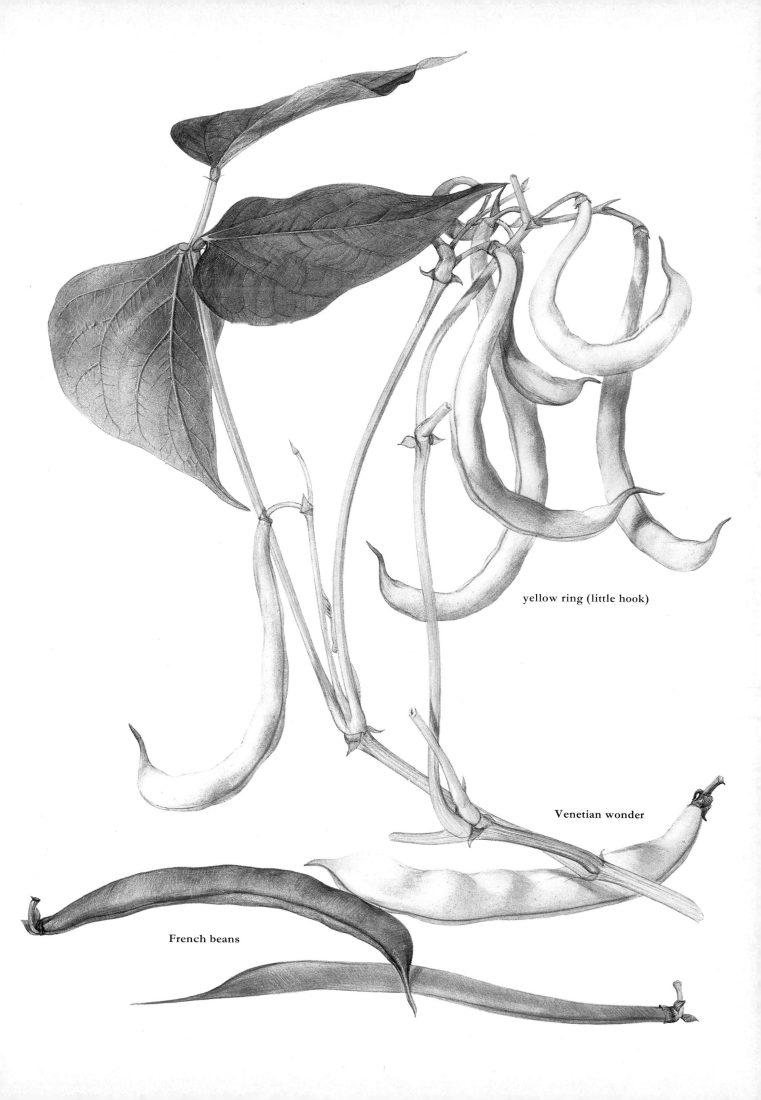

yellow ring (little hook)

Venetian wonder

French beans

Scarlet runner bean
Lima bean

The **Scarlet Runner** (*Phaseolus multiflorus*, but more often called *P. coccineus*), like any of the numerous cultivars of the kidney bean, can be used fresh or dried. When fresh and still slightly unripe, it has a more finely textured flesh and a thinner, more tender skin. Dried, and after immersion in warm water, it presents a more floury and compact meat and a tough skin. Commercially, the white-seeded variety (Spanish White) is nowadays the most common. It has white seeds, larger than those of other varieties, with a softer skin and more delicate flavor. The consumption of unripe pods is limited to a few north European regions. The scarlet runner is used for soups, and is especially good together with corn rocket (*v.* p. 72) or stewed with tomato sauce and various meats, or in salads, particularly with tuna fish and onions.

Within the species *P. lunatus*, commonly known as **Lima bean**, is found a type with small seeds, and another, perhaps a subspecies or variety *macrocarpus*, corresponding to *P. capensis*, characterized by large seeds reaching up to $\frac{3}{4}$ inch in length. To the first type belongs the Sieva or Carolina bean, as they are called in the United States (the "small Lima bean" of the British). To the second type (true Lima bean) belongs the Cape or Madagascar bean. There is also a dwarf Lima bean which grows as a bush and does not therefore require supports. Another type, common in Indochina, *P. tonkinensis*, is probably a form of *P. lunatus*. Yet another variety of Lima bean has large white seeds. The Lima bean was known and used by the pre-Columbian Incas, and around the eighteenth century was introduced to Mauritius and Madagascar, where its cultivation became of great importance. Widely cultivated and valuable from an economic standpoint in tropical regions, it is planted there in rotation with sugar cane. Lima beans are popular in the United States and Great Britain where they are often known as "butter beans." Great Britain absorbs almost the entire production from Madagascar. Because of the delicate texture of the pulp of its seeds and its characteristic aroma, the Lima bean is good for soups or as a vegetable. Its nutritive value and that of the scarlet runner are on a par with that of the common bean.

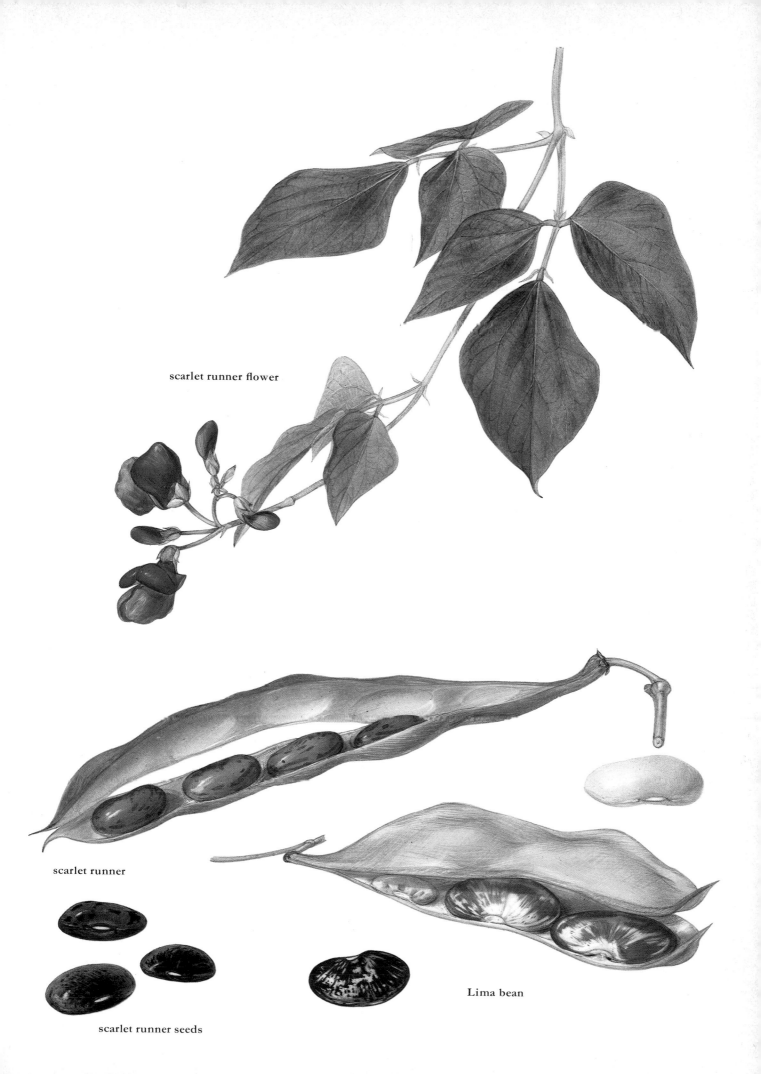

scarlet runner flower

scarlet runner

scarlet runner seeds

Lima bean

Cowpea or *Black-eyed pea*
Asparagus bean

The **Cowpea** is native to South America and widely cultivated in warm and temperate regions. Botanically, it is variously known as *Vigna unguiculata, Dolichos unguiculatus,* or *V. sinensis.* There are several varieties typical of different countries, for example, the "cubia beledi" of Arab countries, the "dan tua" of the Far East, the African "niebe," the "pois chique" of the Antilles, and the American cowpea. Little is known of its introduction into Europe and of its dispersion throughout the world. Cowpeas can be used shelled, either fresh or dried. The very young unripe pods are used in the same way as green beans. Cowpeas can be eaten, after boiling, hot as a vegetable or cold in salads, but they are not recommended for soups because of their strong flavor. The food value of the dry seed is very high: 23–24% protein, 1% fats, 56–57% carbohydrates. As human food it is similar to the kidney bean.

V. unguiculata var. *sesquipedalis* (also considered as a true species *V. sesquipedalis*) is known in many countries as **Asparagus bean** or yard-long bean. The edible part is provided by the long immature pods, used in the same way as green beans. This is an annual, climbing, herbaceous plant, with the stalks reaching up to 9–12 feet in height and therefore requiring poles for support. The flowers are beautiful, with a large violet-blue corolla. This characteristic makes the plant suitable for ornamental use on garden walls and trellises. The pods, when picked still unripe, can be stewed with tomato sauce or, after boiling and draining, seasoned with lemon juice and oil, or sautéed in butter with oil and garlic. Cowpeas and asparagus beans are much less widely used than green beans for human consumption. They are grown mostly as a curiosity or, particularly the cowpea, as a forage plant. There is no valid reason for the limited use of these vegetables for human consumption, since they are excellent and would add an unusual flavor to meals.

Another bean, little used as food, is the *Dolichos lablab* (hyacinth bean) native to tropical Africa, which produces characteristic flattened, deep purple pods. It is grown almost exclusively as an ornamental plant for the decoration of garden walls and trellises.

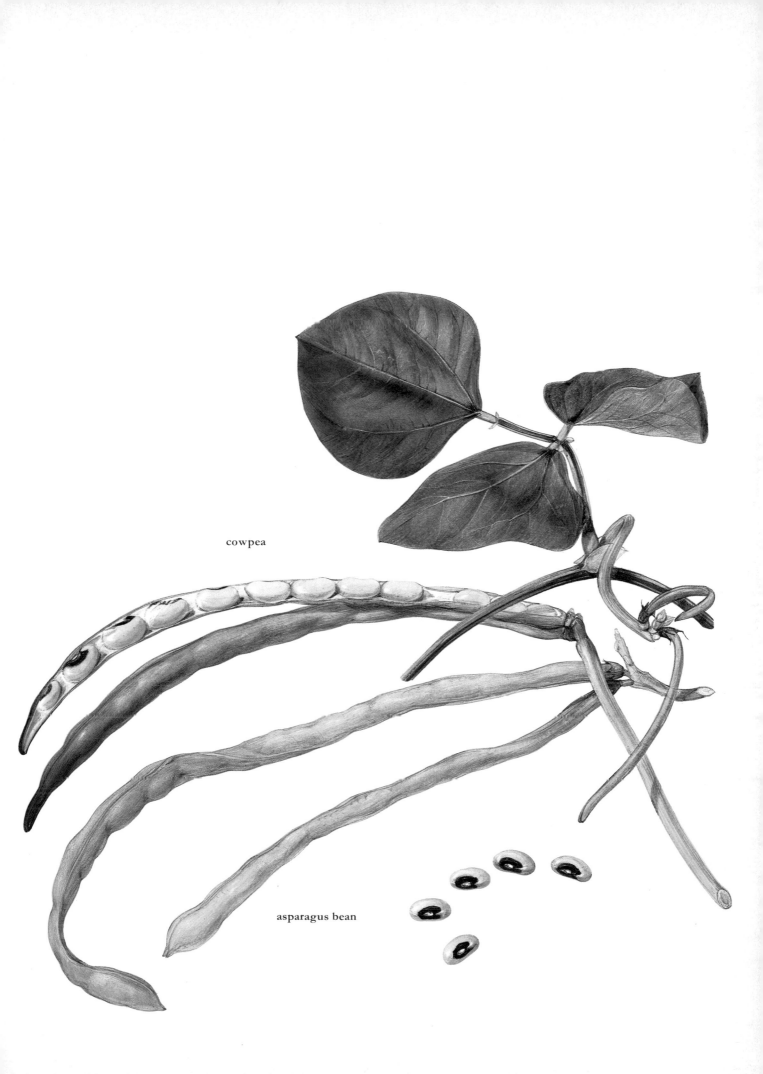

cowpea

asparagus bean

Lupine
Broad bean

Under the botanical name *Lupinus sativus* can be included all the cultivated forms, that is, *L. albus*, *L. termis* (considered as a variety of *albus*), and *L. graecus*, the latter being an almost unknown species. The **Lupine** originated in the Mediterranean basin and can still be found growing wild in Sicily and other Mediterranean regions. Since ancient times the lupine has been a staple food for the poor. It was grown in Egypt 2000 years before Christ and was also widely cultivated by the Greeks and Romans as both food for humans and as forage. In ancient Rome cooked lupines were distributed free to the people on holy days and at festivals. Although of high nutritive value, the lupine is of very little importance today as food; it is used as a snack, more like peanuts, salted almonds, and roasted pumpkin seeds, than as a main dish. The lupine is often grown as green manure to enrich the soil because of nitrogen-fixing bacterial nodules found on the roots. This is done also with other large *Leguminosae*, such as alfalfa (*Medicago sativa*) and lespedza. Some species and varieties are also grown as ornamental plants.

The importance of the **Broad bean** (*Vicia faba*) as food is greater than that of the lupine. This plant is considered native to the Mediteranean basin. A French botanist, Trabut, maintains that the original species could have been a *Faba pliniana* discovered by him near some Algerian villages in the interior. Other types of broad bean have been found near ancient dwellings dating back to the Bronze Age. In Egypt seeds have been found dating back to 2200–2400 B.C. In the Greek and Roman world the broad bean was highly regarded, although in Greece and Egypt there were some strong reservations against this leguminous plant for religious reasons. In the Middle Ages broad beans were one of the staple foods. Today, they are cultivated in the Mediterranean regions, because of their resistance to drought. They are used for green manure, as a rotation crop (that is, a crop which is cultivated alternately with others requiring great amounts of nitrogen fertilizers, such as various cereals), especially the small-seeded varieties which are also used for fodder. Fresh broad beans have 15–16% solid residue, 5% protein, 4% carbohydrates, and 40 calories per $3\frac{1}{2}$ ounces (100 grams). Dry broad beans have a higher nutritive value: 87% solid residue, 21% protein, 53% carbohydrates, 3% lipids, 3% ash, and the highest calorific content after chick peas among leguminous plants: 332 calories per $3\frac{1}{2}$ ounces (100 grams). Broad beans are known to be the cause of a strange illness, favism, with symptoms similar to those of common allergies, but that sometimes can produce coma and even death. This illness, caused by the consumption of the bean or by the inhalation of the scent which is given out by beans grown on marshy ground, cannot be considered a simple form of allergy; it appears only in individuals with hereditary predisposition.

lupines

single lupine

dried beans

broad beans

Pea
Chick-pea
Lentils

Peas belong to the species *Pisum sativum* (or *P. commune*), var. *hortense*. This variety is believed to be derived from the varieties *arvense* and *elatius* also belonging to the species *P. sativum*, and can be found growing wild in Italy, either through having escaped cultivation, or because it is the original native plant. Peas have been cultivated in Europe since very early times. They were well known to the Greeks and Romans, but there is no documentation that they were also known to the Egyptians and Hebrews. Peas have also been used since ancient times by the populations of India, from which country they were introduced into China. During the Dark Ages, peas, together with broad beans and lentils, were considered to be of great importance and represented the staple food of the poor. There are many pea cultivars, dwarf, half-dwarf, pole (climbing); and they can be divided into two large categories, shelling peas and edible-podded or sugar peas. They are cooked either fresh or dried and are used in several types of soup and as side dishes, and are canned or frozen in large quantities. Like other leguminous plants, peas are highly nutritious. Fresh peas have 25% solid residue with 7% protein, 12% carbohydrates, and 80 calories per $3\frac{1}{2}$ ounces (100 grams). Dry peas have a higher nutritive value: 87–88% solid residue with 20–21% protein, 53–54% carbohydrates, 3–4% lipids. They therefore also have a high calorific value: 334 calories per $3\frac{1}{2}$ ounces (100 grams). Their vitamin content is, however, quite low. Dietetically peas, like beans, are a high-energy food source, but if consumed in large quantities they can cause flatulence.

Chickpeas (*Cicer arietinum*) have also been cultivated since ancient times. They were known in Greece at the time of Homer, and in Egypt and India even before that. Today they are widely cultivated around the Mediterranean. The commercial product is the dried seeds which are cooked before eating. They can be boiled, then seasoned with oil, or stewed, or, as in some regions in southern Italy, cooked under the embers. Chickpeas can be the base of several excellent soups such as chickpeas and pasta or chickpeas and rice. Their nutritive value is similar to that of peas, but they have a higher percentage of lipids (4%) and therefore a high calorific value, 340 calories per $3\frac{1}{2}$ ounces (100 grams).

Lentils (*Lens esculenta* or *Ervum lens* or *Vicia lens*), also leguminous, unknown in the wild state, have been cultivated for a long time as confirmed by findings dating from the Bronze Age. They were also known to the ancient Egyptians and in India around 2000 B.C. Lentils were also eaten by the ancient Jews, as the story of Esau, who renounced his birthright for a dish of lentils, shows. From the dietetic standpoint, lentils have the same merits and defects as other leguminous plants but they have a higher protein content (25%). They are used as a vegetable and in the preparation of soups.

peas

chick-peas

lentils

Catalonia or *Asparagus chicory*
Witloof or *Belgian endive*

The many cultivated chicories are all varieties of the same species, *Cichorium intybus*, a herbaceous plant, biennial or perennial, polymorphic, and found growing wild along roadsides and in fields in Europe, in the temperate areas of northern Africa, western central Asia and virtually all over the United States. Chicory plants have a basal rosette of runcinate leaves (lobes deeply incised and recurved at the tip). Sometimes the leaves can be confused with those of the common dandelion (*Taraxacum officinale*). During the summer the flowering stalk emerges from the rosette of basal leaves growing to variable heights from 1 to 3 or more feet, bearing numerous heads of flowers of a delicate blue color (hence the vernacular name, blue sailors) or, rarely, pink or white. Around the Mediterranean where chicory is native, this plant has been used for a long time, first by collecting the wild forms, and then, progressively, through cultivation. Both the nutritional and medicinal virtues of chicory have long been known. The purgative properties of this plant are mentioned in Pliny's writings.

Commercially, chicories can be classified into various groups. The root chicories (Soncino, Magdebourg, and Chiavari) are quite different from the others, both in the way they are treated and because the parts used are the roots. Also included in the group of root chicories is **Witloof** (also called Belgian endive and barbe-de-bouc) even though the part used is not the root, but the blanched leaves. The cultivation of Witloof goes through the following stages: the seeds are sown in July and the plants, including the roots, are harvested before the winter frosts. The plants are prepared by cutting all the leaves to about $\frac{3}{4}$ inch above the base, and the extremity of the root. A bed of fresh manure covered with a thin layer of soil is prepared in a cellar or other closed environment. The plants are then placed on the bed very close to one another and covered with a layer of sand 8 inches thick. The heat produced by the fermentation of the manure (bottom heat), or by a heating system, helps the development of the plants which are ready for the market after 15–20 days. The characteristic hearts of Witloof are much sought after by gourmets for use in salads. When the plants are grown in darkness the leaves are much less pigmented than those grown in light, and are almost completely without chlorophyll, but they are more tender and crisp. Some chicories are blanched in the field, either by mounding soil up around them, or tying the leaves together with reeds or willow twigs. The most suitable varieties for this treatment are those called sugarloaf or full heart. All these chicories are quite large and have big roots which, however, are not often used. Quite different from other varieties of chicories is the **Catalonia** or **Asparagus chicory**, usually known as Catalonia.

The Catalonia is widely cultivated in southern Italy, often in association with woody crops such as the olive. It is the most readily available chicory on the winter markets, and is mostly used as a potherb, seasoned with oil and lemon juice or sautéed after boiling.

Belgian endive

Catalonia chicory

Red Verona chicory
Red Treviso chicory
Castelfranco variegated chicory

The prized wild chicory from the Venetian province, known by the name of "radicchio" also belongs to the group of root chicories, although only its leaves are used. There are three types of "radicchio," the red Verona chicory, with short leaves and rather roundish heart; the red Treviso chicory with long and lanceolate leaves and, therefore, with tapered heart; the variegated chicory of Castelfranco with almost globose heart and green leaves speckled with wine-red spots and streaks. It is not necessary to tie these plants for blanching although it is sometimes done for the Treviso chicory. The internal part of the rosette after the tougher, outside leaves are removed consists of a tender, crisp heart, slightly bitter to the taste but pleasantly aromatic. These "radicchi" are sold with a somewhat long piece of root that should not be discarded unless it is too stringy and tough, as it sometimes is at the end of the season. This root, cleaned of the skin, is perhaps the best part of the chicory, being very crisp because of the white and compact pith.

From a nutritional standpoint the chicories (Witloof, Catalonia, "radicchi," broad-leaved, and escarole) represent good eating. Raw, they supply a considerable amount of vitamins (especially vitamin C), and the bitter elements which they contain are thought to have a tonic and diuretic action. The wild chicory, common parent of the other species, has always been considered a medicinal plant. Chicories have a modest solid residue, 6–7%, with about 1% of protein and 1–2% carbohydrates, no lipids, and only about 13 calories per $3\frac{1}{2}$ ounces (100 grams). With the exception of the Catalonia, which is always cooked, seasoned with oil and lemon juice, or sautéed with garlic and chili, all the other chicories are eaten raw as salads and the heart chicories also in *pinzimonio*, a sauce of oil, salt, and pepper. Witloof hearts are also used in this sauce. The range of flavors is very varied; a strong garlic dressing with oil and vinegar is good for a coarse chicory, although it would ruin the delicate flavor of the Verona radicchio. A very unusual way to prepare the Treviso chicory is to cook it on a grill (broiled). Although these three types of chicory are indigenous to Italy they are well known thanks to the travelers and tourists who celebrate their virtues.

red Verona chicory

Castelfranco variegated chicory

red Treviso chicory

Grumolo
Endive
Escarole

The small **Grumolo** of Lombardy is a broad-leaved chicory, easily recognizable for its shape and bitter taste. The cutting-type chicories are popular in domestic cooking. They are planted close together and cut near the base at regular intervals.

Similar to the true chicories in their use and characteristics are **Escarole** and **Endive**, both belonging to the species *Cichorium endivia* which is believed to be native to India. There is no proof that the endive was known to the ancient Greeks and Romans, but some botanists believe that its use dates back to those times. We know that in France *C. endivia* appeared at first as a medicinal plant and only in the fourteenth century was it considered a food. Within the species *C. endivia* some authorities identify a *crispa* variety with curly, deeply dentate leaves (endive) and a *latifolia* variety with only slightly denticulate leaves, slightly curled at the edges (escarole).

There are many forms of the variety *crispa* with curly, deeply cut leaves: Full Heart Batavian, Broad-leaved Batavian, Salad King, Pancalier, Ruffec, and Green-curled. These are used only in salads. They are sometimes blanched in the field. The various forms of escarole, Florida Deep Heart, Florida Giant, and Florentine Big, can be either blanched for use in salads or cooked like Catalonia chicory (*q.v.*). The nutritional value of these plants is the same as those of other chicories. A special Italian dish is the *calzoni* (pants) stuffed with escarole. To prepare this dish the head of escarole is boiled in a small amount of water, or better, steamed, with fillets of anchovies and black olives; it is then put over pizza dough and baked.

escarole

grumolo

endive

Wild chicory
Bitter chicory root
Black salsify

In the plate opposite, besides another representative of the polymorphic **Wild chicory** are two specimens of the best known "bitter roots": the **Bitter chicory root** (sometimes improperly called white or black salsify), and the true **Black salsify**. The enormously swollen root is rich in reserve products (mostly inulin) and is the part of the plant which is eaten. Soncino and Magdebourg are two of the better-known varieties. The taste of chicory roots, although bitter, is pleasant and full of flavor. Chicory is a winter vegetable. To prepare, the roots should be boiled and either seasoned with oil and lemon juice, or sautéed. The true black salsify (or *scorzonera*) is a completely different species: *Scorzonera hispanica*, a perennial herb found in the meadows and woods of central and southern Europe, Caucasia, the Crimea, and central Asia, is prepared like the other varieties. Its popular name is common viper's grass.

The roots of other plants of the *Compositae* (daisy or thistle family) are also used as above, for example, those of *Tragopogon porrifolius* (white salsify, oyster plant), an annual or biennial plant, quite common in the grassy places of southern Europe and northern Africa, and sometimes confused with the chicories with large roots. Salsify, chicory roots, and black salsify all contain medicinal properties. Inulin is their carbohydrate reserve and, like the Jerusalem artichoke, the roots are thought by many to be good in a diabetic diet. The roasted roots of wild chicory are sometimes used as a coffee substitute or as an adulterant. The roots are sliced, roasted, and then pulverized. This dates back to the mid-eighteenth century soon after coffee became the fashionable drink. It is thought to have been first used in Sicily. It contains laxative properties and has more food value than coffee. True coffee lovers, however, would not allow chicory near their brew, although it is used as an economy measure in many continental households.

wild chicory

bitter chicory root

black salsify

Lettuce

The cultivated **Lettuces**, perhaps the plants most widely used in salads (to such a degree that in some countries salad and lettuce have become synonymous), belong to the *Compositae* (daisy or thistle family) and to the genus *Lactuca*. The majority of botanists agree that the garden lettuce is a variety (*sativa*) of the species *Lactuca scariola* which is found in the wild state in Asia, Europe and northern Africa, and has become naturalized in North America and the Argentine. Some authorities believe that *L. sativa* originated from *L. scariola*; others maintain that this variety is native to a mountain region in Siberia where it is said to grow wild. Whatever the case, lettuce has been cultivated since very early times and was known not only to the Greeks and Romans, but, even earlier, to the Chinese. The Romans were familiar with several different forms that were mentioned by Pliny and Columella, while the authorities of the Dark Ages and of the Renaissance seem to have known fewer forms. Lettuce was introduced from Italy to France and in the sixteenth century the "Roman" lettuce (romaine, cos) arrived in England. At least three principal forms are recognized: head or cabbage lettuce (var: *capitata*), cos or romaine (var: *longifolia*), and the curled or leaf lettuce with leaves somewhat deeply incised, belonging, according to some botanists, to the varieties *crispa* and *palmata*. Head lettuce comes in many forms. The typical round head is a large bud, the development of which is helped considerably by transplanting. Lettuce is primarily a salad plant. It is highly refreshing and contains several vitamins, such as vitamin A, riboflavin, thiamin, and above all, vitamin C. Its calorific value is extremely low, its composition being mostly water, 1% protein, only traces of fats, and 2–3% carbohydrates. One of the lesser known but highly recommended uses of lettuce is in the preparation of vegetable or *minestroni* soups, the addition of lettuce adding a very delicate flavor.

The various seed companies throughout the world list more than fifty cultivars of garden lettuce. Not all of them are equally adapted to all areas, and hence cultivars should be selected for a particular region. Leaf lettuce varieties are not common in commercial markets but are very popular with the home gardener. They are easier to grow, and do well during hot weather, supplying leaf lettuce for salads throughout the summer.

Head lettuce varieties: Butter-head types: Buttercrunch, Bibb, Summer Bibb, White Boston, Dark Green Boston and Matchless; Crisp-head (Iceberg) types: Great Lakes, Iceberg, Imperial 44, Mesa 659, Ithaca and Fulton.

Leaf or curly varieties: Grand Rapids, Green Ice, Salad Bowl, Oak Leaf, Ruby, Slobolt and Greenhart.

Romaine varieties: Cos, Parris Island, Paris White, Dark Green Cos and Mammoth Giant White.

head lettuces

cos lettuce

Corn salad or Lamb's lettuce
Water speedwell
Bitter cress

Valerianella olitoria, the common **Corn Salad** (also **Lamb's lettuce**, *Fetticus*), is one of the most prized salads for use between fall and spring. It is usually expensive, but, because of its small leaves, gives a very good yield and quite a small plant makes enough salad for two or three servings. Seed catalogs generally do not mention this plant, or list only a few varieties such as those with a rosette of compact leaves at the center, and another with big seeds (which are really dried fruits). In old treatises on food plants, many varieties of *V. olitoria* were mentioned, among which were the Etampes green with large round leaves, and a variety with spoon-shaped leaves. *V. eriocarpa* (Italian corn salad) is similar to the *olitoria* and used in the same manner. So also are many other species of this genus which are common around the Mediterranean, but not well known in Anglo-Saxon countries. These salads have practically no calorific value, but their consumption, especially in winter, is thought by many to be useful for their vitamin and mineral salt content, and for the beneficial effects on the body functions (increased diuresis and stimulation of the intestines).

Water speedwell (*Veronica anagallis-aquatica*) known in some parts as cress (but not to be confused with the true cress, *Nasturtium officinale*, v. p. 58), can be found only in a few local country markets. The 4–6 small leaves at the top are used in winter and spring salads because of their subtle flavor. *V. anagallis-aquatica* is a water plant that flourishes even in snowy weather because of the relatively mild temperature of water in comparison to the cold winter air. Its delicate aroma and taste should be enhanced with a light dressing of lemon juice, rather than vinegar. The same applies to corn salad, which resembles water speedwell in its culinary properties.

Bitter watercress (*Cardamine amara*), of the *Cruciferae* or mustard family, is found in humid places, near springs and brooks. It can be eaten alone as a salad, or, as with other plants of the mustard family such as rockets and watercress, used to enhance the flavor of other salads with its aromatic, piquant taste. Its dietetic properties are analogous to those of other *Cruciferae*, particularly those of the garden rocket and of true cress (*Nasturtium officinale*). Bitter cress is believed to have diuretic, antiscorbutic and stimulant properties and in the past was considered to be a medicinal plant like *Cardamine pratensis* (Lady's smock).

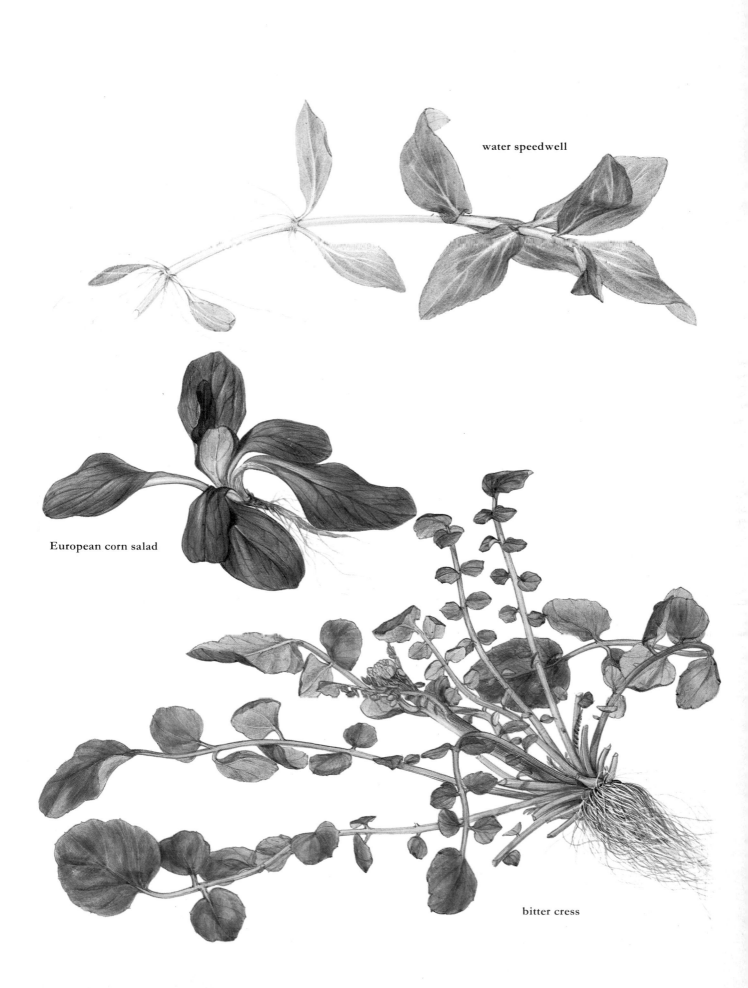

water speedwell

European corn salad

bitter cress

Plantain
Judas tree
English elm

Another little-known salad is the **Plantain** (*Plantago coronopus*), known in the United States as "crowfoot plantain" and in some parts as "buck's-horn" and "Capuchin's beard." When very young and tender the leaves are a good addition to any salad. Although its use is not extensive, the plantain is mentioned in many old classical texts as a vegetable foodstuff. There is documentation of its use in a German book dated 1586; it is also mentioned by sixteenth- and seventeenth-century botanists. Culpeper, the great seventeenth-century English herbalist, commends it "against venomous bites, especially those of a mad dog." Plantain has refreshing and diuretic properties, and is rich in mineral salts and vitamins, especially vitamin C. Unfortunately, it is almost impossible to find this plant on sale. Once it was offered to the Italian public in the so-called *misticanze*, which originated in the Marche region, and were a mixture of little-known species which were a puzzle to botanists. Today, now that overharvesting has destroyed most varieties, all that can be found in the *misticanze* is rocket and cultivated salad. The only way to obtain this plant is to look for it oneself. The many varieties of plantain (Fiori lists about six varieties of *Plantago coronopus* plus the cultivated forms that he includes in the variety *sativa*) grow wild in sandy and saline soil, along the coasts, and are sure to be found in spring along the seashore where there are often several specimens. To be suitable for use, it must be picked before the flowering stalk has appeared and when the rosette of leaves is very young.

The **Judas tree** (*Cercis siliquastrum*) grows in North America, Asia and southern Europe, and yet very little is known about its uses. It has strongly perfumed flowers which may be either pickled in vinegar, rather like capers, or fried. When mixed into a salad the flowers give a very decorative appearance.

It is unfortunate that even less is known of the use of the very young fruits, just after they start forming and are therefore still very tender, of the **English elm** (*Ulmus campestris*). These fruits have a very aromatic, unusual flavor, and leave the mouth fresh and the breath smelling pleasant which makes them a welcome addition to salads. As well as the fruits of the English elm, the fruits of other elms, either wild or cultivated, can be used in the same way.

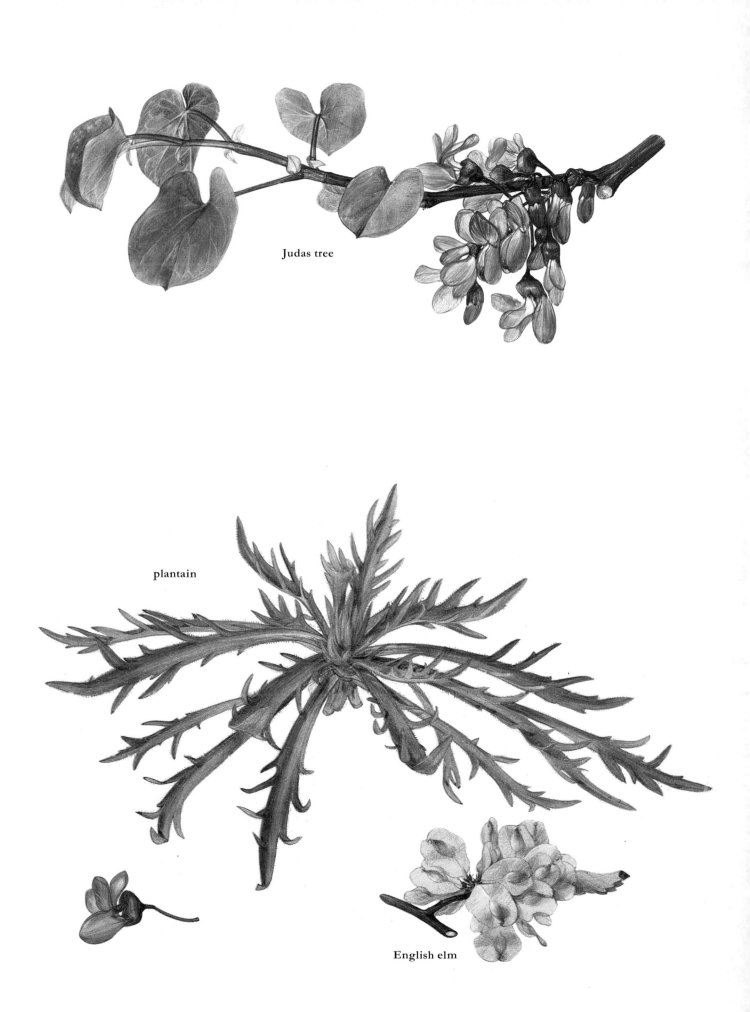

Judas tree

plantain

English elm

Dandelion
Garden burnet

There is more detailed information available about the common **Dandelion**, also called cow-parsnip (*Taraxacum officinale*). It is not cultivated in Europe since the plants found growing wild in fields are more than sufficient for the limited use made of them. The French, with Gallic realism, have named it *pissenlit* because of the unpleasant sticky substance which oozes from the stem when it is plucked. In France, and to a limited extent in the United States, especially during the nineteenth century, the dandelion was so popular that several improved forms, giant, curled, full-heart, and thick-leaved, were selected and cultivated. This plant has a characteristic bitter but pleasant flavor. When very young the more tender central leaves of the rosette can be eaten in salads, or cooked in the same way as spinach. The nutritive value of the dandelion is similar to that of the various chicories: 6–7% solid residue, a very low level of protein (about 1%) and of carbohydrates (also about 1%), and no fats. Its calorific content is only 13 calories per $3\frac{1}{2}$ ounces (100 grams). Dietetically it is also considered to be a medicinal plant for its tonic, diuretic and purgative action, and has been highly recommended for its beneficial effect on the liver.

Another characteristic and little known spring herb is the **Garden Burnet** (*Poterium sanguisorba* or *sanguisorba minor*), a perennial grass belonging to the *Rosaceae* (rose family). It can be used only in the spring or during the fall renewal, when the tissues are tender and the characteristic rosette of pinnate leaves has just begun to form. It is easy to find in grassy places or on barren spots like rocks, walls or ruins. The plant has an aromatic smell which makes it a pleasant addition to salads. There is nothing special about its dietetic properties, but it is a source of vitamin C as well as being refreshing and diuretic. Although little known, it is considered by herbalists to be a medicinal plant with astringent and carminative properties. In the seventeenth century, it was highly spoken of by Culpeper, who recommended "Two or three of the stalks with leaves put into a cup of wine, especially claret" to "quicken the spirits, refresh and clear the heart, and drive away melancholy."

dandelion

garden burnet

Borage
Watercress
Wall rocket
Sea rocket

Borage (*Borrago officinalis*) is a typical plant of the Mediterranean region from whence it was introduced into America and central Europe, particularly Germany, where it has flourished. In Italy it is found mostly in the central and southern regions from Emilia and Liguria southward, in varied habitats: roadbanks, cultivated and untilled fields, ruins, etc. In many parts of France its flowers are cooked as fritters and it is also used in salads and as a flavoring for vegetables. It can be drunk as herbal tea or in claret cup to give a decorative and aromatic effect. It appears toward the end of winter or in the fall and lasts until the beginning of summer. The parts used are the young leaves and sometimes the flowering tops. The less tender leaves can be cooked as a substitute for spinach, or in the preparation of spring omelets. In Italy its use is more limited than in France, except in Liguria and the central and southern regions where it is used in some traditional dishes. Borage is considered more a medicinal plant than a food, although it can be found on sale in some large cities. It contains mucilages and saltpeter and is thought to have diuretic and emollient properties.

Watercress (*Nasturtium officinale*) shares its common name of cress with another plant, water speedwell (*Veronica anagallis-aquatica, v.* p. 52), which grows in the same habitat; it is used mostly as a flavoring for salads, and as a garnish for meat dishes. It is seldom cooked although many excellent recipes exist for its use. Quickly blanched in salted water, drained and dried, it may then be simmered in butter or in a few tablespoons of boiling cream. Like other *Cruciferae* (mustard family) it has a typical pungent flavor due to the presence of chemical compounds generally known as isosulfocyanic glucosides. Its properties resemble those of other *Cruciferae*, stimulant, diuretic, antiscorbutic, etc.; hence it is both edible and medicinal. On the Continent (with the exception of Italy) and especially in France and the United States, watercress is very popular. Better varieties have been selected and are cultivated in special fields. The nineteenth century was a time of great popularity for watercress, but its cultivation in France, according to some botanists, dates as far back as the twelfth century.

Wall rocket (*Diplotaxis muralis*) is never used alone in a salad because of its sharp, piquant taste. It is mostly used as a flavoring, as is another rocket, *Eruca sativa*.

The youngest and tenderest shoots of **Sea Rocket** (*Cakile maritima*) are also used as flavoring. They are fleshy and crisp and have dietetic properties similar to those of watercress.

borage

sea rocket

watercress

wall rocket

Cardoon
Artichoke

There is some confusion regarding the origin of **Cardoons** and **Globe artichokes**. Some European botanists believe that both vegetables were derived from a wild perennial herb (*Cynara cardunculus* var. *silvestris*) that grows in southern Europe and northern Africa. Current American taxonomists think that they are two distinct species, cardoon (*C. cardunculus*) and globe artichoke (*C. scolymos*). Others consider the globe artichoke to be a cultivated form of cardoon. The wild species of cardoon is of medium size, growing up to about 3 feet. It has many thorns and its flowers are much smaller than those of the globe artichoke. The cultivated cardoon (*C. cardunculus* var. *altilis*) is very different from the original form. It is much taller (6–7 feet) with fleshier leaves and fewer thorns. The flowers are deep blue with large inflorescences. Cardoons look even more different when they arrive on the market because they are artificially blanched. Although the cardoon is a perennial plant, it is cultivated as an annual. It is sown in spring in cold frames and the seedlings are transplanted later to the field. At the beginning of the fall, at the height of its vegetative development, it is subjected to blanching through various processes. One of the older methods was to tie the leaves at the top into a bunch and draw the soil up around the base of the plant. Today it is more convenient to cover the plant with canvas or opaque plastic or cardboard packing. The leaves that are gradually forming inside the rosette are white and very tender, suitable for eating raw. But generally cardoons are eaten hot, and are first boiled so that the leaf stalks will be tender. Often they are seasoned with cheese or white sauce, and are also good when breaded and fried. When eaten raw they are excellent if dipped in *bagna cauda* (a hot anchovy and garlic dip, popular in Piedmont). Asti ivory white, Romagna's giant, Tours cardoon, Paris cardoon, and Spanish cardoon are selections of the wild form. They have a delicate flavor and tender stalks. According to Theophrastus the cardoon was known in ancient times and is today very popular in Europe. Both cardoons and artichokes were derived through successive selections from the wild varieties, and have evolved into a quite different species. They are both of considerable economic importance, particularly the artichoke, and their cultivation is widespread.

Cultivated artichokes (*C. cardunculus* var. *scolymus*) are taller than cardoons, although with smaller heads. The leaves are wider and fleshier. The inflorescences are also much larger; they can reach up to 4–5 inches in diameter. The flowers are blue, while those of the wild species are light pink. The artichoke is a perennial plant, as are the cardoon and the wild thistle. But after three or four years of cultivation the production of the artichoke field decreases and it is better to renew it using the shoots that are produced at the base of the plant every year at the beginning of the growing season. The best known cultivars are Green Gold, Paris Green, Lyons Green, the Chioggia or Venice violet, and the Tuscany violet, with truncated-conical heads; the Provence violet, the Breton stocky, the Roman, with almost globose heads; and the "thorny," which has bracts with sharp thorns at the tips. The head of the wild artichoke is also edible. The artichoke may be eaten hot or cold, but either way it must first be boiled vigorously for 30–40 minutes. The lid should be left off the saucepan during boiling as otherwise the vegetable will take on a bitter flavor. The smaller heads, picked at the end of the season, can be preserved in oil. This is a simple process; clean the heads, removing the tougher scales, cut off the tops, then cut the heads twice lengthwise, thus obtaining four pieces for each head. Boil them in a mixture of water, white wine, salt and vinegar. Drain, put in jars, and cover with oil flavored with capers, oregano, or chili peppers. Cardoons and artichokes are very healthful foods. Both are considered medicinal plants, with diuretic and purgative action.

cardoon

Tuscany violet

Roman artichoke

Their composition is as follows: for the cardoon, 1–1.5% protein, 3–4% carbohydrates, traces of lipids, 90% water; for the artichoke, 2–3% protein, 7–8% carbohydrates, traces of lipids, and 85% water. They both contain vitamins of the B complex; the cardoon has a higher amount of vitamin C than the artichoke.

Some gourmets claim that only water should be drunk with the artichoke as wine is said to change its character when drunk with this vegetable. However, a strong white wine, served very cold, such as a Mâcon, should be able to hold its own. Another wine suitable to drink with the artichoke is the very dry *vin gris*, the *Cendrée de Novembre*, from the Jura.

According to the famous physician and naturalist Matteoli, the cultivation of the artichoke was extensive by the second half of the sixteenth century.

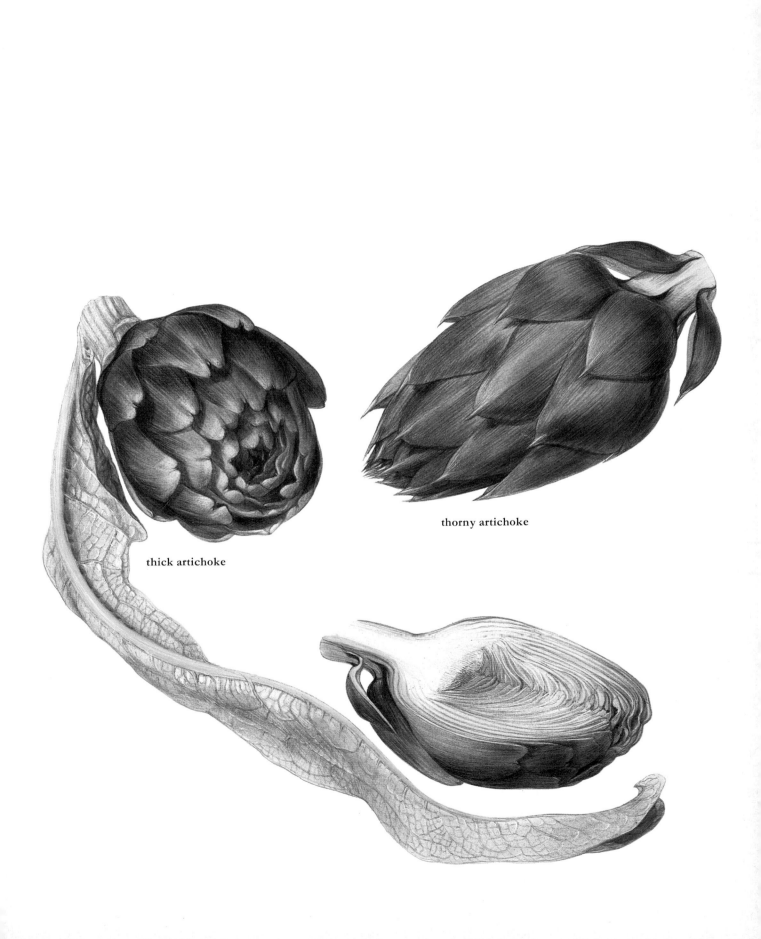

thick artichoke

thorny artichoke

Black cabbage
Brussels sprouts
Savoy cabbage
Common cabbage
Kohlrabi
Cauliflower
Broccoli
Turnip tops
Sea kale

Cabbages, in the broadest sense, have been cultivated since very early times. They are derived from a wild form native to central and western Europe, and western Asia. Some botanists ascribe these wild plants to the variety *silvicola* which grows on rocks. They are all included in the diffuse and polymorphic species *Brassica oleracea* of the *Cruciferae* (mustard family). Today, because of selections started many centuries ago, the cultivated forms differ greatly, not only from the original type, but also from one another. They can be classified simply and concisely as follows:

var.: *acephala*, including the headless cabbages, with long stems, sometimes reaching a height of 6–7 feet, broad green leaves, at times bearing leafy appendices on the primary or secondary ribs. These cabbages are mostly used as livestock feed, and very occasionally for human consumption, as in the case of the **Black cabbage** or Tuscany Black;

var.: *gemmifera*, which produces the **Brussels sprouts**; the sprouts are large adventitious buds, with tightly compact leaves, which develop along the stem at the axil of the leaves;

var.: *sabauda* or *bullata*, known as **Savoy cabbage**, with short stem and leaves crimped, blistered and closely appressed, forming a compact and globose head, usually until flowering time;

var.: *capitata*, or **Common cabbage**, with smooth, pale green leaves (but also red or purple) which are tightly appressed to form an even more compact head than that of the Savoy;

var.: *gongyloides* or *caulorapa* called **Kohlrabi**, with a fleshy, swollen stem, globe-shaped;

var.: *botrytis*, the **Cauliflower**, in which the edible part is provided by the large, hypertrophied inflorescence, still unripe, with fleshy branches which form a generally globular structure, the head being sometimes pointed at the top;

var.: *cauliflora*, commonly called **Broccoli**, with leaves less broad and thick than those of the cauliflower, and less tight floral peduncles, forming a more open head which expands like an umbrella.

Cabbages have been used by man since prehistoric times when he was still living on wild plants and herbs, and had not yet learned the art of cultivation. Later the use of the cabbage became confined to Europe. The Jews did not know this plant, which is not mentioned in the Bible. It was highly regarded by the Romans.

64

common cabbage

Savoy cabbage

red cabbage

Cato was said to use "no other physic" and considered the cabbage to be valuable both as a food and as a stimulant, and as a remedy for many ailments from sore throats to cataracts. However, it is not known which forms were used in Roman times, as the sketchy descriptions left by Cato, Pliny, Columella, and others, are insufficient to define precisely the morphology of the cultivated forms of those days. Possibly they were still similar to the wild varieties, but are now irretrievably lost. In Europe, the ancient Germans made great use of the cabbage. The varieties of greatest economic and commercial importance today are the Savoy, the common cabbage and the cauliflower.

The Savoy and common cabbage show a consistently parallel behavior. In the course of time, selection has brought about great changes in the appearance of these vegetables compared with the wild varieties. The leaves have become very broad and tightly appressed, forming the so-called head, which can be spherical, oblong, or slightly depressed. The more firm and compact the head, the more valuable is the cabbage commercially, as the internal leaves will be smoother, whiter, and more tender. The external leaves are tougher (those of the Savoy being more crimped and blistered), more deeply colored, and often having a soft bloom that gives them a characteristic waxy appearance. A longitudinal section shows that the head is a very large terminal bud. In the spring (cabbages are late summer and autumnal crops, lasting until the next spring) when the many dormant axillary buds start blooming, the head loses its compact shape and breaks down completely. From a dietary viewpoint both the Savoy and the common cabbage, like many plants of the mustard family, have been highly recommended, especially during winter, either raw or cooked. Raw cabbage has a high vitamin content, especially of vitamin C. Cooked cabbage is low in fat, medium-low in protein, a good diuretic agent and, because of its high content of cellulose fibers, effective as roughage in stimulating the intestines. Cabbages also cost less than most other vegetables. It is no longer possible to buy all the different cultivars that were listed in the old treatises. Even the most comprehensive seed catalogs list only a few cultivars of Savoy cabbage, and sometimes they represent very slight differences.

The current leading varieties of the Savoy-type cabbage are Savoy King, Chieftain Savoy, Vanguard, Perfection Drumhead, Asti, and Ironhead. Even vegetables follow the fashion, and each year some varieties are "in" and others "out." Gastro-

broccoli

Brussels sprouts

nomically, the Savoy is the base for many different dishes: soups; meat stews such as the Piedmont *ragù* made with Savoy cabbage and pork meat, or more elaborately with goose or duck; German sauerkraut and Polish and Russian stuffed cabbage. By using only the inner part of the head, it is possible to prepare very good winter salads and coleslaw.

The common or head cabbage cultivars are further subdivided on a seasonal and color basis: early cabbage: Copenhagen Market, Market Victor, Market Topper, Early Jersey, Wakefield, Earliana, Golden Acre, and Stonehead Hybrid; mid-season cabbage: O-S Cross, Harris Resistant Dutch, Market Prize, King Cole and Roundup; later or winter cabbage: Danish Ballhead, Green Winter, Premium Flat Dutch, Surehead, and Danish Roundhead; red or purple cabbage: Red Acre, Ruby Ball, and Red Head.

Both sauerkraut and braised red cabbage are better if simmered for 4–5 hours the day before they are to be eaten, and then reheated very slowly. For cooking purposes other varieties of cabbage, with the exception of broccoli and cauliflower, have similar characteristics to those of the Savoy and common cabbages.

Brussels sprouts are usually boiled or steamed. **Broccoli**, after the basal part and tougher leaves are removed, is boiled and then served with butter or a hollandaise sauce. Some of the various cultivars of broccoli are: De Cicco, Calbrese, Waltham 29 and Green Comet. Some well-known Brussels sprouts varieties are: Jade Cross Hybrid, Long Island Improved, Green Gem, and Catskill. Broccoli has the following composition: 15–16% solid residue, with 5–6% protein, 5% carbohydrates, no lipids, 1% ash and 43–44 calories per 3½ ounces (100 grams). It has almost twice as much nutritive value as Savoy cabbage.

There are also numerous varieties of **Cauliflower** available. Some of the leading cultivars are: Super Snowball, Snowball A, Dominant, Clou, White Horse, Igloo, Jet Snow, Purple Head, Burpeeana, and Self-Blanche.

Cauliflowers have 8% solid residue, 2–3% protein, 1–2% carbohydrates, less than 1% ash, and no lipids. The calorific content is 17–18 calories per 3½ ounces (100 grams). Even after cooking the cauliflower still retains some vitamin C and small amounts of thiame and carotene. It is eaten primarily cooked, or raw pickled in vinegar. While boiling, it is better to use very little water, leaving the head uncovered so that it will cook by steam. After cooking, the cauliflower can be

sea kale

turnip tops

black cabbage

eaten as an accompanying vegetable with a little butter, or served as a dish on its own with a cheese sauce, usually wrongly called *au gratin*. It is also very good when fried in batter, or used in a salad after being only partially cooked. A cauliflower soufflé is also an excellent main dish.

Black cabbage, which is common to Tuscany and central Italy, can be used in soups and stews. It is not much known in England or the United States.

Kohlrabi (*Oleracea caulorapa*) (not illustrated) was once very popular especially in the Alpine regions and central Europe. Its use has now declined so much that it is hard to find commercially. The edible portion of this vegetable is the bulbous part at the top of the stem where the leaves grow.

Turnip tops (*Brassica campestris*) commonly called "greens," are the flowered tops of the turnip. For culinary purposes they are best when sautéed in oil with garlic, after boiling in the same manner as broccoli. They are one of the cheaper winter vegetables.

Sea-kale (*Crambe maritima*) is a large perennial herb of the mustard family, growing wild on the eastern and northern coasts of Europe. It is used as a vegetable in France and England, where several horticultural varieties have been developed, among which the Feltham white is one of the best. It should not be overcooked.

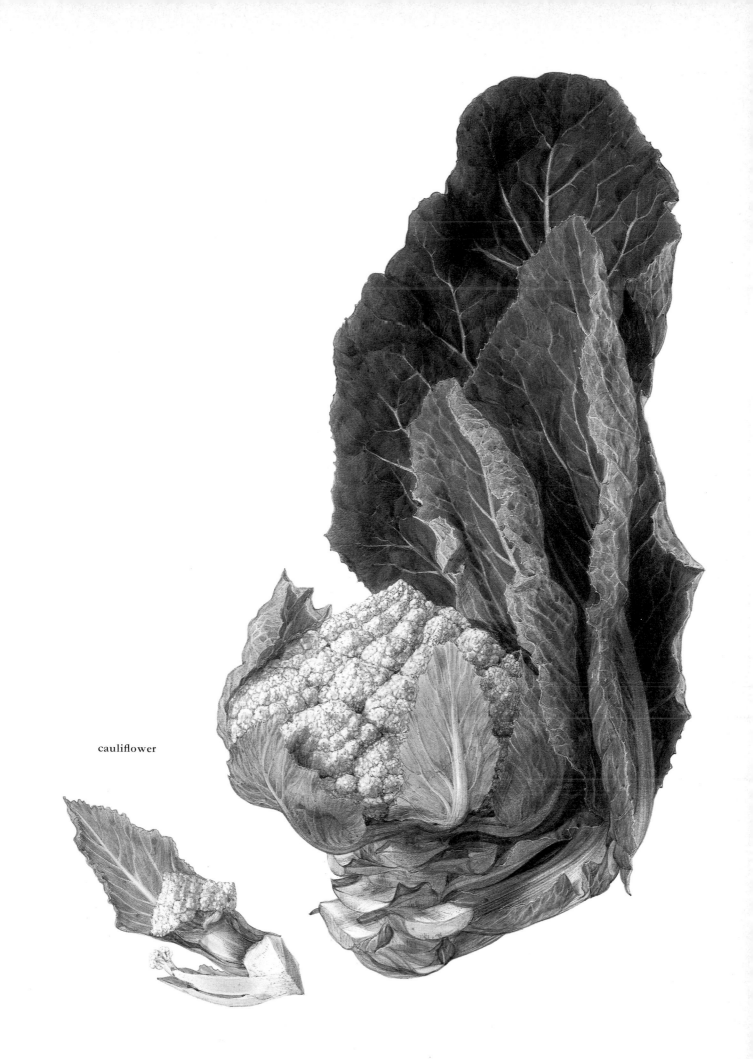

cauliflower

Corn rocket
Hairy bitter cress
Shepherd's purse
Horseradish

Corn rocket (*Bunias erucago*), **Hairy bitter cress** (*Cardamine hirsuta*) and **Shepherd's purse** (*Capsella bursa-pastoris*) are herbaceous plants very common on the Continent, but growing in varying habitats, and with different geographical distribution, so that it is not easy to find them growing together. Corn rocket (one of the many plants known as rockets), found in central and southern Europe and around the Mediterranean, is typical of untilled and rather poor soils. Hairy bitter cress, found throughout the world, except Australia, is common in grassy places, and is considered a weed in vegetable gardens. The cosmopolitan shepherd's purse grows on roadbanks, in waste places, and in gardens. They are all annual plants and only corn rocket is cultivated. The edible parts are the leaves of the very young plants, still in the rosette stage. They make refreshing spring soups or side dishes. Because of its natural life cycle and the farmer's timetable, corn rocket is often available in the fall. It has a characteristic aromatic flavor that goes well with white Spanish beans (Dutch case knife bean) in dishes such as *ris e barland* soup from Lombardy. Like other *Cruciferae*, these three herbs are reputed to have antiscorbutic, diuretic, and stimulating qualities.

The hairy bitter cress is mostly used as a garnish and is not mentioned with other cresses in early herbals.

Shepherd's purse was highly thought of by Culpeper, who recommended it as a cure for jaundice if "bound to the wrists or the soles of the feet." Cotton Mather used to cure toothache by putting it in the ears (inadvisable).

Horseradish (*Nasturtium armoracia* or *Armoracia lapathifolia*) is a perennial herb of the *Cruciferae* which originated in east-central Europe and is now extensively grown. The cultivated and naturalized forms found on the Continent are sterile; they flower but do not produce seeds and are, therefore, propagated vegetatively. The roots are used for consumption. They are thought to have diuretic and antiscorbutic properties and are, from the culinary standpoint, stimulating and appetizing. The root is grated and mixed with vinegar to prepare a sauce especially good with beef, or combined with tomato sauce as a seafood dip. It is used mostly in central Europe, including the Alpine regions, and in Britain and the United States. The leaves of this plant can be used for salads when they are very young and tender. Opinions differ on the history of the horseradish. Some authorities maintain that it was known in very early times, about 1000 B.C., by the Greeks and before the Roman conquest of the British Isles. Other scholars, such as De Candolle, claim that the use of horseradish is comparatively recent.

corn rocket

hairy bitter-cress

horseradish

shepherd's purse

Turnip
Wild radish
Garden radish

The **Turnip** (*Brassica campestris* var. *rapa*, or *B. rapa*) is botanically a close relative of cabbage (*B. oleracea*), rape (*B. napus*) and rapeseed (*B. rapa* var. *oleifera*). The latter, for morphological and commercial reasons, is often confused with colza (var. *oleifera* of *B. napus*). Another variety, sometimes called turnip is the rutabaga, Swedish turnip, Russian turnip or Swede (*B. campestris*, var. *napo-brassica*). The turnip is a biennial plant with a characteristic edible, tuberous root (or hypocotyl) of various shapes in the different cultivars (flattened and disclike or cylindrical). It is believed to have originated in Europe, where it has been grown and used as food since prehistoric times. Together with the cabbage, the turnip has been for a long time the staple food of the peoples of northern and central Europe, and its use declined only after the introduction of the potato. Trying to summarize and simplify the complex and long list of commercial varieties is very difficult. The four main types of turnip and some representative varieties of garden turnip are based on the shape of the root: (1) long types with a root three or more times as long as broad; (2) spindle-shape (tankard) with a root twice as long as broad; (3) round or globe shape; and (4) flat with roots broader than long. One other type, the foliage turnip, forms no swollen root but a cluster of leaves that are cooked as potherbs (greens). Seven-Top and Shogoin are foliage turnips. Popular round turnips are Just Right, Purple-top White Globe and Yellow Globe, Tokyo Cross, and Amber Globe. Flat or flattened globe varieties are Tokyo Market, Early Purple-top Milan, and Flat Milan. The turnip has very little nutritional value: it contains mostly water, 1% protein, traces of fats and 6–7% carbohydrates. It is used especially for the preparation of soups, in Irish stew, and as a winter vegetable.

Wild and garden **Radishes** are considered by some botanists as two varieties of the species *Raphanus raphanistrum*: others believe that the garden radish is a true species (*R. sativus* or *R. radicula*) and the wild radish a variety (var. *niger*) of the latter, while some books list the wild radish as *R. raphanistrum*. The origin of the radish, like that of most cultivated plants, is uncertain, but it was certainly known in China and Egypt in ancient times and also to the Greeks and Romans. Today the coarser wild radish is practically no longer used, but the garden radish is popular in salads or eaten raw as a relish. In France radishes are served as an hors-d'oeuvres with fresh, crusty bread and butter. Three groups of cultivars exist: (1) the familiar red globe-shaped varieties of radish: Champion, Cherry Belle, Red Boy, Scarlet Globe, and Comet, and the Round Black Spanish, a round-type radish with deep black skin that is excellent for storage in moist sand during the winter; (2) the long-root radish: White Chinese (Celestial), All Seasons White, Burpee White, White Icicle, and Summer Cross and long and red: half-long, Naples half-long; (3) numerous globular ones, deeply and totally pigmented, or half and half red and white, Saxa, Perfection, and Champion.

The food value of the radish is almost insignificant. However, it contains some vitamin C, and is good for stimulating appetites.

cultivated radishes

turnip

wild radish

Swiss chard
Spinach
Field poppy
Common saltwort
Goosefoot
Purslane
New Zealand spinach

The species about to be described belong to that complex of plants that could be called "leaf vegetables." Some are well known, others somewhat less, and still others unknown to the majority of people and considered as luxuries.

Swiss chard (*Beta vulgaris* var. *cicla*) was already known to the ancient Greeks as a food plant. Pliny mentions a variety with long midribs which was highly regarded in the Roman world. It is not generally realized that the white beet was originally known by the same name. The chard has therefore been cultivated from remote times, and the quantities available on sale today are enormous compared to the small yields of old-time agriculture. Chard is excellent not only as a vegetable, but also in soups and rice dishes, prepared like spinach, with a piece of butter added at the last moment of cooking. The white ribs of the chard are the best part. They are boiled in a little salted water, drained, and then simmered in the desired seasonings. The green part of the leaves, mixed with sorrel, can also be used in the same manner as spinach.

Spinach (*Spinacia oleracea*) is one of the most healthful of vegetables especially in late autumn and winter, because it has properties uncommon in other winter plants. Spinach belongs to the goosefoot family (*Chenopodiaceae*). It was introduced into Europe by the Moors, around A.D. 1000, and is thought to be of Persian origin. Its intensive and widespread cultivation in Europe started only after the eighteenth century, especially in the Netherlands, France, and England, and later in the rest of Europe and the Americas. Spinach is considered to be so healthful because it is very rich in vitamins: it contains a high percentage of vitamin A and of the B complex, whose components are important in the development and growth of the body, and in the prevention of beriberi and anemia. The amount of vitamin C is also high, as are vitamins E and K. It also contains potassium of oxalate and some iron. Unfortunately the vitamins are soluble in water and fats, and are lost in cooking. For this reason it is advisable to cook greens in the shortest time possible. Although it was once thought that spinach could not be eaten raw it is now much in demand in the United States as a gourmet salad. With regard to protein content, spinach resembles cabbage, providing a fair amount of nitrogen compounds and only a negligible percentage of carbohydrates. The iron content of spinach, almost the same percentage as that found in fish and eggs, used to be considered its most valuable asset, especially as iron enters into the composition of the hemoglobin of the blood. However, recent studies have shown that it is impossible for the body to use the iron contained in spinach because it is present in a form not easily assimilated. Eating spinach is not recommended for those suffering from liver ailments or kidney stones, or uricemia, because of the oxalic acid present in the vegetable, which prevents the utilization of calcium. The calorific content of spinach is quite low and does not differ from that of other cooked greens. In the past

Swiss chard

spinach

common
saltwort

field poppy

it was given credit for its therapeutic properties: it was believed that it could cure diseases of the throat and of the respiratory system, as well as intestinal atony. But now, because of progress in the medical field, this theory has been abandoned. Today this plant is appreciated for its mineral substances which are thought to be good for convalescents. Those who have no health problems can enjoy spinach in many different ways as there are dozens of recipes for it: soufflés, soups, green lasagna, ravioli, puddings, omelets, tarts, croquettes, etc. Spinach with ricotta cheese cake is a great Italian delicacy. Recipes for spinach dishes are so numerous that it could be included in every part of a menu.

The **Field Poppy** (*Papaver rhoeas*) despite its leaves being slightly narcotic, can be cooked and seasoned like spinach, while the plant is still young, or be used as a herb for flavoring soups and salads. The same applies to the **Common Saltwort** (*Salsola kali*), also called sea grape and marsh samphire, which can be boiled when still young and tender. Early botanists used it to cure dropsy, and even leprosy.

Many centuries ago, before the introduction of spinach, **Goosefoot** (*Chenopodium bonus-henricus*), also known as good King Henry, or all-good, was much used in Europe, especially as a cure for scurvy. It was cooked either as spinach, the entire plant, except the roots, being used, or like asparagus, the peeled stalks being cooked.

Common in France and in the United States is another herb, **Purslane** (*Portulaca oleracea*) which can be added to soups and salads. It has fleshy leaves and brittle reddish stalks, with refreshing and diuretic properties. Culpeper employed it to cure venereal diseases, and, mixed with vinegar, linseed oil, and gall, to cure tension pains in the neck. This would certainly be cheaper than modern treatments prescribed for the effects of today's stresses, if one cared to risk it.

New Zealand spinach (*Tetragonia expansa*) is a summer vegetable. As its name suggests, it originated in the Antipodes. The leaves are eaten cooked and taste like the best varieties of spinach. They are a good substitute when the latter is not in season.

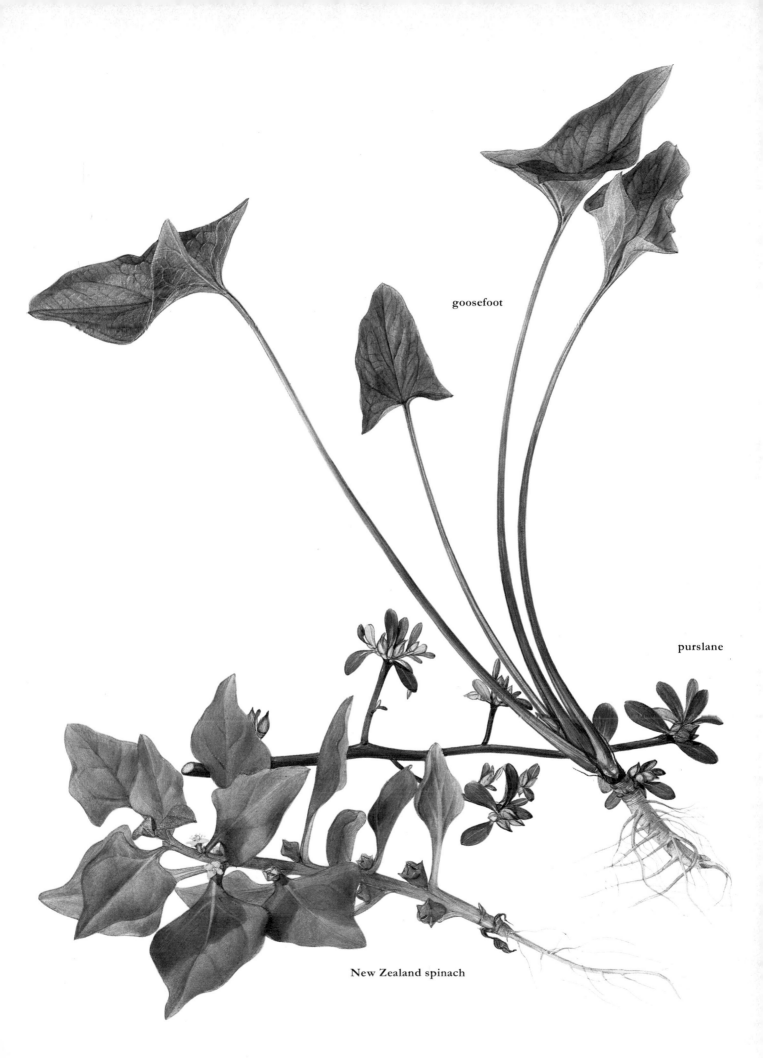

goosefoot

purslane

New Zealand spinach

Beetroot or Red beet

Beta vulgaris (var. *rapa*, form *rubra*), known as **Beets** in the United States, and called **Beetroot** in the British Isles, has been cultivated for many centuries and used not only as food for humans and animals, but also, as in the case of some varieties, for distillery purposes. It is also a medicinal and curative plant, believed three or four centuries ago to be an antidote against yellow jaundice and many other illnesses. The beets described by Horace and Cicero must have been vastly different from the ones used today. Those grown in Roman times were probably more appreciated for their leaves than for the rest of the plant. Our red beet, with the roundish root, cannot therefore boast a long history. Red beets in the wild state grow along the coasts of western Europe and North Africa. The plant is rather slender, and the cultivated varieties differ in the size and color of the root. The stem is so short and condensed that the leaves and the floral scape (the latter is formed during the second year) seem almost to grow out of the top of the root. The cultivated red beet originated in Germany and was then introduced into Italy around the fifteenth century. The yellow beet was favored first and only later was there an increase in the cultivation of the red beets that are the most used now. There are several varieties of red beets and they can be classified into three groups: (1) with round roots, as for example the Naples early with sweet and tasty pulp and wine-red color; (2) with flat-roundish root; (3) with long roots reaching sometimes up to 12 inches. The beets of the first group are the most popular as they are sweeter, tastier, and more tender. Red beets generally arrive on the market already cooked. When prepared at home, they should be neither cut nor peeled because the infiltration of water inside the root during cooking causes a loss of the nutritive substances and color. From a dietetic standpoint, the cooked beet contains up to 10% carbohydrates, mostly in the form of sucrose. This is a considerable amount, not found in other vegetables. The quantity of protein, between 1.5% and 2%, is good, the percentage varying in relation to the chemical composition of the soil and the different varieties analyzed. The high protein content makes the red beet one of the most valued vegetables. Beets also contain mineral salts, such as iron and calcium compounds. The calories supplied by $3\frac{1}{2}$ ounces (100 grams) of beets are 46, more than double the average of other vegetables. The amount of vitamins is, however, very low, and in the case of vitamin C it is reduced to less than half by cooking. The red beet can be regarded as a nutritious plant, although some find it rather indigestible. This depends on the manner of cooking and on the tenderness of the root. Because of the presence of sugar, the red beet is not advised for diabetics. Some excellent varieties for cultivation are: Crosby's Egyptian, Burpee Red Ball, Early Wonder, Detroit Dark Red, Burpee's Golden Beet, Dark Red Massy, Dark Red Globe Early and Dark Red Turnip-rooted Egyptian.

basal leaves

red beet

Onion

The **Onion**, perhaps even more than garlic, has a starring role in the kitchen. Its scientific name is *Allium cepa* and it belongs to the lily family (*Liliaceae*). Like the shallot, it has tubular leaves, that is, hollow inside, and belongs to the subgenus *Schoenoprasum*. The history of the onion is as old as that of garlic. It originated in central Asia (Iran, Baluchistan, Afghanistan), and was already known to the Chaldeans long before the beginning of the Christian era. In ancient Egypt it was so highly valued that it was an object of worship, and its consumption was immense, as it was in the Greek and Roman worlds. During the Renaissance the onion was often cited in the works of many physician-botanists of the time, from Fuchs to Lobel, to Pier Andrea Mattioli. Its popularity has never declined. Commercially, the classification of onions is very complex because of the large numbers of cultivars and the small differences between them.

There are several classes of onions, based on color of the bulb, place of origin (Bermuda, Spain), when harvested, and whether or not a bulb forms. Onions may be grown from directly sown seed, sets (small bulbs) or southern grown transplants.

Spanish onions are usually yellow, and include Yellow Sweet Spanish, Nutmeg, Ebenezer, Stuttgarter, Buccaneer, Yellow Globe Hybrid and Yellow Utah. Red onion varieties such as Red Bermuda, Ruby and California Early Red are popular for garden culture. Crystal white wax, White Sweet Spanish, Milan Coppery and White Portugal are typical white varieties. Stuttgarter and Ebenezer are the most popular varieties for growing from sets. There is also the Florence Long, with an elongated bulb, not much known outside the Continent.

Increasing in popularity in recent years are those onion varieties that are picked when very young or else do not form a bulb. These onions are called scallions or green or, in Britain, spring onions. For green onions, White Sweet Spanish, White Portugal, Japanese Bunching, Southport White Bunching and Evergreen Long White Bunching are excellent varieties. The green onions are picked when young and tender, with their leaves, and used as garnishes, in relish trays and in salads.

To weaken the flavor, which can be too strong, the pieces can be kept under water for a few minutes. Peeling the bulb under water will prevent the eyes from watering. The cooked onions can be used boiled or baked and seasoned with butter, to be used as a vegetable with meat or fish or in a sweet and sour sauce. The onion is often an important ingredient in soups and stews. The leaves of young onions or of sprouting bulbs can be used instead of being thrown away. Another use is to add a boiled and finely ground onion to meat loaf. Onion rings, floured and deep-fried, are excellent with steak. The young bulbs, or those from the small and flattened varieties, for example, the Italian *borrettane*, are also very suitable for pickling.

In old herbals it is recommended to mix the onion with vinegar in order to "take away all blemishes, spots and marks on the skin."

The chemical composition of the onion is as follows: solid residue, approximately 1%; protein, scarcely 1%; carbohydrates, about 6%; ash, around 2%. Onions produce 28 calories per $3\frac{1}{2}$ ounces (100 grams). From the dietary standpoint, the onion is not only a much valued flavoring, but is thought to be a diuretic and stimulant of the intestines. The vitamin content is modest.

Florence long

red onions

white onion

Milan coppery

small onions *or*
borrettane

Garlic
Shallot

At the mention of **Garlic** (*Allium sativum*) sensitive people might turn their heads away in disgust. This is more likely to happen in Anglo-Saxon than in Latin countries, where it is the king of herbs and is used extensively with meat, fish, and other vegetables. The Latin genus name, *Allium*, is probably derived from the Celtic word "all," meaning hot, burning, which is exactly the sensation that garlic produces on the palate. Among the several different hypotheses about the place of origin of garlic, the most likely is central Asia. Garlic has been known and cultivated in China from time immemorial and, according to Herodotus, was widely used by the ancient Egyptians. From Egypt it was introduced to the Greeks and Romans, with whom it was extremely popular, especially among the poor. Because of the tiny amounts used in cooking, it is unnecessary to report data on the very small content of protein and carbohydrates in garlic. This herb is used almost exclusively to season foods. Its aromatic properties are due to a crystalline amino acid called alliin contained in its oil that converts to allicin by enzymatic action, thus releasing the characteristic odor. Because of this essential oil, garlic has various properties: first, it is a purgative acting upon the liver and gall bladder; its use against intestinal worms has been known since very early times. Furthermore, it has considerable antiseptic properties which have recently been confirmed and recognized as due to allicin. In conclusion, besides being very important in the preparation of food, garlic is thought by many to be a truly medicinal plant; it is said to promote hypotensive and cardiovascular activity and a beneficial, soothing, antiseptic and expectorative action on the respiratory system. Pliny had great admiration for it, and believed it to be a cure for consumption. Mohammed recommended it as an antidote to the bites of snakes and scorpions. It was said to reduce lethargy, and Aristophanes told of athletes eating garlic before exercising in the stadium. Culpeper, who used it to cure almost everything, including the plague, advised that "it be taken inwardly with great moderation; outwardly you may make more bold with it," believing that it accentuated characteristics already present in a person's personality; "in choleric men it adds fuel to the fire; in men oppressed by melancholy, it will attenuate humour. . . ." Even today, health-food addicts and those who wish to see a return to nature believe that a cold will soon be cured if the soles of the feet are rubbed with cut cloves of garlic. This has been known to work, but the smell permeates everywhere. Wreaths of garlic hung outside the door were supposed to ward off witches in medieval times. It is now used a great deal pharmacologically.

In cookery garlic is often used raw, to be added, finely sliced, to salads or rubbed on slices of crusty bread which are then spread with oil or butter and eaten as fantastic but strong-smelling sandwiches. It is also used in many dishes and sauces, from the simple spaghetti to *osso bucco* (veal shanks). When adding it to food which is being fried in oil or butter it should be put in only at the last moment and not allowed to fry at all, as this would make the dish too pungent.

The **Shallot** (*Allium ascalonicum*) has never been found in the wild state; therefore its place of origin is unknown. It is very similar to the onion in the shape of the bulb and in the tubular leaves. De Candolle and other botanists believed it to be derived from the onion. The shallot was not known in ancient times. Its citation by Pliny derives from a wrong interpretation of a sentence of Theophrastus. Some more recent authors gave credit to the legend that the shallot had been brought to Europe by the Crusaders. The only sure fact is that it was known around the twelfth or thirteenth century. From the commercial viewpoint there are two types of shallot: the common shallot with pear-shaped bulb about the size of a walnut, and the Jersey shallot with more compressed bulbs, sometimes larger in width than in length. Its flavor is more delicate than the onion's and it is more easily digestible. It is used as a seasoning, and may also be preserved by pickling.

garlic

shallot

Leek
Grape hyacinth

Although Linnaeus considered it a "good species," today the **Leek** is commonly believed to be a variety (*porrum*) known only in cultivation, of *Allium ampeloprasum*, a species with all its different varieties widely spread throughout the Mediterranean region, in stony and arid terrains. Some types are believed to be native to some small Mediterranean islands, such as the *melitense*, typical of Malta, and the *hemisphericum*, typical of Lampedusa. It is thought by some botanists to be a cultivated variety of oriental garlic. The cultivated leek is generally a biennial plant. During the second year in the spring following the period of vegetative winter growth, it produces a large flowering scape, up to 3 feet in height, which bears on its top a beautiful globose inflorescence. Several cultivars are known: among them the Monster of Carentan, the very long winter (Paris), the very big Rouen leek, the long Mezières, Giant of Verrières and Broad London. The ancient Egyptians and the Romans used a perennial form of leek and it is said that the Emperor Nero ate leek soup every day to make his voice sonorous and clear for delivering orations, as the leek was believed to help the vocal cords. Ancient authorities, Camerario for one, showed that the plant, before reaching the present state of development, used to have a clearly distinct bulb, while now the bulb of *Allium porrum* is much less pronounced. The leek was cultivated all over France, particularly in Arras during the Middle Ages, and is still very popular there, while in Italy it is grown and valued only in the north, particularly in Piedmont and Lombardy. The leek is a vegetable for fall-winter-spring consumption, very good as an ingredient for soups and as a stewed side dish. Its nutritive value is modest (2% protein, 7% carbohydrates, traces of fats), but it is good from the dietetic point of view (although slightly indigestible for some) chiefly for its antiseptic and diuretic properties. It is an excellent appetizer when made into a quiche with narrow bacon slices rolled around each leek.

The use of the **Grape Hyacinth** (*Muscari atlanticum* or *Leopoldia comosa*) is characteristic of the cooking of the regions surrounding the Mediterranean, especially Greece. Today, however, it can easily be found in northern markets and is exported in quantity to North America, probably because of the large Italian population established there. The bulbs of the grape hyacinth, which constitute the edible part, have a slightly bitter flavor. It is necessary, therefore, to boil them in a large pot of water with a few drops of vinegar. Afterwards, they can be preserved, either pickled or in oil served as antipasto or as a relish. They are thought by many to have diuretic qualities and to be helpful in stimulating the appetite.

grape hyacinth   leek

Asparagus
Butcher's broom
Hop

The edible part of the **Asparagus** (*Asparagus officinalis*), a genus of the *Liliaceae*, is provided by the "spears" or young sprouts, very fleshy and tender, which are cut as soon as they grow to 6–9 inches. Cultivated asparagus is derived from a wild form still commonly found in sandy places, woods, and along river banks in south-central Europe, western and central Asia, and in northern Africa. The plants can be started from seeds, or, better, from the so-called "crowns," the subterranean stems (rootstocks) which are provided with a cluster of white, fleshy roots. The spears, always sold at very high prices, arise from the crowns in the following spring, or, because of forced growth, also in the fall and winter. Asparagus has a long historical record. Proof of its use in ancient Egypt has been found on old bas-reliefs. It was also used by the Greeks and Romans. Two hundred years before the Christian Era, Cato described its cultivation, which was not very different from that of today. Its use seems to have disappeared in the Middle Ages, except in Arab countries. It started again in Europe during the reign of the Sun King, Louis XIV of France, spreading especially in regions characterized by fertile and sandy soils where it grows best. Later, through repeated selections, asparagus has evolved from the forms still close to the wild species, with thin, green spears, to those with fleshier and larger spears, variously pigmented. The commercial names of asparagus are derived primarily from the places where it is intensively cultivated and from the color of the spears. So there are the Argenteuil asparagus, which is white and considered to be the best, the purple Holland asparagus, the white German asparagus, the Bassano del Grappa with green spears, the purple Genoa asparagus and the Mary Washington of America. Its uses in cookery are varied: to make soups (chopped or creamed), or more simply in the classical way, boiled, with the spears tied in a bunch in the saucepan with the tips above the water, and afterwards seasoned with butter and parmesan cheese or oil and lemon juice, or a Hollandaise sauce. They are often eaten with the fingers. Dietetically, asparagus has little nutritive value. The edible portion represents only 10%. Of this, the solid residue is approximately 14–15%. The protein content is less than 1%; the carbohydrates are about 6–7%, and there are no lipids. The calorific value is 52 calories per $3\frac{1}{2}$ ounces (100 grams). This is one of the most expensive vegetables to be found. As a substitute for garden asparagus the spears of *A. acutifolius*, which are very aromatic, can be used. This asparagus is sometimes preferred by gourmets because of its stronger flavor. It is excellent in omelets, or seasoned with oil and lemon juice. Another substitute is the pungent and rather bitter **Butcher's Broom** (*Ruscus aculeatus*), with narrow tapered points, or the shoots of the **Hop** (see p. 214).

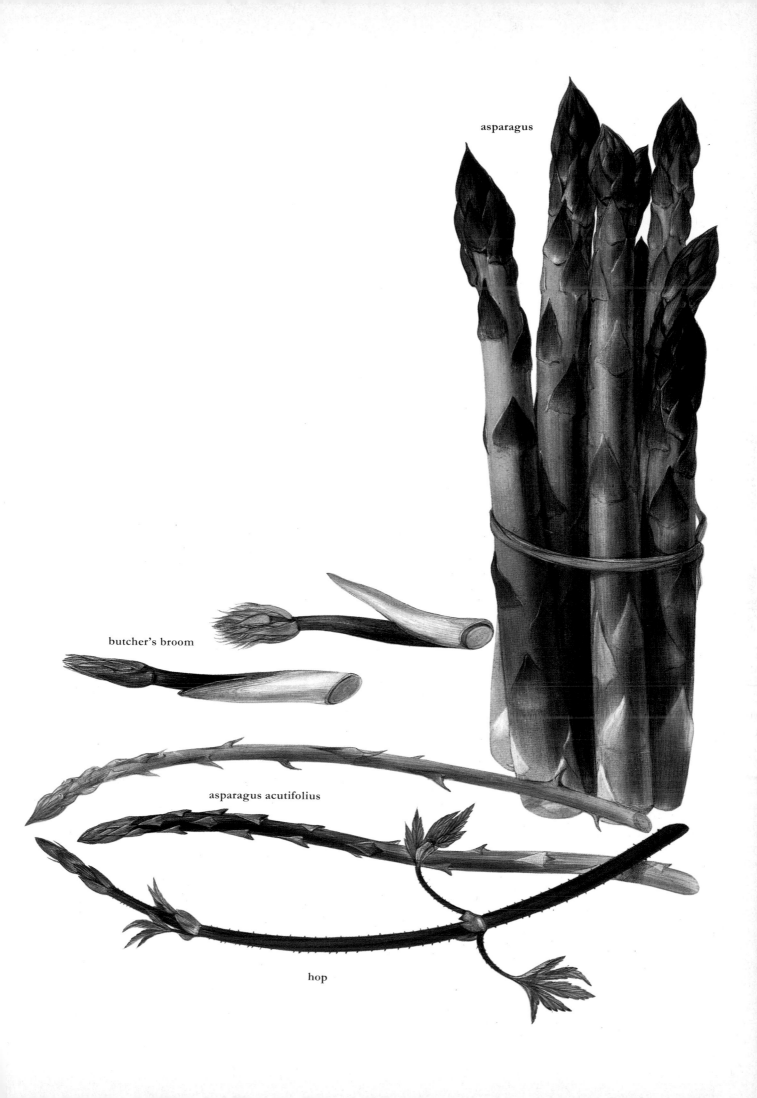

asparagus

butcher's broom

asparagus acutifolius

hop

Tomato

The **Tomato** originated in South America, but its botanical name *Lycopersicum esculentum* was once applied to an Egyptian plant, and only later transferred to the American fruit. The first names given to the tomato, in the sixteenth century, "Peruvian apple" or "Apple of Peru" would seem to indicate a Peruvian origin. Most botanists agree with the theory that Peru was an important area of early cultivation. The term "tomato" by which the plant is known in many European languages (French, Spanish, German, English), derives from an ancient Mexican word, *tomatl*. The more romantic French name of *pomme d'amour* that was given to the tomato when it first came to Europe, has remained as a little used synonym in English, "love apple." It was introduced into Europe by the Spanish and Portuguese, who used it as a vegetable. Its cultivation quickly spread throughout the Mediterranean and, more slowly, in the northern part of central Europe. In the second half of the eighteenth century, it was listed in the catalogs of a famous Parisian horticultural firm as an ornamental plant. Now, it is grown all over the world, and because of the highly refined techniques of hothouse cultivation, is available throughout the year at a relatively moderate price, compared with other out-of-season vegetables. The wild parental form is thought to be *Lycopersicum cerasiforme*, which grows wild in Peru, the Antilles, and Texas. The many cultivars known today are derived from this wild species through a long succession of hybridizations and selections. Commercially the large, round, smooth or ribbed tomatoes are suitable both for immediate use and for the canning industries, and the pear-shaped tomatoes, among them the classical San Marzano, are also good for the table or for canning, especially when peeled. However, the cherry tomatoes, strictly related to the *L. cerasiforme*, which represent the original form, have been little cultivated in the past, but are now becoming popular in the United States. These tomatoes have red or yellow skin when completely ripe. Golden Jubilee is one of the most widely used in the United States.

Among the large number of tomato cultivars some of the most popular ones are Burpee's Big Boy, Burpeeana Early, Beefsteak, Manalucie, Rutgers, Tropic, Valiant, Ramapo, Fireball, and Jetster. Presto, Small Fry, Basket Pak, Tiny Tim, Red Cherry, Yellow Plum and Yellow Pear are popular small-fruited tomatoes. The tomato can be eaten raw when still slightly unripe, as a salad flavored with a little garlic or a pinch of oregano, or cooked in many different ways. Commercially it is used to make tomato paste, catsup and tomato juice, which is widely drunk, both on its own, and mixed with alcohol. The raw tomato has a modest nutritive value, water representing the largest part of its weight, more than 90%; protein less than 1%; carbohydrates 4–5%, and ash 1%. The calories in $3\frac{1}{2}$ ounces (100 grams) are 23–24. From a vitamin standpoint $3\frac{1}{2}$ ounces (100 grams) of tomatoes provide 1 mg. of vitamin A, traces of thiamine and riboflavin, and a moderate amount of vitamin C (30 mg). The tomato is also easily digestible, and its bright color helps stimulate the appetite.

Prince Borghese

beef-heart tomato

salad tomato

San Marzano

yellow tomato

Eggplant or *Aubergine*

Eggplant (*Solanum melongena*) belongs to the *Solanaceae* (potato family) and is said to have originated in India. No wild plant, however, has ever been found, or if it has it is now unknown, so that the cultivated eggplant seems to be an improved form of either *S. insanum* or of *S. incanum*, both species being native to India. The existence of Sanskritic terms referring to this plant show that it has been known in India since very early times. Unknown to the Greeks and Romans, it appeared in Europe in the fourteenth century, probably via Africa, where its cultivation was supposedly introduced and spread in the Middle Ages. In the thirteenth century it was mentioned by an Arab physician. Furthermore, modern travelers now find the eggplant growing in the region of the Nile and in Guinea. From Europe its cultivation spread to America. Old documents show that it was cultivated in Brazil in 1658. In Italy the eggplant appeared toward the end of the fourteenth century, and by the fifteenth and sixteenth centuries had spread throughout the country. The classic areas of growth are around the Mediterranean, as a warm climate is needed, and it is therefore not well known in the north. It is still grown in the warm regions of India and also in Japan, and in North and South America. Its cultivation requires warmth and constant and abundant irrigation. In addition, the eggplant is very hardy and is not usually afflicted either by parasitic insects or disease. It is a perennial plant, but is cultivated as an annual, growing to about 24 inches; the stem is lignified at the base; the leaves coarse, ash-gray, whole or simply lobed, sometimes spinescent on the main rib. The flowers are star-shaped and very beautiful, of a typical blue-violet color, with five sepals and five petals and the stamens joined at the center of the corolla. The edible fruits are large berries, varying in shape from round to oblong, and in color from white to purple. They contain numerous seeds for which reason the fruit should not be allowed to become overripe; the fruit is attached to the plant by the fruit-stalk and the persistent calyx, both of which are often covered with sharp spines which can hurt one's fingers.

Eggplants can be cooked in numerous ways, but cannot be eaten raw. Two classic recipes for aubergines are "Ratatouille" from Provence, and "Imam Bayeldi" ("Swooning Imam") from Turkey. Ratatouille is a vegetable stew of coarsely chopped aubergines (eggplants), onions, zucchini, red and green pimentoes, garlic, and a few crushed coriander seeds, cooked in olive oil. To make Imam Bayeldi the aubergines are stuffed and simmered slowly for 3 hours in olive oil which should almost cover them. They are then left (with the lid still on the pan) to cool for 24 hours, and eaten cold as an hors d'œuvre. The story goes, that when his thousand wives served this dish to him, the imam swooned with ecstasy. It is certainly a delicious way to prepare eggplants. They can also be sliced, lengthwise or transversally, and breaded (or tossed in flour) and then fried. A very famous dish is eggplant parmesan, a combination of eggplant, tomato, cheese, and oil. Before cooking, sliced eggplants should be sprinkled with salt and left, covered, for 30 minutes to draw out the excess water. They must then be thoroughly dried in a cloth. Eggplants are not very nutritious, the solid residue being only about 8%. Protein 1%; carbohydrates 3%; no lipids. Some authorities claim that the unripe fruits may contain potentially dangerous amounts of solanine, and therefore should be avoided. However, this is not the normal practice. On the contrary, the young fruits which are much more tender than the ripe ones, taste far better. The cooking process is believed to eliminate the solanine.

Some of the better varieties are Barbentane eggplant, Giant New York eggplant and Chinese eggplant.

Naples early purple

white short eggplant

purple long eggplant

purple thick eggplant

eggplant flower

Pepper

The genus *Capsicum*, to which the **Pepper** belongs, is so called because its fruits resemble a box (Latin, *capsa*) which encloses the seeds; according to other authorities it is related to the Greek term *capto*, meaning "I bite," for the acrid and pungent flavor of the several varieties of fruits. As always there is a difference of opinion about the number of species that should be recognized within the genus. Some botanists tend toward a high number (24–25 species), but others, equally competent, suggest that the cultivated peppers should be ascribed to only two species: *C. annum* which includes the sweet table peppers, and *C. frutescens* which includes some of the varieties used for seasoning. Peppers originated in South America, probably Brazil, and have also been cultivated for several centuries in other parts of the American continent. They were introduced into Europe after the discovery of America. They are annual or perennial herbaceous plants, but woody at the base, of modest size, with typical dichotomic ramification, and leaves with long petioles. The flowers are formed by five white petals: the fruits are hollow berries of varying shape. It is in relation to the shape of the fruit that some botanists have proposed a classification, interesting commercially as well, which would subdivide the peppers into three groups of varieties: (1) peppers with smooth fruits and curved peduncles so that the fruits appear pendulous; (2) with more or less deeply lobed fruits and curved peduncles; (3) a group which includes forms and varieties with smooth fruits and erect peduncles. To the first group belong most of the peppers used as condiments, such as the various ordinary long red, or the similar cardinal, the Mexican long black (with long, very thin, red fruits), and the Cayenne pepper. The latter, however, is ascribed to the species *C. frutescens* or *C. fastigiatum* or *C. minimum*, a perennial species, but delicate, and unsuitable for growing in Mediterranean climates except in the southern regions. The first group also contains the cherry peppers known as *ceraselle* in southern Italy. Some authorities ascribe these to a separate species, *C. cerasiforme*. The varieties with curved peduncles and lobed fruits include almost all the sweet table peppers which can be divided into four groups; typically square fruits; fruits tapering, like a child's top, at the apex; long, conical fruits, sometimes smooth, and sometimes contorted; and finally, not illustrated since they are no longer cultivated much, the flattened peppers known as tomato peppers. Among the best known and currently favored cultivars are the various Nocera and Asti "square" types, with yellow or bright red fruits, and the new California Wonder, Yolo Wonder, and Midway, the latter very early and edible both unripe, when it is a bright dark green, and ripe, when bright red. Also excellent for their fragrant sweet aroma and their crispness are the long peppers of "bull horn" or "of Spain" type, and the top-shaped peppers, with particularly fleshy fruits. The third category includes forms with erect peduncles; this group includes the Chinese with conical yellow or red fruits, prized not only as a condiment but also as an ornamental fruit; the small "bunched" peppers with red, oblong, horn-shaped fruits; some other cherry peppers with spherical fruits but erect peduncles; the chili peppers, and many others. The very popular, ornamental forms also belong to this third category.

In the United States, Bellringer, Bell Boy, California Wonder, Merrimack Wonder, and Worldbeater are leading varieties of sweet or green peppers for salads, and to be cooked with various stuffings.

There are two very beautiful ornamental cultivars which have been grown in Italy: the *cornetto di corallo* (coral horn) with small, brightly colored, oblong fruits, and the *lampion* (lantern) whose fruits look very much like Chinese lanterns. Sweet peppers are eaten either raw, dipped in oil; in *pinzimonio*, an oil, salt and pepper sauce, or in salads separately, or mixed with other vegetables. They can also be cooked in many different ways: in combination with other vegetables, such as tomatoes, eggplants and onions, or in the very tasty Sicilian *caponata* with eggplants, olives, and capers; they can also be stuffed or fried. However, a classic recipe that brings

94

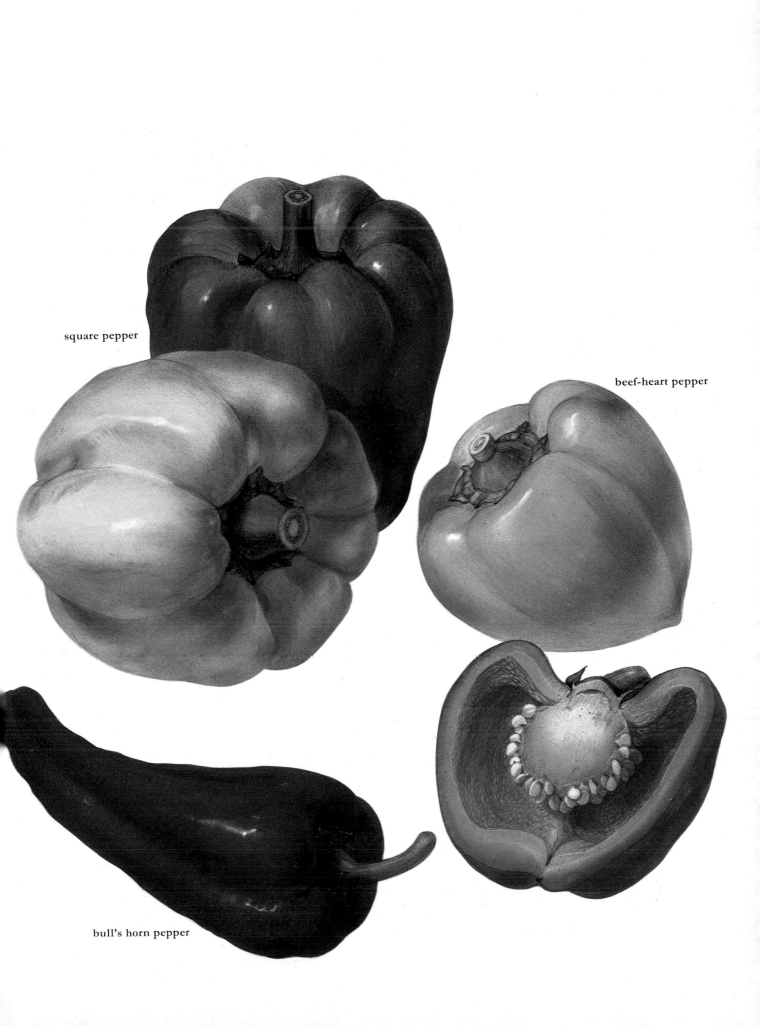

square pepper

beef-heart pepper

bull's horn pepper

out all the flavor characteristic of peppers is to charcoal broil them, then remove the membranous skin, and season them with a few drops of olive oil, and if desired, a little garlic. Peppers are also suitable for preserving in vinegar or, after boiling in water and vinegar, in oil. The best ones for this are the long green peppers, known commercially as "cigarettes," or the old cultivars, now hard to find, with very depressed fruits (tomato peppers). All the cultivars with particularly fleshy tissues are suitable for preserving. Nutritionally, sweet peppers (but to make sure that they are sweet they must be freed from the internal septa that have an acid and burning flavor) are low in calories, only 18 per $3\frac{1}{2}$ ounces (100 grams), because their solid residue is only 7–8%; it contains chiefly carbohydrates (3–4%). Both the protein and the ash are less than 1%; there are no lipids. Peppers contain vitamins A, B, C, and E. The small hot peppers are used exclusively as a condiment and for seasoning salami, meats, vegetables, and pasta. The pungent taste is due to the presence of an alkaloid called capsaicin. Hot peppers are considered to have a rubefacient and hyperaemic effect, and, eaten in moderation are said to be beneficial for the digestive system.

sweet red pepper

common long red pepper

hot red pepper

cherry pepper

Cayenne pepper

Celery
Celeriac
Parsley

If the great authors of classical Greek literature had not mentioned the humble **Celery** (*Apium graveolens*) in their works, it would be difficult to imagine that in ancient Greece it was considered worthy of crowning the heads of athletes. Another custom in Plutarch's time was to use celery for funeral wreaths. Celery only became a table vegetable during the Middle Ages, when specialized cultivations began to be organized on a large scale. Today celery is widely grown because of its many culinary uses. It does not provide many calories, although it is rich in mineral salts, vitamins, and, like parsley, iron. Raw celery, although agreeable to the taste, is not easily digestible. It is better served cooked, as it has considerable diuretic properties and is therefore helpful for those suffering from kidney stones, and for arthritic and nephritic conditions. It also has a favorable effect on the functioning of the bile. The various types can be grouped in two large categories: the common celery, in which the leaf stalk becomes extremely developed; and the **Celeriac** (*A. graveolens rapaceum*), called also German celery or turnip-rooted celery, in which the rootstock increases in size near the collar, becoming turnip-shaped, with the leaves almost lying on the ground. Among the most common varieties are the Stuffed White Pascal with short, large, full leaf stalks, very resistant to cold; Giant Pascal; American Stuffed White, very hardy, with very white stalks; the stuffed summer celery and the stuffed winter celery with very large, stuffed stalks; Fordhook and Golden Self Blanching. Among the various celeriacs two of the best are Verona Celery and Alabaster, which develop thick, tasty roots that keep well during the winter. The best roots are those of medium size, without secondary roots, and with a modest clump of leaves.

Parsley is an herb, known to the ancient Romans as is clearly indicated by its Latin genus name *Petroselinum*. During past centuries parsley was used more as a medicinal plant than as a garden vegetable. Today it is considered primarily as a seasoning or garnish for soups, salads and sauces. It has become almost indispensable, being used constantly in everyday cookery. It is rich in minerals, primarily iron salts, and, in a smaller degree, sulfur salts; also it is rich in vitamin C. Its most important properties, besides its functions as a seasoning, are its appetite-stimulating qualities. Among the most common cultivated varieties, the three best known are the common parsley with rather small but very aromatic leaves, Naples parsley with large leaves and thick stalks, and curly parsley with typically curly leaves, called Extra Curled Dwarf.

In medieval times parsley was thought to belong especially to the devil, and Good Friday was said to be the only day of the year on which it could be sown successfully, and then only if the moon is rising. There is an old country saying in England: "Only the wicked can grow parsley."

celery

celeriac

parsley

Coriander
Garden poppy
Caraway
Cumin
Dill

Coriander (*Coriandum sativum*) is an aromatic herb belonging to the parsley family (*Umbelliferae*). Its name, used by Pliny, comes from the Greek and means bedbug. It was given to this plant because of the odor produced by it when struck or broken. The coriander is grown for its seeds which must be dried out before use in order to lose the nauseating smell. These seeds, like those of the anise, can be used as an aromatic seasoning, and for the extraction of an essence for making liqueurs. The tender leaves give a pleasant aroma to certain types of salad, although care must be taken not to use too many.

The **Garden Poppy** belongs to the genus *Papaver* (*v.* p. 78), whose young plants can be used as a substitute for spinach when cooked. To the same genus belongs *Papaver somniferum*, commonly known as **Opium poppy**. This produces the dangerous drug, collected by incision of the still unripe fruits (capsules). Another variety of the opium poppy is the *hortense* whose seeds are used to flavor breads and cookies all over the world.

Caraway (*Carum carvi*) is another plant grown since ancient times for its seeds, which are used to flavor cakes, breads, cheeses, and soups. The latter are prepared with the young leaves of this plant. The distillation of the seeds yields an aromatic oil that produces the typical flavor of Kümmel liqueur.

The seeds of **Cumin** (*Cumin cyminum*), as well as other aromatic *Umbelliferae*, have been used for many centuries but today they are not so popular. They are mentioned in Saint Mark's Gospel, but their golden period was probably during the Middle Ages when they were highly valued as a spice for flavoring cakes and breads, especially among the Germanic peoples. In the Netherlands, they are still used to give a characteristic flavor to some typical cheeses. Cumin is also a fundamental ingredient of certain liqueurs and a seasoning for several types of pickled vegetables.

Dill (*Anetum graveolens*) is one of the plants used in both medicine and the kitchen since ancient times. Its seeds are used for seasoning pickles and vinegar; they can also be put into cakes, sauces, soups, and various other dishes as flavoring. The young leaves and the tenderest shoots are used in the same way and also to add zest to salads and cooked dishes. The young stems can be eaten raw, when seasoned with oil, salt and pepper.

coriander

póppy

caraway

cumin

dill

Fennel
Chinese or *Star Anise*

Fennel was widely known in ancient Greece, and the name of a region, Marathon, where it grew profusely, was derived from the Greek name for fennel, *marathon*. There is even earlier information about this plant of the parsley family, in a papyrus dating back to 1500 B.C. A description of fennel can also be found in the works of Pliny, who described it as a medicinal, rather than a food plant, which, together with other essences, was used in an infusion for the eyes. However, not until the sixteenth century could some small and sparse cultivations of this sweet-smelling herb be found in Europe, particularly in central and southern Italy. Today a wild fennel (*Foeniculum officinale*) is recognized as native to the Canary Isles and naturalized for several centuries around the Mediterranean, and also a sweet fennel (*F. vulgare*) whose taste has made it one of the most popular garden vegetables. The wild fennel, known in England as Florence fennel, is mostly used in liqueurs and pharmaceutically. The roots and seeds of the wild variety have diuretic and digestive properties, and the seeds are also used for the extraction of an essential oil. Sweet fennel, besides being used for its seeds, and eaten in large quantities as a condiment or a source of the essential oil, may also be eaten raw or cooked as a vegetable. The edible portion is provided by the leaves and the white and fleshy bulbous stem. Sweet fennel has little nutritive value, having almost the lowest number of calories of any vegetable. Carbohydrates, protein and lipids hardly reach 1% each. Vitamin C is also scarce, while there are only traces of vitamin B_1 and niscin. Fennel is essentially composed of water, cellulose, and a volatile oil, anethole, diffused in the entire plant and particularly in the seeds. It is therefore because of its fragrance and flavor that this plant is considered to be so appetizing and refreshing, to such a degree that its use, once confined to Italy, is now spreading across the Continent and even farther afield. All types of fennel can be eaten raw or cooked, and in the latter case they should be briefly parboiled to make them more tender and digestible. After being drained, they can be stewed with butter, or served *au gratin*. Fennel is thought to act as a stimulant, a tonic, a digestive, and an appetizer.

An interesting species of the magnolia family is the **Star** or **Chinese anise** (*Illicium anisatum*). It is native to the Far East where its cultivation still flourishes, particularly in China. Its fruits are believed to have therapeutic properties due, partly, to a volatile oil, containing anethole, which may have a sedative effect on the nervous spasms caused, for example, by coughs and asthma. The fruits are used in liqueurs, especially anisette, an ancient liqueur which is still very popular.

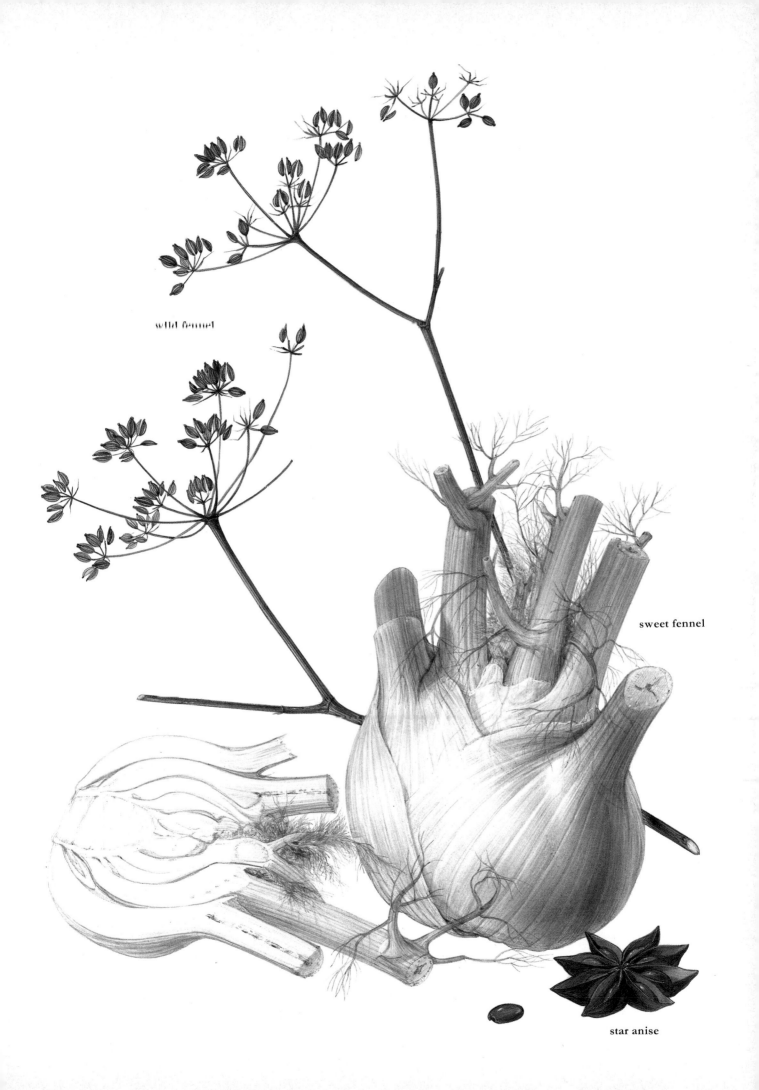

wild fennel

sweet fennel

star anise

Carrot
Sea fennel

The uses of the **Carrot** for food date to the sixteenth century when some better varieties were obtained from the wild form. Before that, going back to the Greeks and Romans, this species grew wild in scattered locations and was listed among the medicinal essences. At the present time the carrot is an important garden vegetable as shown by the continuously growing number of cultivars recently introduced. *Daucus carota* botanically belongs to the *Umbelliferae* (parsley family). In cultivation it is considered an annual plant, but its natural cycle is really biennial. This means that the root is developed during the first year, while flowers and seeds are produced during the second year. As is known, the edible part of the carrot is supplied by the conical, thick and fleshy root. The very numerous cultivated varieties are divided into two large groups: according to either the color of the root (red, yellow or white) or its size (short, medium or long). Undoubtedly, the best quality carrots are the orange-yellow ones of medium or short size. Their market value depends upon the development of that characteristic internal, hard and woody part, called "heart," which is practically inedible; the less developed the heart, the more prized the carrot. Some of the best cultivars today are Goldinhart, Nantes Half-Long, Danvers Half-Long, Gold Pak, Burpee's Oxheart, Royal Chantenay, and Little Finger. Carrots are used in the kitchen throughout the year in many varied ways. They can be eaten either raw or cooked, alone or together with other vegetables. They are often used in vegetable soups and make an excellent base for various sauces. Carrots have considerable medicinal and nutritive properties, having a large amount of sugar and being rich in vitamins, particularly in alfa-beta-gamma carotene, which is responsible for the typical coloration. The beta carotene, also called provitamin A, is transformed into Vitamin A, thus becoming part of the growth vitamins. The beta-carotene content of one pound of carrots is about $4\frac{1}{2}$ times the minimum daily requirement of the human body. There is a considerable amount of vitamins B_1 and C, which helps to increase the body's resistance to certain illnesses. Carrots also contain an essential oil, rich in vitamin E and carbohydrates. Conversely they are low in protein and lipids. Cut, dried, and roasted, carrots can be used as a coffee substitute. When fresh, they can be squeezed to obtain a drink similar to tomato juice, and in India are used to make small, sweet cakes.

Sea Fennel (*Crithmum maritimum*) also belongs to the *Umbelliferae* (parsley family). This species can often be found growing wild on the seashore along the Mediterranean and along the European coasts of the Atlantic. Today, sea fennel has appeared among cultivated vegetables, although its consumption is, at present, still limited. The edible part is supplied by the leaves which, cut into small pieces, have a flavour vaguely reminiscent of that of fennel, but more bitter and brackish. They are generally used with oil and vinegar to prepare an agreeable salad dressing.

carrot

sea fennel

Crookneck squash
Chayote
Yokohama squash

The collection of squashes, pumpkins, and other plants of the gourd and melon family (*Cucurbitaceae*) in this and in the following plates, may seem profuse. However, the sometimes curious variety of forms and bright hues of the plants of this family makes an interesting and colorful display. The species of the genus *Cucurbita*, belonging to the *Cucurbitaceae* are herbaceous plants of great size, with long, vinelike shoots bearing tendrils. *Cucurbita* plants are monoecious, that is, with unisexual flowers borne on the same plant: the staminate (male) flowers have a five-lobed, campanulate corolla, golden yellow, with three stamens united by their anthers; the solitary pistillate (female) flowers, have an inferior or semi-inferior ovary in the varieties *turbaniformis* or *pileiformis*, formed by three carpels and with a short, three-lobed style. The fruit, like that of the other plants of the gourd family, is a large berry, sometimes with a very tough skin or rind, called more specifically a "pepo." Within the cultivated forms of the genus *Cucurbita* are distinguished four principal species as follows:

Malabar squash (*C. ficifolia*), a perennial plant of large size, with black seeds, grown only in the tropical regions, usually for ornamental purposes.

Crookneck squash, cushaw, Canada crookneck squash (*C. moschata*), with flabby leaves, and with the calyx tube very short or not present.

Winter squash (*C. maxima*), with stiff, round-lobed leaves, and with the calyx tube campanulate.

Pumpkin (*C. pepo*), with deeply lobed leaves.

An important feature distinguishing *C. maxima* from *C. pepo* is provided by the peduncle which is cylindrical in the former while it is particularly short, obtuse, and many-sided in the latter. The illustration shows two interesting forms, one well known with long, club-shaped fruits; the other, less common, with round and depressed fruits, of *C. moschata*, winter crookneck squash. The terracotta color of the rind is typical of these squashes, as is, in the sectioned fruit, the orange color of the flesh and the characteristic neck stuffed with a compact tissue, while the spongy tissue containing the seeds is limited to the upper part. The upper part is so named because, in interpreting the parts of a fruit, the original position of the ovary from which the fruit is formed must be remembered. These forms of *C. moschata* are best when fried in oil or baked. Their fine, silky pulp makes them unsuitable for boiling. In recent years a new cultivar of *C. Moschata*, the butternut squash, has become popular in the United States.

The **Chayote** (*Sechium edule*) is a strange vegetable, also of the *Cucurbitaceae*. It is a perennial, climbing plant, with shoots sometimes several yards long. The fruit, spiny outside and of the size of a large pear, contains only one seed which has the unusual property of germinating while still inside the fruit. The composition of the chayote is similar to that of zucchini: 90–92% water, 1% protein, 3–4% carbohydrates, and traces of lipids. The culinary uses are also similar, but more varied. The chayote can be stewed, stuffed, fried, boiled, or cooked in many other ways. It is also possible to use the young shoots in the same manner as asparagus, and even the tuberous roots, rich in starch, formed by plants living in regions where they behave as perennials, are edible.

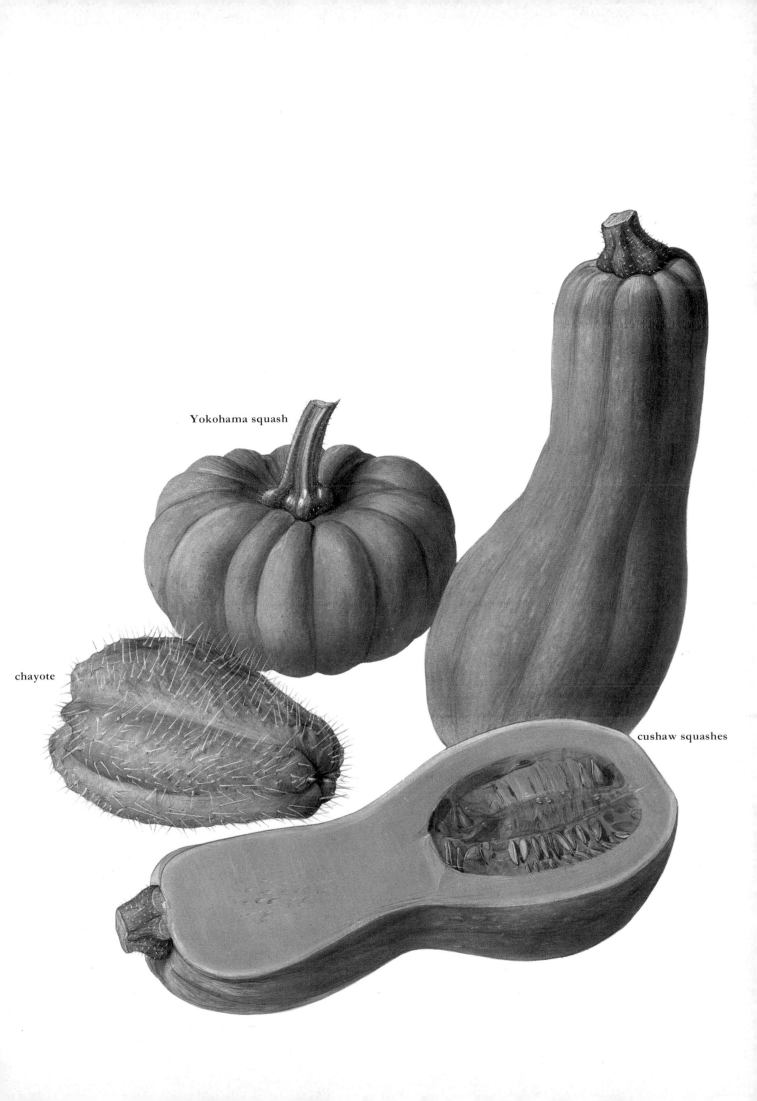

Yokohama squash

chayote

cushaw squashes

Naples stuffed squash
Scallop gourd
Bottle or Club-shaped gourd

This illustration shows another typical and well-known representative of *Cucurbita moschata*, the **Naples squash**, whose cultivation is very common in southern Italy and other Mediterranean regions. As can be seen from the plate, this is another cultivar that produces cylindrical fruits, but stouter and less club-shaped than the preceding forms, and with different colored skin: bronze, or greenish, or brightly variegated. The flesh is a beautiful orange-yellow, even brighter than those in the previous illustration. The uses and nutritional attributes of the Naples squash are the same as those already described for the other forms of *C. moschata*. It is quite good in soups, but, because of its sweetish flavor it is advisable not to use a great amount. The largest fruits of this squash can reach up to nearly one yard in length and 10 pounds in weight.

Also shown, more as a matter of curiosity and a colorful addition than for their interest as edible fruits, are two representatives of *C. pepo*, to be eaten only when completely ripe. Certain cultivars of *C. pepo* that are commonly known as summer straightneck and crookneck squash are very popular and appetizing vegetables. The **Scallop gourd** (*C. pepo* var. *melopepo*), a polymorphic species, is interesting for its ornamental uses. Some cultivars of *C. pepo melopepo* are known as pattypan or custard squashes, and are also excellent baked or boiled, and mashed with butter.

A similar use can be made of the young fruits of the known forms of *Lagenaria*, the **Bottle gourd**. In the past these fruits were used to make bottles and gunpowder flasks; today they are used exclusively as ornaments. The fruits of *Lagenaria vulgaris* of the *Cucurbitaceae*, the so-called bottle gourd or **Club-shaped gourd** (*cocozzelle*) are very popular because of the varieties of their shapes and colors: some are metallic green, others have dark green variegations. This is not, however, the same plant as the cocozzelle bush squash or Italian marrow of the United States which is a form of true zucchini. The dry fruits can be decorated with paints or by fire branding. The unripe fruits can be eaten, stewed, or added to soups; the variety *cougourda*, with long, tapering fruits, is particularly suitable for this use. The bottle gourd is also useful for decorating and shading patios and arbors.

bottle gourd

Naples stuffed squash

Naples stuffed squash

winter crookneck squash

scallop gourd

Brazilian pumpkin
American pumpkin
Ohio or *Hubbard squash*

This plate illustrates a further assortment of varieties together with representatives of *Cucurbita maxima*. The two forms of *C. pepo*, the **Crookneck squash** and the **Brazilian pumpkin**, should be eaten when fully ripe, and therefore can be stored, although not for too long, for the fall and winter seasons. Both can be stewed or, more generally, cooked in the same way as chayote (*Sechium edule*).

In the United States there is a winter form of *C. pepo* called the acorn or Des Moines squash. It is 4″–6″ long and 3″–4″ thick with a dark green ribbed skin. It is often cut in half and baked and served as a side dish. Table Queen and Table King are good cultivars of this variety.

Much more interesting is the cultivar of *C. pepo* commonly called **American pumpkin**, although it is in Italy that it is most cultivated. Its uses and culinary qualities are similar to those of *C. moschata*. Pumpkin cultivars are much in demand for making the famous American pumpkin pie, and are also used at Hallowe'en, for the making of jack-o'-lanterns.

In the plate are also shown some specimens of winter squash (*C. maxima*) with roughly tapered or spherical shapes. Squashes are easily hybridized, so that the range of colors and forms that can be obtained is very wide and it is difficult to tell one variety from another. Some of these tapering or oval squashes are ascribed to the variety *ohioensis* and are commonly called **Hubbard** or **Ohio squashes**.

The stouter and roughly spherical specimen pictured in the center of the illustration could also be considered as one of the Mammoth squashes or Whale pumpkins, often of very large size; they can weigh more than 25–30 pounds. Because they have less flavor and a very watery consistency, they are used almost exclusively to feed livestock.

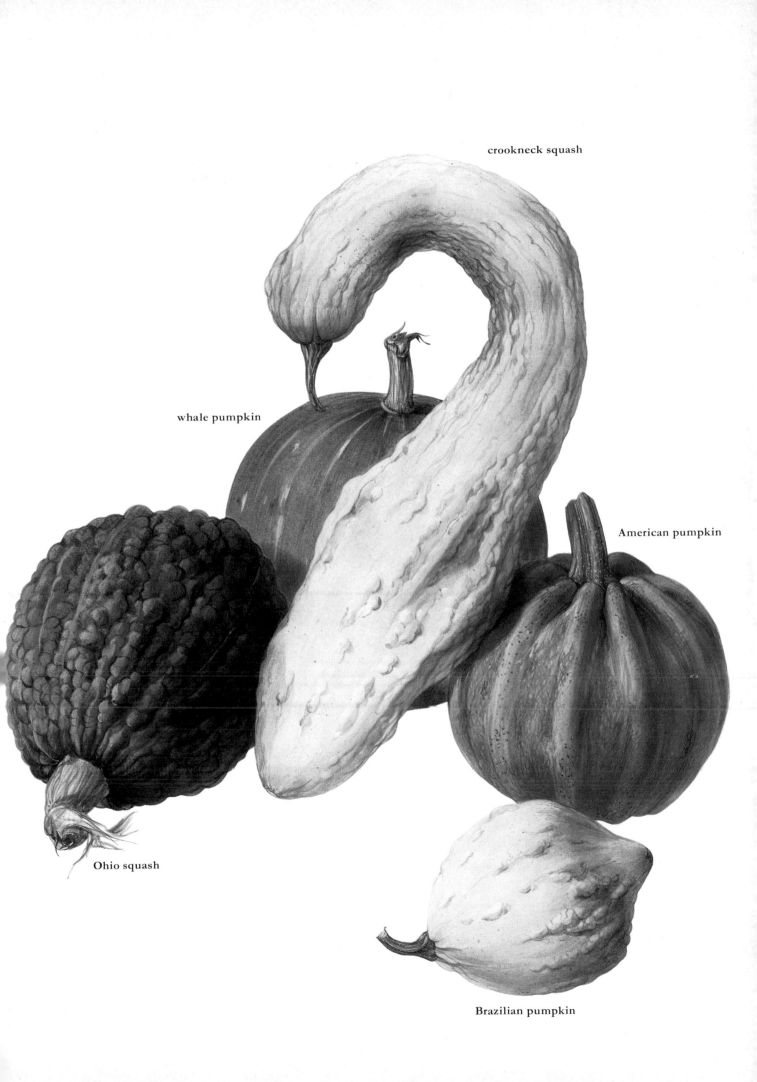

crookneck squash

whale pumpkin

American pumpkin

Ohio squash

Brazilian pumpkin

Sea or Chioggia squash
Turban squash

In this plate, in addition to a third specimen of the category of the Hubbard or Ohio squashes, some of the most classic and best known examples of *Cucurbita maxima* are shown: the characteristic **Sea** or **Chioggia squash**, with a typical coarsely wrinkled rind, generally metallic gray or greenish, and the equally distinctive **Turban squashes** (var. *turbaniformis* or *pileiformis*). In the last few years a form of turban squash with rather small and brightly colored fruits, the expanded part bright red, and the tapering part lemon yellow, has become very popular as ornamentals. The sea squashes have very mealy flesh, good for various recipes: they can be boiled, baked or puréed, and also used in minestrone soups, and an unusual risotto. Sometimes the unripe fruits of these squashes can be used in relishes and preserves.

The area of cultivation of squashes and pumpkins is vast and embraces all the warm regions of the world. In the past, squashes were in great demand among poorer people and in country areas, but now they are thought little of. This is a pity as they are inexpensive vegetables, and very digestible. They are simple to prepare. Squashes contain almost 95% water, 3–4% carbohydrates, traces of protein and lipids.

another Ohio squash

sea *or* Chioggia squash

turban squashes

Zucchini or *Courgette*

Zucchini (*Cucurbita pepo*) belong also to the *Cucurbitaceae*. In Britain they are called **Courgettes**. Their fruits are eaten when unripe, and since the younger ones are preferred they are often sold still bearing the corolla. Zucchini are annual herbaceous plants with sturdy running stalks which can easily grow up to 3–4 feet or more in length. The leaves, large, hispid, wrinkled, and lobed, are supported by long, thick, completely hollow petioles. Like the majority of *Cucurbitaceae*, zucchini bear staminate and pistillate flowers separately on the same plant. They are therefore monoecious plants with unisexual flowers. The pistillate (female) flowers have small ovaries just behind the flower that develops into the fruits. The staminate (male) flowers have large and showy corollas with petals fused together, and are a beautiful golden-yellow color. They can be distinguished from the pistillate flowers because they have longer and thinner peduncles and, of course, no ovaries. These flowers are sometimes sold in continental markets in little bunches. They are good dipped in a batter of milk and flour and then fried. The fruits of the cultivars used when still unripe, called by the Italian name, zucchini, are for the most part smooth and cylindrical, sometimes also globular. They are in general, uniformly dark or light green; but some cultivars are variegated; among these is the so-called "Italian striated." Some botanists, including Naudin, have subdivided the polymorphic category of the exponents of *C. pepo* into seven groups. Today, within the zucchini, there are numerous, very popular cultivars. Some of the best known are the Apulia striated, the green round, the Bolognese or the Faenza gardener with long ovoid fruits; various new American varieties with cylindrical, dark green fruits, such as the Ambassador, the various Black Jack, Store's Green, Super Diamond, and others. Dietetically, zucchini are highly recommended. Boiled and seasoned with oil and lemon juice they are easily digestible and therefore good for convalescents or people on strict diets. The solid residue of zucchini is 6%; a small amount of protein, no lipids, carbohydrates 2–3%, ash 1%. There are only 8 calories in $3\frac{1}{2}$ ounces (100 grams). Zucchini are thought to have a considerable diuretic action and to be effective against constipation because of the mucilage they contain. If the thought of boiled zucchini seasoned only with oil and lemon juice appears unappetizing, the numerous other ways in which they can be prepared must be remembered. They are very good after being dipped in batter or in egg and bread crumbs and fried; stuffed; stewed separately or with other vegetables such as eggplants, tomatoes, potatoes, peppers, etc. A typical dish of southern Italy is *tenerume*: the very young shoots, together with flowers and leaves, are picked, cleaned, boiled and then sautéed with garlic and chili pepper.

zucchini flower

Ambassador zucchini

green round zucchini

Cucumber

The **Cucumber** (*Cucumis sativus*) is another member of the *Cucurbitaceae*. Some botanists believe it to be a close relative of the watermelon. Like other plants of the *Cucurbitaceae*, the cucumber is an annual herbaceous plant, with branching and angular stems, palmate three- to five-lobed leaves, and the tissues generally rough and hispid to the touch. The flowers, unisexual, are borne at the axil of the leaves and are greenish yellow in color. The edible portion of the plant is given by the unripe fruits that have the same general characteristics as the fruits of other plants of the *Cucurbitaceae*. They are large berries, with a hard epicarp when ripe, and are more properly called "pepo." In particular, the cucumber fruits have a typical elongate shape, rounded at the extremities, and are often provided with hispid, superficial tubercules. According to several authorities, including Naudin, who devoted his career to the study of the *Cucurbitaceae*, the cucumber, although never found in the wild state, is native to India, and, more extensively, to tropical Asia. It is one of the food plants used by Oriental populations for more than three thousand years; one proof of this long use is, for example, its Sanskrit name, *soukasa*. From the Far East the cucumber came to eastern Europe many centuries ago. Its presence in ancient Egypt is the subject of some controversy. According to some botanists it was already there at the time of the Twelfth Dynasty. It is mentioned in the Bible, and it is believed that the Hebrews imported it from Egypt to the Promised Land, where it became one of their most popular foods. It was known to the Greeks and was used extensively by the Romans. Tiberius was extremely fond of cucumbers. Columella described their cultivation in his book *De re rustica*. The cultivars of cucumbers used in the past were numerous, from the "Russian cucumber" with small, smooth, ovoid fruits, and the Holland Yellow, with elongate fruits, to the various long green, and the small Paris Green which are particularly suitable for pickling. At present, agricultural trends toward large monocultures of garden vegetables have also affected the cucumber, especially in relation to the earliness of the crop and the resistance to parasites. Many of the old cultivars have disappeared, with the exception of Paris Green, and have been replaced by new cultivars, such as Victory, Ohio MR 17, Sunnybrook, Pioneer, Marketer, West Indian Gherkin, Straight Eight, Marketmore 70, China (Kyoto), and Mariner (all female).

Cucumbers are almost always eaten raw, and rather unripe. The very young fruits, used whole, are suitable for pickling, but mature fruits may also be used in this way. They are usually eaten in salads, but in some Slavic countries they are cooked in various ways with meat. From the standpoint of food value the cucumber is very rich in water and is therefore a most refreshing vegetable, but almost completely lacking in nutritive value: the amount of nitrogen compounds is less than 1%; lipids are almost completely lacking, and carbohydrates are scarce (2–3%). It has some vitamin C, thiamin, and riboflavin. Among the good and bad qualities of this vegetable, it should be added that it is found by some people to be very indigestible.

cucumber

Morel
Truffle

Morels and **Truffles**, while not true mushrooms, will be considered together for the purposes of this discussion since they have many of the same characteristics and uses. Technically, true mushrooms are *Basidiomycetes* (club fungi) and the mushroom itself is the "fruit," a basidiocarp. The morels are therefore not mushrooms. The edible, above-ground portion is an ascocarp and so they belong to the sac fungi, the *Ascomycetes*. This is also true of *Tuber* species (truffles) and *Helvella*, called the "false morels."

Morels are provided by "fruiting bodies" or macroscopic portions of the mushroom which are collected and used, and which are often identified with the entire mushroom while they actually represent only a fleeting, although important stage in the plants' life cycle. Mushrooms have another, more perennial and obscure life, in the form of "mycelium," a tangle of very thin, microscopic filaments, extending underground, particularly in the genus *Morchella*, but also in the less known and less rich *Mithrophora* and *Verpa*. The best-known species of the genus *Morchella* (morel) are: *M. deliciosa*, *M. rotunda* or *esculenta* (yellow morel), *M. conica* (brown morel), and *M. vulgaris*. Other morels of the genus *Mithrophora* and *Verpa* are: *M. hybrida*, *V. bohemica*, *V. digitaliformis*, *V. agaricoides*, and *V. fulvo-cincta*.

Although they are usually thought of as something exotic and esoteric, **Truffles** are nothing but mushrooms that produce their fruiting bodies underground. They have a symbiotic relationship with such trees as the hazelnut, beech, poplar and willow. Morels and truffles cannot be cultivated in the same way as mushrooms. At best, their diffusion may be helped by planting acorns which have been collected under oak trees around which truffles are found.

These acorns stand a good chance of being "contaminated" with truffle spores, so there is a strong probability that truffles will form around the little oak plants that will develop from these acorns. Truffles are found with the help of specially trained dogs and, in some areas, hogs. The best known truffles are: (1) the white or Alba truffle (*Tuber magnatum*), so called because it is considered worthy of the *magnati*, that is, the very rich. It is found only in Italy, in Piedmont (Langhe and Monferrato) and in Emilia (in the Apennines in the Parma, Modena, and Bologna area), and universally considered the best among the truffles; (2) the black truffle, or Spoleto or Norcia truffle (*T. melanosporum*), found in France, especially in the Garonne and known therefore as *Truffe de Périgord*; in Spain, in Germany (Baden) and in Italy in Piedmont, Lombardy, Trentino, and in the Apennine areas of Umbria and the Marches. Other, but less valued truffles are *T. mesentericum*, *T. aestivum* (red-grained black truffle), and *T. borchii*. No American species is considered edible. The white truffle has a penetrating, slightly garlic-smelling odor. It is very good raw, and excellent, sliced very thin, for flavoring risotto, pasta, meats, eggs, cheese fondues, and especially as "truffles parmesan." The black truffle, however, is best cooked: for example, in *tartufi alla nursina* in which the truffles are finely sliced in layers with cheese and butter, seasoned with basil, nutmeg, oregano, and bay leaves, and then baked. They are also used to flavor many pâtés. Truffles should never be washed or peeled. If it is necessary to wash them, it should be done in dry white wine. To preserve them for a few months, they should be put, covered with white wine, into hermetically sealed glass jars, and boiled for two hours.

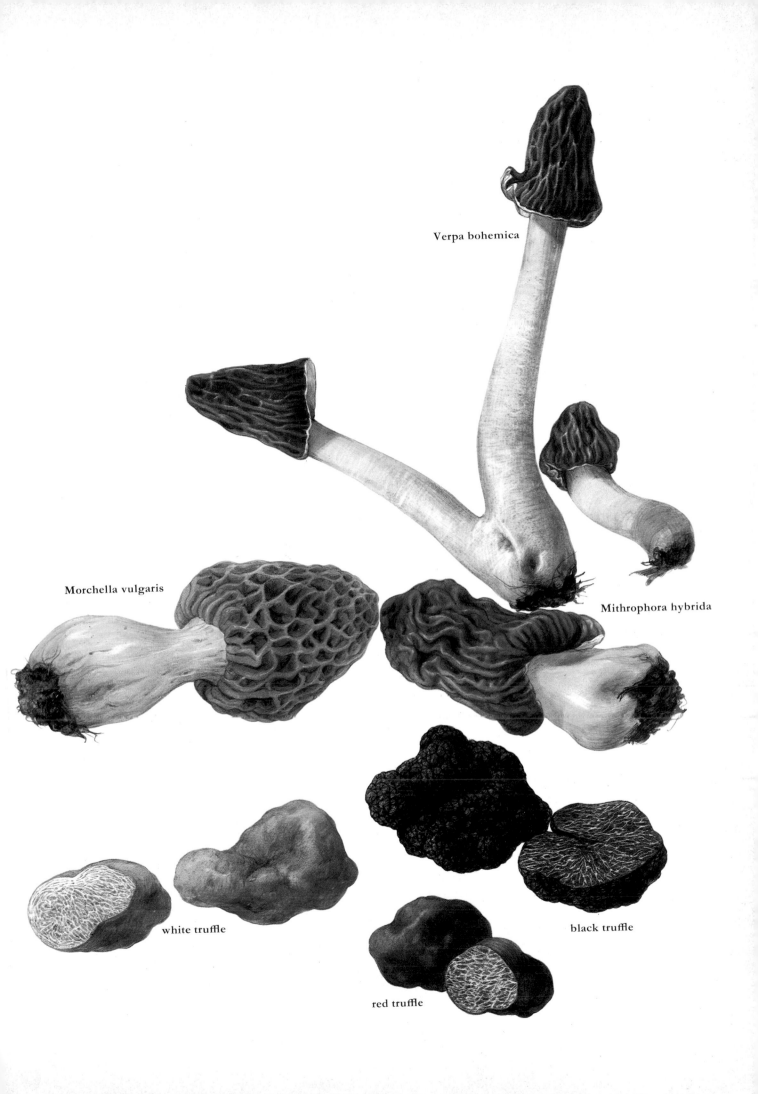

Verpa bohemica

Morchella vulgaris

Mithrophora hybrida

white truffle

black truffle

red truffle

Caesar's mushroom
Field mushroom

Caesar's mushroom (*Amanita Caesarea*), so called because it is considered worthy of an emperor, is undoubtedly, with truffles and the boletus, among the best mushrooms available. Its price is always high. This mushroom is easily recognizable, at least when completely developed. It could possibly be confused with the poisonous *Amanita muscaria* although they differ in color (which is brighter in *A. muscaria*, except under heavy rains), and *A. muscaria* also has numerous warts on the cap. To these characteristics, which unfortunately are not completely clear-cut, it must be added that in *A. muscaria* the stem and gills are white and not sulfur yellow as in *A. caesarea*. The volva is not large and membranous but reduced to a series of circular scales. When the fruiting bodies are very young and still completely enveloped in the universal veil, it is essential to tear off part of this veil to be sure that the color of the cap is the beautiful warm color of *A. caesarea* and not the greenish or white of the deadly *A. verna* and *A. phalloides*. Caesar's mushroom is widely distributed in Europe, Asia and Africa. It can be found in the roots of broadleaved trees, and appears in the late summer and in the fall. It was certainly known and used by the ancient Greeks and Romans. Like the truffle, the boletus, and others, it is a symbiotic mushroom, whose mycelium forms an association, known as mycorrhiza, with the roots of the tree; therefore it cannot be artificially cultivated. Caesar's mushroom can be eaten in many ways, either raw as a salad after being marinated in lemon juice for four hours, or it can be stewed or broiled. For the latter recipe the caps are stuffed with a mixture of finely minced mushroom stems, onion, parsley, bread crumbs, salt, and pepper. Add oil and some curls of butter and cook at a low heat for about fifteen minutes.

The **Field mushroom** (*Psalliota hortensis*, *P. campestris*, *P. arvensis*), although easily recognizable, can sometimes be confused with the poisonous *Amanita verna*, but if it is remembered that *A. verna* always bears a volva which is lacking in the *Psalliota*, lethal mistakes will be avoided. Furthermore, in *Psalliota* the color of the gills is shaded from rose to brown and the spores are dark purple, while in *Amanita* the gills and spores are both white. Unlike the symbiotic truffle, field mushrooms are saprophytes, that is, organisms living at the expense of dead substances such as straw, vegetable wastes, and manure. Because of this they can be artificially cultivated in airy caves, cellars or sheds, and on substrata such as horse manure. This is why field mushrooms are so abundant and available on the market all the year round. They can also be eaten raw but only if the very young fruiting bodies are used. They may be stewed, sautéed, or preserved in oil.

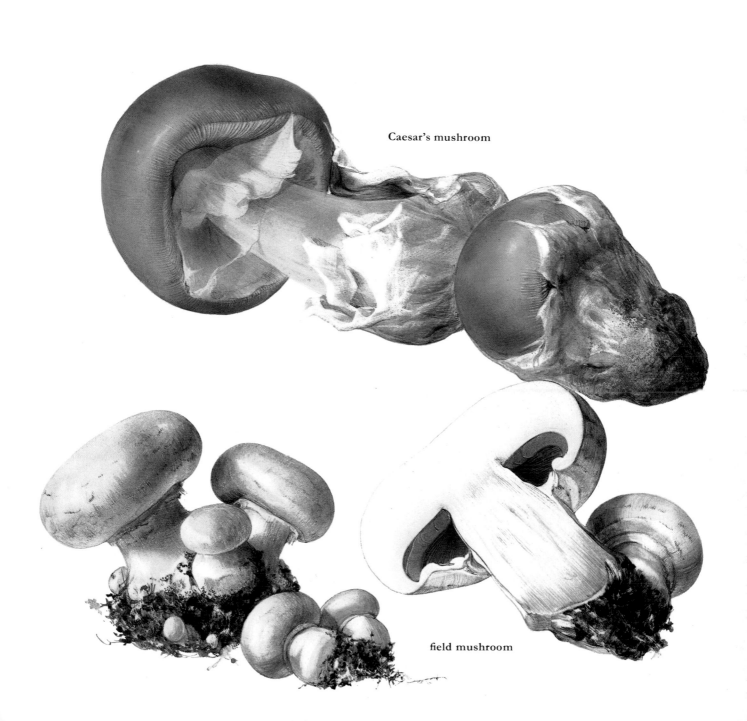

Caesar's mushroom

field mushroom

Parasol mushroom
Chanterelle
Horn of plenty

The **Parasol mushroom** (*Lepiota procera*) is common in many different habitats, woods, pastures, meadows, etc., particularly if the soil is sandy. It is practically cosmopolitan. It appears in summer and during the fall, especially in October. This is a most elegant looking mushroom, and the largest known. It can reach a height of 15–16 inches with a cap diameter of 8 inches. The name *Lepiota* comes from *lepis*, squama or scale, because the cap is covered with many small scales; *procera* is from the Latin *procerus* which means tall. The flesh of the young mushroom is white and tender, delicately flavored, and very fragrant. Although its characteristic appearance makes it impossible to confuse with poisonous species, it is unknown, in many regions. Yet *L. procera* is an excellent edible mushroom. However, only the cap should be used as the stem is tough and fibrous. The cap, which is better if from very young specimens, when it is just starting to open, is delicious either broiled or breaded and fried as a cutlet. From the nutritional viewpoint its value, like that of other mushrooms, is limited. Water represents about 85% of its weight; the content of nitrogen compounds is about 4–5%, and that of lipids is small. Its calorific value is very limited, but it should be remembered that appetizing flavor is an important factor in human diets. Mushrooms can also be included in the diets of those who have to keep their calorie intake low.

The **Chanterelle** (*Cantharellus tubaeformis*) also appears during the summer and fall, growing in coniferous woods. It is cooked in the same way as *C. cibarius* (*v.* p. 124). It can also be dried and reduced to powder for seasoning purposes, or preserved in oil. The nutritional value is minimal. It is commonly called "funnel-shaped" chanterelle.

Craterellus cornucopioides, commonly called **Horn of plenty**, grows best in the coolest and most humid parts of both broadleaf and coniferous woods. It appears from August to November, and is widely distributed in Europe, Asia, North America and Australia. It has almost identical characteristics with the chanterelle, and can also be dried and reduced to powder, or preserved in oil. It has the great advantage of not being easily confused with poisonous species because of its distinctive black color.

parasol mushroom

horn of plenty

funnel-shaped chanterelle

Boletus
Oyster mushroom
Girolle

Together with the truffle and Caesar's mushroom, the **Boletus** (Ceps) is undoubtedly a most highly prized mushroom. The genus name *Boletus* derives from the term "bolites" that the Greeks and Romans used for the edible Amanitas and later for all the best edible mushrooms. Afterwards, the term came to be applied only to the boletus. These mushrooms are very common in both coniferous and broadleaf woods such as chestnut, oak, and beech. They are symbiotic, living in mutual association with tree roots. Their presence, therefore, shows one facet of the ecological importance of these woods. Unfortunately like all symbiotic mushrooms they cannot be artificially cultivated, despite occasional statements to the contrary in misleading advertisements. Boletes are found throughout the world: in Europe, in some areas of North Africa, in North America, and Australia (*Boletus edulis*); in Europe and Australia (*B. aereus*). They appear from June to November, and their presence is closely related to the seasonal climatic trends: a hot and humid summer increases the production enormously. Boletes can be used in many delicious dishes. The caps can be broiled, and the whole mushroom, either fresh or dried, can be used in many different ways. The dried mushrooms, previously softened in water, are particularly good for flavoring risotto, pasta, veal cutlets, and stuffing *vol-au-vent*, etc. The very young fruiting bodies are excellent preserved in oil.

It is essential to avoid all species of boletus with red tube mouths (underside of the cap) as they are usually poisonous.

The **Oyster mushroom** (*Pleurotus ostreatus*) does not enjoy the same reputation and prestige as the other mushrooms already described, and yet there is no doubt about its value. Its flesh is a little tough even in the youngest fruiting bodies, but it is precisely this "gumminess," together with the typical scent, that gives Oyster mushrooms their particular sensory qualities. They are almost always stewed. Served with salt cod, pork loins, or sausages, they are excellent. The youngest fruiting bodies can be preserved in oil. The Oyster mushroom is so called because of the suggestive color and shape of the cap. It appears from fall to winter which explains one of the common names used on the Continent, "chilblain." It grows on dead or dying stumps and trunks of poplars and mulberry trees, and can also be cultivated on logs of poplar trunks. The simplest technique consists in "seeding" the logs with a few caps that have been allowed to become mushy in water. Other, more refined techniques are now quickly developing commercially.

Cantharellus cibarius is another well-known and widespread Chanterelle, commonly called "little cockerel" or **Girolle**. It is common in woods where it forms spots or rings, and is found in many parts of the world: Europe, Japan, North Africa, America, Australia, appearing between June and October. It is best prepared stewed, and cannot be cultivated.

girolle

boletus

oyster mushroom

Apple

The cultivation of the **Apple** (any tree of the genus *Malus*) probably dates back to the beginning of the Stone Age, according to findings in Switzerland and Austria in the mid-nineteenth century. An interesting fact to be observed in these findings is that the apple discovered by the archeologists had been cut into two to four parts as if even at that time they were used as dried fruits or stored for the winter. In the time of Ramses III (twelfth century B.C.) the apple tree was cultivated along the fertile Nile Valley. In the sixth century B.C. Sappho in Greece, and a little later Hippocrates, and Theophrastus, wrote about a fruit which could be related to our apple. In the Roman world the species is mentioned by Cato, Varro, Pliny, and Palladius, who in the fourth century A.D. wrote of 37 varieties, a really considerable number for the period. At the beginning of the seventeenth century, the apple tree was imported into North America, and a little later to South Africa and Australia. Its spread followed the routes of other fruit trees, thanks to the widespread colonization of those times. There are thousands of varieties of apples today, and they are generally classified on the basis of their time of maturation (summer, autumn, winter) and their color, size, flavor, and so forth. The many varieties can be divided into two groups: those to be eaten fresh, and those to be used for cooking. The apple is one of the most prized table fruits, but it can be used in many other ways. It is made into jelly, preserves, apple butter, and compotes. The juice is made into cider and can be distilled to produce Calvados or apple jack. Pure apple juice is very popular today. In medicine its disinfectant and therapeutic qualities are highly valued. The apple must be considered a true and proper food, containing carbohydrates, vitamins, salts, and water. The carbohydrates, about 10%, are present in the form of glucose and fructose, that is, in the simplest forms, which are easily assimilated by our bodies. The vitamins contained in the apple are vitamin C, which is considered an antiscorbutic and has a general nutritive function and a specific action on the mucous membranes of the digestive system, and several of the B vitamins. The mineral salts found in apples are calcium, iron, phosphorus, and potassium. A ripe apple contains a considerable amount of water, about 85%, which makes this fruit a favorite thirst-quencher, both for immediate thirst that could be relieved by water, and also for that at a cellular level. The apple's reputation as a healthful fruit is well deserved: apples are highly digestible because they contain pectin, which helps the normal digestive processes after a meal. But for people suffering from acidity it is advisable to cook them, preferably by baking to retain all the flavor. The syrup obtained from apples is used to relieve chest colds and whooping cough; it is said to reduce fevers, soothe irritation, and benefit the kidneys, bladder, and liver. Apples are good for children suffering from some kinds of gastro-intestinal disturbances: because of their natural antitoxic, acidifying action they can modify the intestinal environment by reactivating the bacteria that grow there. The old saying "An apple a day keeps the doctor away," has a lot of truth in it. Apples also have astringent action due to their tannic acid content. Gastronomically, the apple is a most versatile fruit: excellent raw, it is really delicious baked, stewed, in fritters, in pies, and strudels, and especially flambéed with kirsch or other spirits after being cooked. The numerous varieties can be divided into four categories: cooking apples, eating apples, cider apples, and drying apples. The principal categories are the first two, but it is difficult to make a sharp distinction between them because some table apples are also very good for cooking. The table varieties are in turn divided according to the time of maturation. *Summer apples.* Some of the varieties for sale in the summer are as follows: Red Astrachan is probably the earliest variety, appearing during the first half of July. It is not very large and has yellowish green skin with red spots or streaks; the pulp is sweet, slightly acid, aromatic and firm. Summer Rambour which ripens between August and September is large with smooth, light green skin spotted with red, and has good

Starkcrimson delicious

Golden delicious

Delicious

Rose of Caldaro

juicy pulp. Yellow Transparent and Duchess are also good early varieties. *Fall apples*. The English Cellini is of medium size with a thin, yellow skin with greenish spots and streaks; its pulp is sweet-tart and mealy and it cooks well. The Autumnal Gray Rennet is also of English origin; the fruits are rather large, elongate, and angular, with wrinkled dark skin spotted with gray, and with very juicy pulp. Like the previous variety, it is very good when cooked.

For winter storage, these cultivars are highly regarded: Stayman (Stamared), Rome Beauty (Cox Red Rome, Gallia Beauty), Baldwin and Wealthy.

Winter Apples. Annurca mostly grown in Campania, Italy, has a slightly flattened shape with very resistant skin (and so is usually exported), is dark red in color, with crisp, tasty pulp. Yellow Beauty of American origin has yellow skin speckled with gray and with red shades on the side that has been exposed to the sun; the pulp is juicy, tender, sweet, and aromatic.

There are many other excellent apple cultivars for eating raw, and for cooking: Delicious (also Red Delicious, Starking and Richard, Starkcrimson), Cortland, York Imperial, Jonathan, McIntosh, Granny Smith, Golden Delicious, Grimes Golden and Yellow Newtown.

Jonathan

Calvilla

Granny Smith

Abundance

Stayman

Rennet

Pear

The cultivation of the common **Pear** tree (*Pyrus communis*), from which, over the centuries, have developed most of the forms cultivated today, goes back to very ancient times. According to paleontological findings, its cultivation could date back to 35 to 40 centuries ago. It seems to have originated in western Asia and around the Caspian Sea. It has been known for many centuries in Europe. Both the Greeks and Romans prized it highly. Homer names the pear tree in listing the plants growing in Alcinous's garden. Some centuries later Theophrastus, Cato and Pliny also mention it. Theophrastus has handed down some extraordinary information. He considers separately the wild and cultivated species, and, for the latter, describes the methods of propagation by seeds and by grafting, and the methods of cultivation. He also wrote a long and knowledgeable dissertation about the usefulness of cross-pollination, so we know that even in those times the pear's cultivation was widespread. Later, Cato identified six varieties, and Pliny nearly forty, although Virgil had written of only three. The varieties of the pear have been continuously increasing, especially since the mid-eighteenth century. Today more than five thousand varieties can be listed, some of them spread throughout the world, others found in only one country, or even limited to a small locality. Although the cultivated varieties are numerous, the fruit industries try to restrict cultivation to those varieties that offer the best commercial guarantee, because of their limited requirements and adaptability to their environment, or their resistance to disease, or ripening period. Commercially the latter is an extremely important characteristic. Pears are one of the fruits most in demand not only when fresh because of their flavor, the abundance of vitamins and the percentage of carbohydrates which make them so nourishing, but also as preserves, jelly, candied or canned fruit, etc. However, this fruit ripens and is harvested during an extremely short period of the year, so supplying the market for many months with fruit harvested long before is a problem to be overcome. It is a horticultural achievement that fresh pears are available during winter and even spring, when the trees have not even begun to bloom. The logical result of this desire for around-the-year consumption was the large-scale development of cold storage, requiring two well-defined stages: first, the harvesting of the pears when still unripe, then their storage under conditions that slow down the processes of maturation. The farmer's experience plays a decisive role during the first phase, since there are no instruments that can determine the degree of ripeness.

In the second stage it is necessary to provide a constant temperature during the long stay in the cold rooms, proper humidity level, so that there will be no weight loss in the stored product, and periodic ventilation and purification of the air. At the end of this waiting period in cold storage at a temperature of $30°–33°$F $(1°-+1°$C$)$, with a maximum of $35°$F $(2°-3°$C$)$, the pears that are not yet ripe undergo a supplementary maturation of twelve days in a temperature of approximately $65°$F $(18°$C$)$. This process should ensure that the pears will finally reach the consumer in perfect condition, with no trace of their early harvest showing in their appearance. With these methods the variety Abate may be stored for eight to nine weeks, a Bartlett for three months, a Comice for over four months, and the varieties Clarigeau and Anjou can be eaten even six to seven months after they have been picked from the tree. A considerable part of the fruit's production is used in the food industry for canning, either in syrup or in their own juice; preserves and jelly, candied or dried pears, etc. The fruits used for these purposes are harvested at a particular degree of maturity and carefully chosen. The varieties that are most suited to commercial purposes are the Bartlett and the William, because of their remarkable aroma and delicious white pulp without granulation. Other valued varieties are the Butter Hardy, which is very good for fruit salads, and Bolsc, Clapp Favorite, Dorset, Gorham, Kieffer and Seckel. An Italian speciality, *mostarda cremonese*, a relish made with semi-candied fruits in a sugary syrup flavored with mustard, requires pears of small size, whole and colored red

Argentine William

Comice

Kaiser

assa crassana

Abate

or green. Like other fruits, pears have a certain importance from a nutritional and dietetic standpoint because of the vitamins they contain. They are also a good source of energy, supplying nearly 40 calories per $3\frac{1}{2}$ ounces (100 grams), and a considerable amount of mineral salts. The usable carbohydrates can total up to 11% and the three principal vitamins present are, in decreasing order, vitamins A, B and C respectively with 800 international units, 300 and 100 milligrams per kilogram. Another element they contain is iodine which helps to keep the thyroid healthy in its function of relating the oxidation processes and the metabolism of the body. It is believed that pears may also be eaten by persons with severe kidney malfunctions because of the very low amount of sodium they contain. A pure complexion and shiny hair are thought likely to be the result of a regular consumption of pears.

early Butter Morettini

butter Hardy

Butter William

Max Red Bartlett

Quince
Loquat or *Japanese medlar*

The many varieties of **Quince** (*Cydonia oblonga* or *C. vulgaris*) obtained over the centuries appear to be derived from a form native to Iran and the Caspian regions, where it is still found in the wild state. This theory is supported by the fact that the cultivated plants growing there have a moderately edible fruit with a sweetish flavor. In spite of the most advanced techniques of modern agriculture, in the areas of southern Europe where the quince is cultivated it is still not edible fresh but must be cooked a fairly long time. The cultivated varieties can be divided into two groups: to the first belong the cultivars producing round fruits; to the second, those producing oblong fruits. The varieties belonging to the first group are generally chosen for commercial purposes such as confectionery, preserves and jams because they are better suited for processing. The most common varieties are: Angers, very hardy with large fruits; Fontenay, smaller than Angers; Portugal, perhaps the best variety, with large golden-yellow fruits; Vrania, native to Serbia with large, irregularly shaped fruits, and Orange, originating in Armenia, which is very good for industrial processing. In Italy the quince is widely cultivated in the south, where delicious *cotognate* or quince marmalade (from *cotogna* = quince) is made. Its golden-yellow flesh is acid, hard and rather unpalatable, but when cooked and sweetened can be made into various kinds of preserves and jams, either alone or mixed with other fruits, such as apples and pears.

The **Loquat**, also called **Japanese** or **Chinese medlar** (*Eriobotrya japonica*), imported from Japan at the end of the eighteenth century, was for a long time grown in France purely as an ornamental. It was not until the middle of the nineteenth century that horticulturists became interested in the fruit, although it must be admitted that the spread of this species is mostly due to the fact that its fruits ripen extraordinarily early, at the beginning of the year. Today there is nothing unusual in having winter fruits in summer and vice versa, but in the past to have early fruits in the middle of winter was considered exceptional and somewhat luxurious. This is why the loquat became so popular, despite the fact that it is not one of the tastiest fruits. It should be picked when perfectly ripe, so that the sugary content and juicy and refreshing pulp are at their best. Generally it is eaten fresh, but it can be used to make delicious preserves and many types of confectionery. It can also be put, like some candied fruit, into various relishes, or used as the basis of a pleasant liqueur tasting of bitter almonds. As a whole the loquat is poor in nutritive qualities, although it is thirst-quenching and easily digestible.

Advance, Premier, Tanaka, Olivier, and Pineapple are cultivars of the loquat, which is grown extensively in the southern states of America, and in Australia and southern Europe.

quince

loquats

Service tree or Sorb apple
Wild rose
Medlar
Azarole

The **Service tree** (*Sorbus domestica*) is not of great importance since its fruits, the sorb apples, do not compare with those of the many other plants of the extensively cultivated rose family. There are two cultivated subspecies of service tree: the apple form (*malifera*), with roundish fruits whose shape resembles the apple's, and the pear shape (*pyrifera*), whose fruits are morphologically the same as those of the pear. Many varieties of these two subspecies are known. Sorb apples, as they are sometimes known, cannot be eaten immediately after picking as they, like the medlar, have a sour taste and a firm and hard pulp. They must therefore undergo a period of after-ripening until the beginning of decomposition changes their color and gives them a more agreeable flavor.

The **Wild Rose** (*Rosa selvatica*) and other botanically close species such as the red rose (R. *gallica*) are fruits of little use and are used almost exclusively to prepare pleasant preserves and syrups which can act as a gentle laxative, and are thought to be generally helpful for sickly children. Bulgaria's most famous export is rose petal jam.

The **Medlar** (*Mespilus germanica*) is also of little importance as a fruit. It is never planted in orchards, but only singly, usually as an ornamental plant, near country houses or in parks. Because of the slight commercial demand for the medlar it will probably drop out of cultivation and eventually disappear, at least in urban areas. Several varieties are, however, cultivated in Britain. Immediately after picking, the fruits have a pinkish white pulp: hard, sour, strongly astringent, and therefore inedible. To become edible they must be spread for some time over straw where they undergo the beginning of a decomposition process that will make the pulp soft, changing its color from green to brownish, while the tannic compounds are transformed into sweet, tasty substances. The medlar has always enjoyed a certain reputation because of its diuretic and astringent properties. It is used in jams and jellies, and sometimes as a table fruit.

The **Azarole** (*Crataegus azarolus* of the *Rosaceae*) is another plant of slight or even no commercial importance, being grown only in scattered locations in southern Europe where the fruit, due to a favorable climate, can fully mature. In Spain and France the fruit of the azarole does not reach the size of the Italian varieties. The plant produces fruits with a globose shape, red or yellowish-orange. The fragrant and sugary pulp has a slightly acid flavor, so that the fruit can be eaten fresh. It has wider uses in the production of confectionery and jelly, especially in northern Italy, where for climatic reasons it is not possible to eat the azarole fresh as it always needs a fairly long after-ripening period.

service tree

wild rose hips

azarole

medlar

Watermelon

The botanical name of the **Watermelon** is *Citrullus vulgaris* or, according to other botanists, *Cucumis citrullus* or *Cucurbita citrullus*. Watermelons are commonly believed to have originated in North Africa, and this theory is very widely accepted today, but opinions in the matter differ. Linnaeus believed they were native to southern Italy, while others claimed that they were of Indian origin. Watermelons are produced by annual, creeping, herbaceous plants of modest size, 6–10 feet, which may seem surprising considering the fruit's dimensions. The leaves are deeply lobed; the rather small, greenish-yellow flowers are unisexual, as is generally the rule within this family. Each plant can produce a variable number of fruits, three to four, or even more. The pulp is generally red, although varying in shade. At one time watermelons with yellow pulp were also grown. The seeds, very numerous, are brownish, blackish, variegated, or totally black. The watermelon has evolved with the changes in style that are characteristic of many popular vegetables (and are due not just to frivolous reasons but, for example, to increasing productivity and, above all, stronger resistance to disease). The fruits typical of the pre-World War II period or of the early forties and fifties have now completely disappeared. Today the watermelons on sale are divided into three fundamental types of cultivars: (1) relatively small fruits, 6–10 pounds, spherical, with dark green rind, and very sweet red pulp, ripening early, for example, the New Hampshire Midget, Sugar Baby, and Summer Festival; (2) fruits spherical but larger, generally around 20–40 pounds, also with sugary red pulp and a uniformly colored rind, dark green and covered with a soft bloom, such as the new Black Diamond or Florida Giant which can weigh up to 40 pounds, or striped on a light green background; (3) the most popular watermelons, having large, ovoid fruits, and rind uniformly variegated as in the Charleston Gray, or with stripes varying greatly in both shape and shades, darker color on a lighter background, as in the famous Klondike Striped or Blue Ribbon, Dixie Queen, Tom Watson, Klondike R7, and Congo. Also with ovoid fruit but smaller, is the recently introduced Sweet-Meat with very fragrant, sugary pulp and, an important factor, very few seeds. As is generally known, watermelons are eaten above all as thirst-quenchers in very hot weather, but often they are used as a dessert, or even at the start of a meal as an hors-d'œuvre. They make a refreshing addition to fruit salads, and the varieties with firmer pulp can be used for making jam. Because of the large amount of water in the fruit it does not affect people with weight problems. The solid residue is only about 5%, and the carbohydrates a modest 3–4%. The calorific value is therefore very low. Watermelons are useful for their vitamin content and as a diuretic, although some people find them difficult to digest.

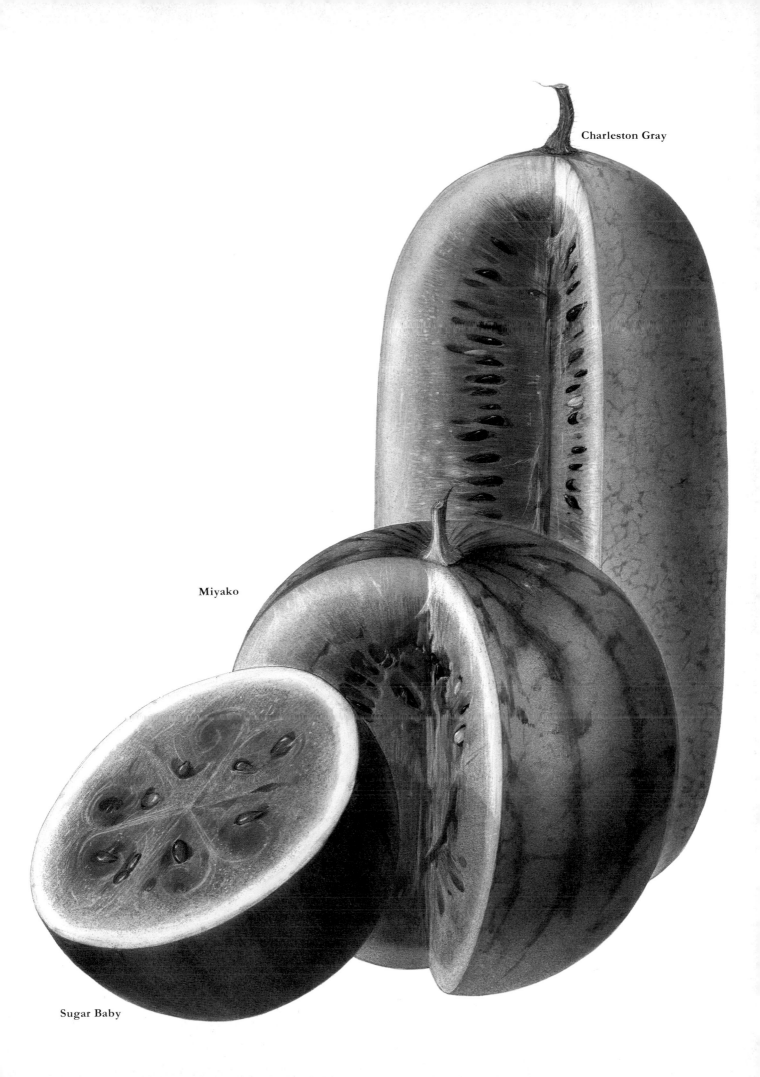

Charleston Gray

Miyako

Sugar Baby

Melon

Nothing is positively established on the origin of the **Muskmelon** and **Cantaloupe** (*Cucumis melo*), although some authorities believe them to be native to Asia, while others claim to have found a wild plant in the Sudan, producing rather small fruits, which could be the melon's ancestor. It is certain, however, that they were cultivated in very ancient times. Examination of records from the first century A.D., found in Alexandria and now in the Louvre, seem to show that melons were represented, together with other fruits, in a cornucopia on a vase-painting. They are also depicted on bas-reliefs and etchings, proving that they were undoubtedly grown in the Nile Valley at the time of the Pharaohs. It seems, however, that they were not cultivated in Europe until the Middle Ages, except perhaps in southern Spain which was occupied by the Moors. Introduced from the Orient via Armenia, the melon appeared in the fifteenth century, brought by Charles VIII to France from Naples in 1495. The name "cantaloupe" is quite recent, dating back to the middle of the eighteenth century. It is thought to be derived from Cantalupo, a district near Rome where the Pope had a villa. Melons are produced by annual, herbaceous plants, of modest size and similar to the watermelon except for the leaves, entire, with rounded or fan-shaped margins. Commercially, they are divided into two categories: netted or nutmeg melons (the common muskmelon) with the rinds covered by a densely meshed net, and cantaloupes with deeply grooved rinds. Among the great number of cultivars of netted melons, which are constantly evolving for reasons of plant health and increased immunity to disease, some important species are Farmers Netted with round fruit and sweet yellow flesh, and Golden Delight, oblong, slightly ribbed, with crispy salmon-tinted pulp. Within the cantaloupes are found Fordhook Gem, a climbing variety with fragrant soft greenish flesh; the Charentais with yellowish green, slightly ribbed skin, and orange, sugary, fragrant flesh; the Bellegarde with green skin and orange-red pulp. Some botanists also include as cantaloupes the winter melons, which could be classified separately. They have sweet, white flesh, and smooth rind irregularly striped with faint lines. They are harvested while still unripe and stored in cool, dry, airy places where they will keep until Christmas or later. In southern Italy it is the custom to keep them hanging on walls protected by a roof-gutter.

Other excellent melon cultivars are Delicious, Saticoy, Hearts of Gold, Honey Rock, Crenshaw, and Gold Star. In addition, there are several other melon cultivars with pale yellow skin (honeydews) and ribbed yellow skin (the casabas). Honey Mist, Honey Dew Green and Tam-Dew are selected honeydew cultivars while Golden Beauty and Sungold are casaba cultivars.

In the United States melons are commonly eaten for breakfast, or for dessert. In other parts of the world they are eaten as a dessert, or as an hors-d'œuvre; either alone or with the thinly sliced Italian smoked ham, known in all countries as "prosciutto." Charentais melons are often filled with a sweet wine such as Barsac, Marsala, Port or Madeira. Winter melons can be sprinkled with a little ginger and sugar.

Choosing a perfect melon requires a certain degree of skill. The smell of the fruit must be right; by tapping the rind one can tell whether it is well-fleshed or hollow. There should be a "crown" around the stem indicating that the melon is ripe and sweet.

Their nutritional qualities are similar to those of the watermelons.

netted melon

cantaloupe

winter melons

Plum

Apricots, cherries, **Plums**, peaches, and almonds are names with different etymologies; but the genus name *Prunus*, given by Linnaeus, is common to all these trees that produce some of the most prized types of fruits. Although in Roman times *Prunus* probably indicated only the plum tree, with the passing of time it became usual to include in the same genus many species found mostly in temperate regions. Some representatives of this genus also grow in South America in the Andes. Today the plum is cultivated to some extent everywhere in Europe and in the United States. The biggest producers are the east European countries. Among the thousands of cultivars throughout the world are found the characteristic mirabelles with very small fruits; the Florentia and the Shiro, both juicy and sweet, but with slightly tart skin; the good Reine Claude (or "greengage") and the Santa Rosa. There are many American varieties such as Damson Beauty, Italian Prune, Burbank, Sugar, and Stanley. Plums are eaten fresh or dried (prunes), but a large part of the harvest is used by the canning industry for preserves, jams and sweet pickles. Some varieties are also distilled to make brandy such as the Balkan slivovitz. Prunes preserved in brandy, and kept for several months, are excellent. Plums are harvested when their characteristic fragrance is strongest; the first fruits to be collected are those that are going to be preserved or candied. The late varieties are used for drying: the fruits are laid in the sun and then baked in special ovens at a particular temperature. The skins acquire the beautiful brownish color and sheen which make them so valued commercially.

The mirabelle is a small, golden-yellow plum with a very penetrating perfume. It has a sweet flavor and is used stewed or to make jam, and commercially in the manufacture of spirits. The Sloe is another species of the *Prunus* family, but is hardly edible, being extremely sour. There are two regions in France where it is celebrated; in Angers where it is distilled to make a famous liqueur, and in the Haute-Saône where it is grown for jam and distilling. The laxative action of prunes is well known. Culpeper, the great seventeenth-century English herbalist, spoke highly of plums as fruits belonging to Venus. As well as recommending the fruits "both in health and sickness, to relish the mouth and stomach . . ." he also wrote that "plum-tree leaves boiled in wine, are good to wash and gargle the mouth and throat" and that the leaves boiled in vinegar would also cure ringworm! Taken in excess, however, the versatile plum could cause colic. Because of the organic acids in plums, they have been recommended for those with gout and uricemia. They are high in carbohydrates but their vitamin content is negligible.

Each species of *Prunus* contains a large number of cultivars. Throughout the centuries, man has always placed great importance on the nutritional and commercial value of plants, and has also succeeded in obtaining particular varieties valued for their flowers or leaves and therefore used as outdoor ornamentals. Early in their cultivation it was probably almost exclusively the sugar content of the ripe fruit that led gardeners to think of its high energy value. But when man began to analyze chemically the various components of the single species, he discovered numerous mineral salts and, more recently, vitamins. This discovery brought both hope and dissension. Today, science tries to show each kind of food, including fruit, in an impartial light, emphasizing the calorific or mineral or vitamin properties, which can be present at various levels simultaneously. It is impossible to discuss in a general way the precise composition of fruit. The sugar content of a cherry differs considerably, for example, from that of a peach. But a fairly accurate average can be obtained. It can be seen that fresh fruit contains more water than anything else, 80–90%; the amount of assimilable carbohydrates is also high, about 12%. Mineral salts, protein and lipids have approximately the same values, 1% or less. The rest of the weight is made up of nonassimilable substances (2–3%) and various vitamins which, however, are not always present. With the exception of a few very rich fruits, they are not generally found in great quantity. The vitamins of

mirabelle

Saint Peter

Florentia

Ruth Gastetter

Shiro

the B complex are often scarce or even absent, while a satisfying amount can be provided of the groups A and C. Contrary to general belief it is not true that fruit is an inexhaustible source of vitamins. Mineral salts which are present in small amounts cannot be compared in quantity with those provided by, for example, milk, meat and cheese. Fruit does, however, have a beneficial effect on the human body, because of its assimilable sugars and the number of calories produced. Another important factor is the presence in fresh fruit of some organic acids, such as tartaric, citric, and oxalic. Fresh fruit is considered by some to be useful for cases of acidosis and rheumatic disturbances.

Stanley

Saint Clare

sugar

Burbank

Reine Claude

Santa Rosa

Cherry

The great many varieties of **Cherries** of the *Rosaceae* that are grown today can be divided into three groups, each including fruits of very different flavors. The first group encompasses at least a thousand forms derived from *Prunus avium*: their common characteristic is the sweet pulp of the fruit. The less numerous representatives of the second group are thought to have developed from *Prunus cerasus*. Their pulp has a slightly sour taste. Finally, the third class contains almost a hundred varieties originating from hybridization of the two previous species, so the fruits are morphologically similar to *P. avium*, while their acid taste makes them closer to *P. cerasus*. The geographical distribution of the two species is as follows:

P. avium (sweet cherry) grows in the wild state in western Asia, in the area between the Caucasus, Iran, and Asia Minor; in Europe between Scandinavia and the Mediterranean, and in North Africa. *P. avium* is thought to have originated in the Caucasus and Asia Minor; later, certainly before the introduction of agriculture, it spread throughout Europe. Evidence of the fruit of this tree, in the form of pits, was found in neolithic ruins in Switzerland and Italy, and in some prehistoric dwellings in Scandinavia.

The other species, *P. cerasus*, known as the Morella cherry, from which the sour variety derives, grows as a wild plant in nothern Anatolia which is believed to be its place of origin. From this region, like the preceding species, it spread toward the west, and grows in Greece and Italy. More is known about the sweet cherry than about the sour variety. It is certain that this plant was known and cultivated in Egypt about six or seven hundred years before Christ, at the time of the Twenty-sixth Dynasty. And it was also known to the Greeks; both Theophrastus and Athenaeus wrote about it. The Roman world has even more evidence of its uses, as is proved by the many authors, poets, and historians who spoke about *P. avium*. Among them were Varro, Ovid, Pliny and Palladius. The latter mentioned no fewer than ten varieties of this plant, which for those times was quite exceptional. Little is known, however, about the sour cherry, and what information exists is uncertain. Its fruits may be among those painted in the Pompeian frescoes, or it could be the plant mentioned by Virgil in a passage of the second book of the Georgics. It seems certain, however, that *P. cerasus* was then used as stock for grafting. Later, the cherry crossed the ocean landing in America soon after Columbus's discovery, thus increasing the already large number of Euro-Asiatic plants that arrived there during that period. Today the United States, Romania, Germany and Italy have the largest production of cherries. A good number of the many varieties which have been obtained through cultivation appear on the market each year toward the end of spring and the beginning of summer. The profusion of shapes and colors is immense. As has previously been said, there are only two varieties, sweet and sour. Depending on the consistency of the flesh, the sweet cherries are divided into "tender" and "hard," the Heart Cherry, and the White Heart Cherry. The former are of regular size, with deep pink to red skin and flesh tender and watery, attached to the pit (of variable color); yellow to pink to blackish-red. The "hard" cherries are heart-shaped and large, with dark red or yellowish-red skin, and firm flesh. The juice is colorless. The *P. cerasus* is mostly globose in shape, usually dark red, with juicy, rather sour flesh. Some of these variable characteristics determine a further division of this group: the Amarelles with light red skin and flesh, and slightly acid taste; and the Morellas or Grottos, smaller than the previous type, sourer, and either dark or light in color. All the many forms of this fruit reach maturity in a relatively short time, so that it is essential to harvest the product at the right moment, when the color characteristic of the variety is almost at its peak. In the last days they increase considerably in weight and sugar content. Interestingly, in the last two weeks the weight increase is as much as a third of the total weight. Cherries are mostly destined for immediate consumption

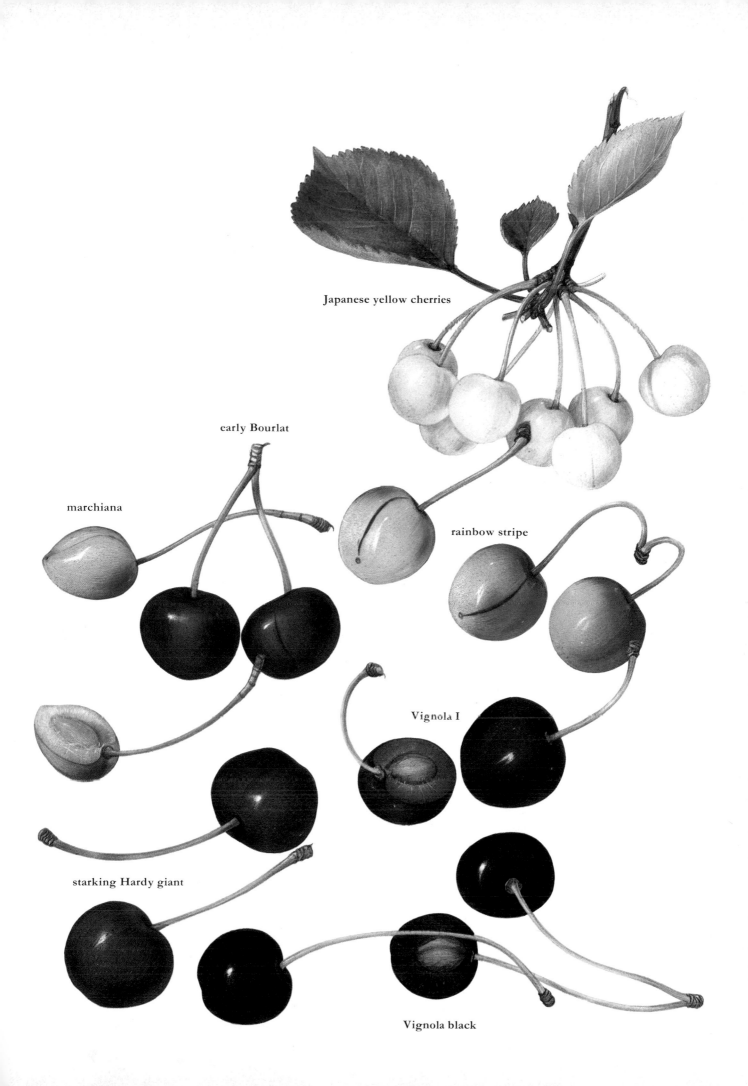

Japanese yellow cherries

early Bourlat

marchiana

rainbow stripe

Vignola I

starking Hardy giant

Vignola black

as fresh fruit, but a fair amount is used in the canning industry and in distilleries for the making of liqueurs and brandies. For preserves, confections and similar products, the sour cherries are preferred, especially when they are not too ripe. Often varying amounts of red currant are added to preserve the color, and also a little apple jam or pectin to obtain the right consistency. For jelly-making some currant and apple juice is added to a clear cherry juice and the mixture is boiled until the right consistency is obtained. Cherries are very important in the spirits industry. The most famous products are various cherry brandies; Maraschino of Zara, in Dalmatia, and Kirsch and Ratafia. Kirsch is a characteristic liqueur smelling of bitter almonds. To make, the fruits, freed from the pedicels, are fermented together with the smashed pits. The liquid thus obtained is distilled two or three times to obtain up to 40–50% in volume of alcohol. Kirsch is often used in desserts with cherries, and is also excellent with pineapples. One hundred kilograms of cherries yield about $2\frac{1}{2}$ gallons (10 liters) of brandy. There are several ways to prepare Ratafia; one is to soak the ripe cherries with the stones in alcohol for a certain number of days; the liquid is then filtered and a syrup of water and sugar is added. Sometimes a few strawberries, raspberries and black currants are mixed in with the cherries. Maraschino is made by pounding the fruits and crushing the stones. After honey has been added the mixture is left to ferment, before being distilled. Sugar is then added. Cherries are also used to make beverages and syrups; the Amarelles are usually preferred. The nutritional value of cherries is relatively low. However, at least in some varieties, it is perhaps slightly higher than that of other plants with fleshy fruits of the drupe type, as they contain a large amount of sugar, an average of about 10%.

red morellos

black morellos

section of
red morello

wild cherries

Peach

The **Peach**, also of the *Rosaceae*, is one of the fruits of greatest economic value. Peaches can be eaten either fresh or dried, used to make preserves and jelly, and canned. Although the cultivation of the peach tree has great agricultural and industrial importance because of its fruits, in the last few years some varieties have been grown exclusively as flowering plants, to obtain blossoming branches for use as ornaments. The peach tree (*Prunus persica vulgaris*) is believed to have originated in China, where it still grows in the wild state, and to have come to Europe through Persia. In China the peach was known two thousand years before Christ. From Persia (now Iran) it was introduced to the Greco-Roman world, perhaps by Alexander the Great. The Spanish introduced it into Latin America during the sixteenth century and in the next century it came to California. In the nineteenth century the plant reached Australia, but it was not until early in the twentieth century that it arrived in southern Africa. Today the peach is one of the most widely cultivated fruit trees throughout the world, wherever the soil and climate are suitable. It seems to occupy a place in order of importance second only to the apple. The two countries with the highest peach production are the United States and Italy. There are many cultivated varieties. Their classification is based upon the shape of the leaves: the size, color, and shape of the flowers, and, in particular, upon some characteristics of the fruit; shape, color, more or less evident pubescence, consistency of the flesh and its degree of adherence to the stone; morphology and corrugations of the latter. But from a practical standpoint, the most important classification is based upon the period of ripening of the fruit. Taking into account the climatic conditions of both countries, which vary considerably, the fruits of the indigenous varieties reach maturation from the end of May to the end of October. There are thus "very early" varieties, which appear toward the last days of spring, "early" or July varieties, August or "medium" varieties, "late" or September varieties, and finally "very late" varieties.

In the United States, peaches are often classed as clingstone or freestone. Clingstone varieties, with a firm flesh adhering to the stone, are often early bearers and are used mainly for canning: Tuscan, Phillips Cling, Chinese Cling, Sullivan Cling, Walton, Peak, Sims, and Libbee. There are hundreds of freestone cultivars which have juicy pulp and a free stone: Alberta, Halehaven, and Golden Jubilee are outstanding. Other good cultivars are Redhaven, Dixired, Dixigem, Sullivan, Early Alberta, Keystone, Rio-Oso-Gem, Jerseyland, Sunhigh, and for home garden culture the best tasting of all, Belle of Georgia.

The sugar content of the peach is not normally higher than 9%, while the amount of mineral salts is considerable. The vitamin value is far greater than in other fruits, especially of vitamins A and C. Peaches make many excellent desserts; baked and stuffed with almonds, butter, and ground macaroons, or stewed with wine or lemon, in pies, flans or shortcakes, and in the famous Peach Melba. It is said that once, when Madame Récamier, the great French beauty of the early nineteenth century, was ill, and refusing all food, her life was saved by a dish of peaches in syrup and cream, which brought back not only her appetite, but the will to live.

Hale

Glohaven

Lugo beautiful

Loadel

Nectarine
Apricot

A particular group of the peach family is that of the **Nectarine**. Nectarines were already known in England at the end of the sixteenth century. The name is believed to be derived from "nectar," the drink of the gods, to which this fruit was compared because of its superb flavor. Nectarines (*Prunus persica* var. *nectarina*), are classed as fuzzless peaches with an even richer flavor than the *P. persica*. There is an old, but inaccurate, country belief that the nectarine evolved from a peach, which was crossed with a plum. Starwyck, Queta, Gold Mine, Lord Matier, Armking and Cardinal are standard varieties of nectarines.

Contrary to what the Latin scientific name, *Prunus armeniaca*, might suggest, the **Apricot** is not originally from Armenia. This region was only a stage in the long journey from the Far East. The apricot has been found in China as a wild plant for at least four thousand years, and although it has been recently observed in a wild form in Turkestan, Tien-Shan is considered to be the first Chinese place of origin. Alexander the Great is believed to have introduced the apricot to the Greco-Roman world, as well as the peach. A variety remarkable for its size was found growing in Armenia in great quantities, and was called by the name of the region itself, Armenian peach. However, it was the Arabs who spread the cultivation of the apricot throughout the Mediterranean, although it was not until the fifteenth century that it became popular in Europe. Only in the eighteenth century did the plant become part of the cultivated flora of the United States and South Africa. Today the apricot is recognized, in its many varieties, as an excellent fruit, especially because of its vitamin content and mineral salts. Despite the sweetness of the flesh, the usable sugars do not go over 6–7%. The level of potassium, however, is high. It is essential to eat this fruit when it is fully ripe in order to get the most out of its high content of vitamin A, which is a hundred times more than the average amount contained in other fruits. Vitamin A helps the body to combat infection and plays an important role in guarding against night blindness.

Important cultivars of the apricot are Blenheim, Tilton, Early Montgamet and Wenatchee Moorpark. The famous and particularly succulent musk apricot grows in Spain, the south of France and North Africa.

Apricots have traditionally been used to make excellent preserves and confectionery. However, the use of dried apricots is surprisingly recent. The commercially preferred varieties for drying come from North Africa and California. Syria exports to many markets, especially in Germany, a typical paste made with apricots dried in the sun and lightly wrapped in long canvas strips. In the United States canned apricots preserved in syrup have become increasingly popular. In England, apricots are also used to make apricot wine, and are distilled to make a liqueur-brandy. In the Auvergne in France, apricots are made into a special jam which is exported all over the world, and are one of the most utilized fruits in that country in confectionery and pastry-making.

Some people eat the kernels found inside apricot stones. This could lead to serious poisoning if the bitter varieties are chewed over a period of time. The poisonous compound is amygdalin, which upon hydrolysis releases hydrogen cyanide.

In eastern countries the apricot is known by the beautiful name of "Moon of the Faithful."

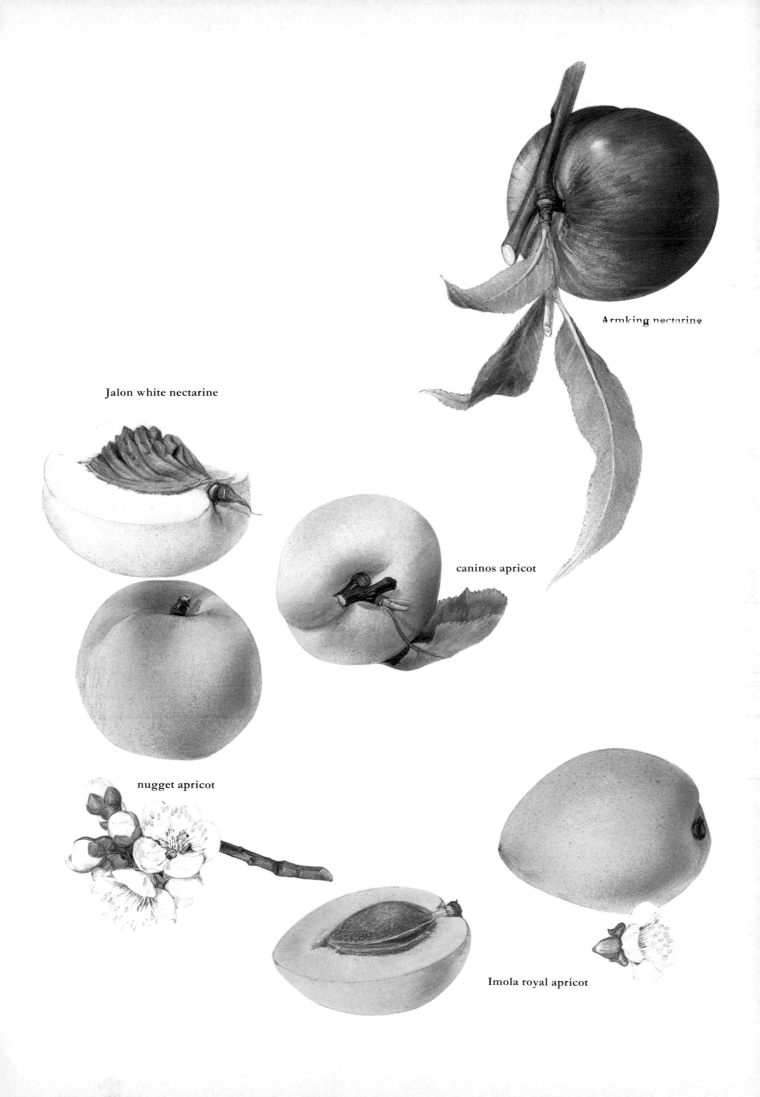

Armking nectarine

Jalon white nectarine

caninos apricot

nugget apricot

Imola royal apricot

Raspberry
Blackberry

The **Raspberry** grows wild throughout most of Europe, from Italy and Greece to Scandinavia, in eastern Asia and in North America. Some fossils found in Swiss lake dwellings indicate that it was known several centuries before Christ. More recent information, apart from a single testimony from Propertius, comes from England where the raspberry was cultivated by the middle of the sixteenth century, and where it was also called hindberry. The British species, *Rubus idaeus*, was later introduced from England to the United States, but as it could not adapt to the new climatic conditions it was soon replaced by a more productive and hardy native species. In Italy, the raspberry is little cultivated, although in the rest of Europe, especially in the northern countries, and also in the United States, it is prolific. In France the best specimens are to be found on the Côte-d'Or, and, perhaps surprisingly, in the environs of Paris.

The raspberry has the same vitamin properties as oranges and lemons and a higher energy value than the latter. The available carbohydrates are about 12–13%, while the vitamin content is 25 mg per $3\frac{1}{2}$ ounces (100 grams) for vitamin B_1, and 30 mg per $3\frac{1}{2}$ ounces (100 grams) for vitamin C. Also present are calcium, magnesium and iron salts. The raspberry, besides being tasty and most refreshing, is a good laxative with considerable diuretic properties. It is rich in pectin and is therefore one of the best fruits for jams and jelly. Raspberries can be eaten fresh, or with sugar and plain or whipped cream. In "charlottes" or "summer puddings" they are indispensable.

The **Blackberry** (*Rubus fruticosus*) is a shrub commonly found along hedges, in woods and in untilled fields of most of the northern hemisphere and also in South Africa. Its fruits, blackberries, can be picked in late summer and in the fall. They were undoubtedly eaten by the first inhabitants of this planet, according to paleontological findings. Historical evidence is provided by Aeschylus and Hippocrates, four or five hundred years before Christ. Today the blackberry is cultivated as a fruit plant in Britain and in some regions of the United States, especially along the Pacific coast. It is represented by different species and varieties that have been shown to be better adapted to the local climate and soils. The blackberry is a nourishing and refreshing fruit, containing about 85% water and 10% carbohydrates. The human body benefits from eating blackberries because of their content of vitamin B_1, and mineral salts, especially calcium, which is present in a higher percentage than in other fruits. Besides being eaten fresh, plain, or with sugar and cream or wine, blackberries can be used in jams, pies, preserves, and syrups. According to popular medicine they are also a good remedy for diseases of the mouth and throat. This belief goes back many years. Culpeper recommended them for quinsies, snake bites, kidney stones and various other ailments, and even said that if the leaves were boiled with lye, and one's hair washed with the solution, it "maketh the hair black."

blackberries

raspberries

Red and Black Currant Gooseberry

Currants have been grown in Italy for at least four centuries according to an entry in a Florentine recipe book, circa 1550, and according to which a "grape of the monks," with similar characteristics to those known today for some species of *Ribes*, was grown on Mount Vernia. It now seems certain that the name *Ribes* is derived from the Arabic *ribas*. This term identified a rhubarb grown by the Arabs in the Lebanon as a medicinal essence. When, shortly after the beginning of the eighth century, the Arabs conquered Spain and found themselves without their *ribas*, they looked for something similar, and finding the gooseberry, called it *ribas*. It is strange that today the old Arabic term has been preserved only in Italian in the common name of one of the species, while it has disappeared in other western languages. In French this plant is called *groseillier*, in Spanish *grosellero*, and in English it is called *currant*. The *Ribes grossularia*, known in Italy as spiny grape (*uva spina*), is the English *gooseberry* and is called in German, *stachelbeere*.

The **Red currant** (R. *rubrum*) is native to northeastern Europe as far as the Arctic Sea, and the steppes of northern Asia as far as Siberia and eastern Manchuria. It produces red, semitransparent berries with a pleasantly sour taste. Part of the production is eaten as fresh fruits; the rest is used commercially in the preparation of jelly, preserves, syrups, and currant wine. The berries contain citric, malic and ascorbic acid, equal parts dextrose and levulose, and are therefore considered a refreshing medicinal essence. They have also been recommended for cases of dysentery. The jelly and syrups, which are particularly refreshing in the summer, also have an emollient action. Besides many varieties with more or less red fruit, many forms obtained by cultivation have colors ranging from yellowish to white. Prominent among the latter is the delicious Holland White which is very good for desserts. At Bar-le-Duc in France, red and white currants are used to make a famous preserve.

The **Black currant** (R. *nigrum*) is a species closer to the gooseberry than to the red currant. The fruit is black and the flesh reddish and sweetish and not particularly good. In Italy it is almost totally unknown; one can find some fairly extended cultivation only in the south, especially around Naples, but in Germany, England and France it is widespread, where it is also used in a very good liqueur, called Cassis. The therapeutic properties of this plant are thought by some to be great in cases of arthritis, gout, dropsy, and many other complaints. They are not limited to the fruit, but are also common to the stem and the leaves. In some parts of the United States black currants are believed to cause "pine forest disease" which can decimate whole forests, so they are little cultivated there. This disease is called "white pine rust" in the British Isles. Some centuries ago black currants were thought to breed worms in the human stomach.

The **Gooseberry** (R. *Grossularia*) is a species native to Europe, western Asia and northern Africa. It is a spiny shrub that produces sourer fruits than those of the currant, of variable size, green, yellow, white or red, with a juicy flesh. It is hairy or smooth depending on the variety. The gooseberry is becoming less and less common in parts of Europe and the United States, where it is losing its popularity. In France and especially in England, it is very much in demand. European varieties have very large fruits that are excellent for jams and preserves. Gooseberry wine can be made by fermentation of the fruits of R. *grossularia*, and often has a high alcoholic content.

The most important American species is R. *hirtellum*. As mackerel is traditionally served with a gooseberry sauce in France, its French name is *groseille à maquereau*.

red currant

white gooseberry

black currant

red gooseberry

white currant

Strawberry

One of the most popular fruits in the world perhaps, for its flavor and its scent, is the red **Wood** or **Wild Strawberry** which can be found in the shade of pine or beech woods, hidden among other wild plants. The wood strawberry (*Fragaria vesca*) in its wild form is unequalled for its flavor. But the commercial demands of modern living require far greater amounts than the limited quantities of this excellent fruit that can be collected growing wild. Today the strawberry has to be large, uniform, and able to withstand transportation, storage, and freezing. It must also be on the market for some months. Therefore new varieties have been cultivated from the original five or six species. However, they are rarely as good as the wild species. There seems to be a difference even in color between cultivated and wild forms. This difference between the two types is supposedly caused by a different ratio of two important pigments. Strawberries contain various types of sugars, fructose and sucrose being the most abundant. Also present are citric, tartaric and salicylic acids, vitamins B_1 and B_2 and above all, vitamin C. Strawberries represent a rich source of ascorbic acid (vitamin C) whose production is stimulated by sunlight. It has been ascertained that the quantity of vitamin C in the ripe fruits is increased in relation to the length of time in which the plant has been in the sun during the last few days before picking. The amount of vitamin C remains almost unchanged in the undamaged fruits for two or three days after the harvest, but if the fruits are cut or damaged, the vitamin C content decreases rapidly. Therefore strawberries should be eaten as soon after picking as possible. The considerable vitamin properties are mostly lost in cooking, so that strawberry jelly, jams and preserves, although good, have only a fraction of the natural vitamins. To reduce the damage to a minimum, strawberries destined for commercial use must have a good taste and aroma and a bright red color. *F. chiloensis*, the Chilean strawberry, and *F. virginiana*, the native American strawberry, along with *F. vesca*, have produced many of the commercial strawberries used today.

It was only in the thirteenth century that the strawberry began to be grown in gardens. It was supposedly brought into France by a sailor named Freziers, from whom it received its French name, *fraise*. Plougastel in Brittany is still one of the most important centers in France for the strawberry's commercial cultivation.

When cooking the fruits times and temperatures must be very precise, as it is a delicate procedure. The strawberry has been recommended in cases of gastritis and some afflictions of the bile ducts. But it is also possible for allergic reactions to be induced in some people when the fruit is eaten in great quantities. In medieval times strawberries were considered to be a cure for almost everything, and it was commonly believed that a lotion made of the roots could even fasten loose teeth, presumably by strengthening the gums.

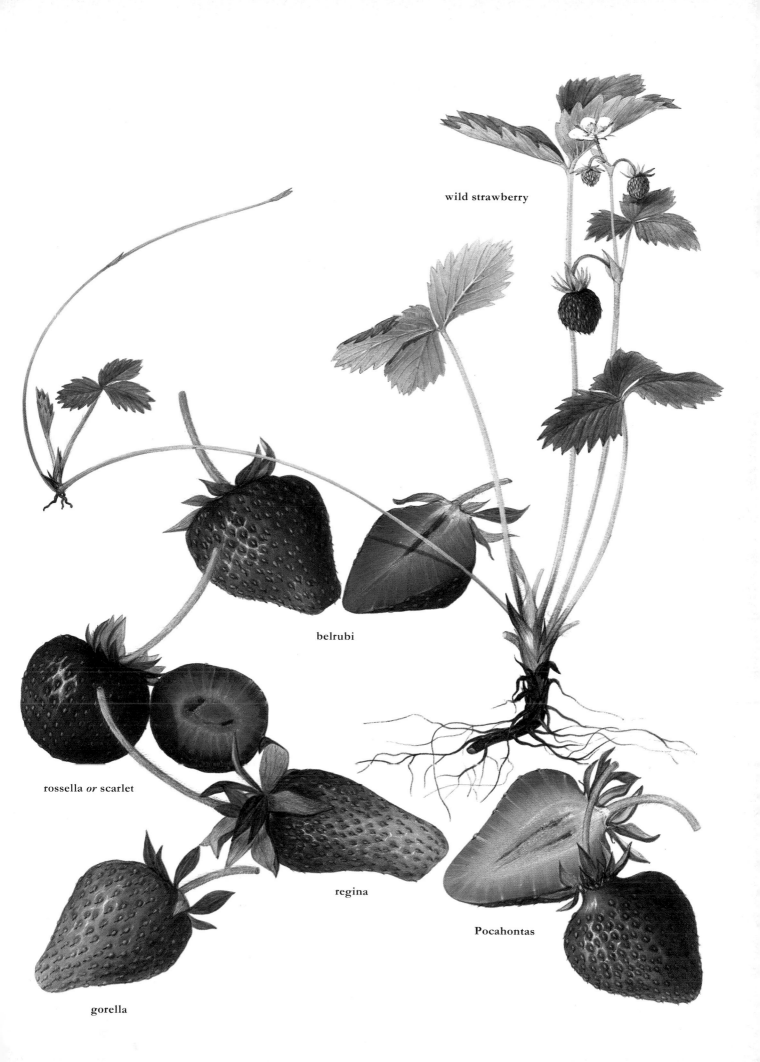

wild strawberry

belrubi

rossella *or* scarlet

regina

Pocahontas

gorella

Grape

Viticulture had its beginnings somewhere around the Caspian Sea in the area generally considered the place of origin of *Vitis vinifera*, our most common **Grape**. It goes so far back in time that the vine is thought to have been already established throughout the world even before the coming of man. The most ancient Greek and Egyptian sources give evidence of the grape's cultivation, and it is mentioned in Genesis 9:20, 21: "And Noah began to be an husbandman, and he planted a vineyard. And he drank of the wine and was drunken. . . ."

Grape culture then spread to other parts of the Near East, then to Greece and Sicily. Grapes were planted by the Romans on the Rhine about the second century A.D. The Greeks, and later, the Romans carried them to Gaul and Provence. At the same time that grape growing was spreading westward, it was also moving to India and the Far East. As new colonization occurred, grapes were carried along until today they are cultivated on all continents and islands that are suitable climatically.

Cato, Virgil, Varro and other Latin authors have written much about the grape. Its cultivation suffered a decline after the fall of the Roman Empire, around the second century A.D., until the rise of the city-states (e.g. Florence, Siena, Pisa, etc.) in the later Middle Ages. After the discovery of America, wild species were imported from the new continent and from them new varieties were obtained. Some centuries later these wild species saved the European grape industry which was then ravaged by disease. In the last decades of the nineteenth century a parasitic insect, the Phylloxera, invaded most of the European vineyards, destroying them in great number. Connoisseurs of wine still refer nostalgically to "pre-Phylloxera vintages." Fortunately it had been discovered that the American varieties were resistant to this insect, so European grape-growers began extensive planting of American rootstock on which, later, shoots of European varieties were grafted. Viticulture has so progressed during the twentieth century that it is now one of the most prominent harvests in existence. Throughout the world Europe clearly occupies first place with an area of about 17–18 million acres reserved for viticulture, in a total world figure of 75 million acres. In Europe, Italy leads in acreage followed by Spain and France. The cultivated varieties are very numerous, and there are also many characteristics that bring them into one or the other of the two groups into which they have been subdivided: table or dessert grapes and wine grapes. Both types are, however, good for eating. Grapes also have digestive and therapeutic properties which are rare in other types of fruit, and are considered to be very nourishing. A grape is formed by the pulp, which is the most important part, enclosed by a thin, membranous skin, and enclosing seeds (grapestones). Water, in which all the various substances are dissolved, is the greatest component of the pulp. A good percentage of carbohydrates is present, 18–20%, in the form of glucose and fructose, both of which are easily assimilable and provide many calories, which explains why grapes, although poor in protein and lipids, are considered to be so nutritious. They also contain potassium, iron, sodium, calcium, magnesium, and phosphorus, which have a refreshing action maintaining the balance of the kidney's functions and helping the elimination of waste and excess acids. Grapes are also fairly rich in vitamin C, while the B complex is present in larger amounts in the white or lighter-colored grapes. Their therapeutic properties are also numerous, as shown by the grape-cure (ampelotherapy) of the eighteenth and nineteenth centuries, once very common every fall, but today viewed with skepticism. All that is natural is automatically underrated in this modern world of pills and machines. Wine is the result of the alcoholic fermentation of the must, the juice pressed from fresh, or even partly dried grapes. Wines differ vastly according to the different varieties of grapes, the composition of the soil, the climatic conditions, and the various treatments to which the must and the grapes themselves are subjected. According to their color, wines are classified

cornicella

muscatel

California grapes

table *or* dessert grapes

as red, rosé and white, while according to their use they are called "table" or "dessert" wines, "blending wines," "sparkling wines," etc. Wine has been known since very early times, and is considered a high-energy food: in relation to its content of alcohol and sugars it can supply from 600 to 1,000 calories per liter, a very high figure indeed. It has been claimed by some medical authorities that people who habitually drink a half to one bottle of red wine per day have a longer life-span.

In certain remote districts grapes are still crushed by the feet, but it is now more usual for mechanical presses to be employed. The harvest time varies according to the variety, but usually takes place during a spell of warm, dry weather. Very good vintages are stored for about three years in heavy wooden casks (although in hot countries, such as Algeria, the casks are lighter), but lesser vintages are put into metal or japanned casks.

Wine should always be handled with respect, even if it is a cheap vintage, commonly called "plonk" or "plonque." A cheap or young wine is vastly improved if the cork is completely removed from the bottle at least three to four hours before it is to be drunk. This "softens" the wine and takes away any acidity. Never be afraid of extravagance in using a good wine in cooking. Good food is worth good wine.

In most religions man's discovery of the vine is attributed to divine intervention.

sangiovese

trebbiano of Empoli

lambrusco *or*
Northern Fox grape

Cornel
Strawberry tree
Jujube
Whortleberry

Among the many species belonging to the genus *Cornus*, the **Cornel** or cornelian cherry (*Cornus mas*) produces the best fruits. It is native to south-central Europe and western Asia, and has been known for many centuries. Today the cornel has limited cultivation. It cannot compete, for quality and quantity, with other fruit trees. Its fruits which have an acid taste, are pickled, like olives, to make a pleasant-tasting preserve with a bland astringent action because of their tannic and gallic acid content. The fruit can also be eaten fresh, or used to prepare alcoholic drinks. It is sometimes preserved in honey or used to make a jelly.

The **Strawberry tree** (*Arbutus unedo*) is one of the most typical plants of the Mediterranean landscape. It has been known at least since Greek and Roman times. Theophrastus, Theocritus, Virgil, Ovid and Pliny have left a wealth of information about this plant, which is also called cane apple or dogwood. The fruits, arbutus berries, are tasteless but slightly sour. They are used for preserves, in the preparation of a drink similar to cider, and for the extraction of alcohol.

The **Jujube** (*Ziziphus jujuba*) is said to be native to the eastern and central part of the mountains of China and of northeastern India, but some botanists believe it to be native to Syria. In China, it was cultivated in the third or second century B.C. Its cultivation gradually spread so that no fewer than 43 varieties were known in the seventeenth century. It was introduced from China into the Philippines and later spread through Persia, Arabia and Asia Minor, arriving on the shores of the Mediterranean a few centuries before Christ. In Europe there are only a few cultivated varieties while in Asia they are prolific. The fruits are picked when they have reached their typical rust color, but must be left to wither for some time, so that the pulp becomes spongy and sweet. They are now used to sweeten medicine and are very soothing to sore throats and chests.

In the temperate regions of the northern hemisphere, in pastures and woods, it is common to find the **Whortleberry** or bilberry (*Vaccinium myrtillus*), called huckleberry in the United States. The fruits are believed to have been used for human consumption since prehistoric times, even perhaps, twenty-five to thirty centuries before Christ. The berries of this shrub are used alone or, in north European countries, especially Germany, as a side dish for game or meat, or as a dessert. They are, however, most suitable in the preparation of sweets, preserves and confectionery. In central Europe a whortleberry wine is made which is pleasant to taste and also recommended as an astringent and antiseptic for the intestinal tract. Besides the black whortleberry, there are other species of *Vaccinium* in the United States and Canada. They produce large fruits, $\frac{3}{4}$ inch or more in diameter, which are used not only in their native countries, but in recent years have also been exported to Europe, especially to Britain.

164

whortleberries

cornel

strawberry tree

jujube

Fig

The area of growth of the wild **Fig** (*Ficus carica* of the *Moraceae* or mulberry family) is much larger now than in the past. The fig is to be found in a vast uninterrupted area stretching from eastern Iran to the Canary Isles, through the Mediterranean countries. It is believed to have come from Syria. Later, especially through the Phoenicians, it spread to China and India, and relatively recently, was introduced to America and South Africa. Its cultivation goes back to very early times. Drawings of figs, dating back to several centuries before Christ, were found in the Gizeh Pyramid; the plant was undoubtedly known in Babylon, and is mentioned three times in the Odyssey. Aristotle, Theophrastus, and Dioscorides speak of the fig as a plant cultivated for a long time, whose fruits, especially when dried, were highly prized. The Latin authors, Cato, Varro and Columella, also left much information. Pliny writes that in his day there was a square where the Romans assembled, in which grew a fig tree in memory of the one under which, according to legend, Romulus and Remus were found suckling milk from the she-wolf. He adds that whenever the tree died of old age, the priests would be careful to plant another of the same race. Today the cultivation of the fig is extensive, particularly in Spain, Turkey and Italy, but more limited in the United States. In Italy the cultivation is rarely specialized; more often the fig is intermixed with grape vines and olive, almond, and citrus trees. There are at least seven hundred varieties which basically derive from a single species, *F. carica*, and from the subspecies *sativa*, which is commonly called domestic fig. There is also a wild species or caprifig, whose fruits are not edible, being dry and stringy. The fig produces only one (uniferous figs), or two crops (biferous figs); in the latter case the figs of the first crop, early figs, mature at the beginning of summer; second-crop figs appear toward August or September. Depending on the color of the skin, there are white, purple and red figs. They are usually eaten fresh, and have a pleasant taste, but are less nutritious than is commonly believed (80% water, 12% sugars). Part of the fresh fruit crop is canned for preserves, or used in spicy relishes. The greater amount of figs is sold as dried fruits which increases their nutritional value considerably, as the sugar content becomes five times greater than in the fresh fruit, and the amount of water is reduced to a quarter. Dried figs are an important commercial product as they can be exported to countries with unsuitable climates for their cultivation. The dried product is very good when stuffed with walnuts or almonds, and small pieces of orange or citron. Figs can be baked after being covered with confectioner's sugar or honey, and can also be used to make an alcoholic drink, very popular in Arabic countries, and, after roasting, as a coffee substitute. All apricot recipes are suitable for figs.

breba

black fig

white fig

Pomegranate
Rose apple
Brazilian cherry
Jambul
White and Black mulberry

Within the *Punicaceae* or pomegranate family, and the *Myrtaceae* or myrtle family, are some fruits of relatively minor importance that are, however, typical of these families. The **Pomegranate** (*Punica granatum*) is undoubtedly known to many people who have perhaps tasted it, if only out of curiosity, at least once. Probably native to Persia, this tree has always been connected with religious ceremonies or rites, during which both the flowers and fruits were used, because of their rather mysterious qualities. This was originally the custom among the Phoenicians, and later among the Greeks and Romans. Today it is grown more as an ornamental plant than as a fruit tree although the fruits have a pleasantly acid taste and can be eaten fresh, or used in the preparation of syrups, especially grenadine, and an alcoholic drink, as well as a jelly.

The fruit of *Eugenia jambos* is called **Rose Apple**. This is a species originally from India and is today grown extensively in Florida. Its name derives from the delicate fragrance of roses that is noticeable when the fruit is eaten. The rose apple is about the size and color of an apricot, with one to three seeds inside.

The fruits of the Pitanga or **Brazilian cherry** (*Eugenia uniflora*) are regarded as a curiosity. This plant produces sour fruits, spherical, $\frac{3}{4}$–1 inch in diameter, bright red in color and not too fleshy, with a large stone.

Another fruit belonging to the genus *Eugenia* is the **Jambul** (*E. jambos*, also called jambu), a name derived from India where it is said to have originated, and where it is still widespread and very popular, especially with Buddhists. The jambul is a tree that often grows to over 30 feet high; it has coriaceous, dark green and shiny leaves, small white flowers, and olivaceous green fruits whose size and consistency are similar to that of the olive. The fruit, like that of the Brazilian cherry, although having an agreeable taste, is not popular with Europeans and Americans.

Among the various species of the genus *Morus*, the **White Mulberry** (*M. alba*) and the **Black Mulberry** (*M. nigra*) are the most interesting. The former originated in the central and eastern parts of the mountains of China, where it is thought to have been cultivated for at least five thousand years for the rearing of the silkworm. The black mulberry appears to have originated either in the southern part of the Caucasus, or in the mountains of Nepal. They were both known to the Greco-Roman world, but only the black mulberry, having a better fruit, was spread and cultivated, while the other species, although having edible fruit but of a poorer quality, was used exclusively for silkworm culture. As a fruit tree the black mulberry is grown today in Iraq and Turkestan, where seedless varieties with large seedless fruits have been obtained. The berries have a pleasant flavor; their sugar content is 9% and they are generally eaten fresh. They can also be used, traditionally, to make a mildly astringent syrup, and the juice is sometimes used to color wines.

pomegranate flower

pomegranate

section of pomegranate

black mulberry

white mulberry

Pineapple

One of the earliest stories concerning the introduction of the **Pineapple** to Europe concerns the Emperor Charles V of Spain, who, seeing for the first time this strange fruit brought from America by Columbus, was so fearful of its oddity that he refused to taste it, in spite of his courtiers' assurances of its delicacy and fragrance. This anecdote, whether or not it actually occurred, clearly shows the astonishment of the Spanish toward the fruit's peculiar form. But by then Europe had become used to the pineapple and soon a profusion of names was found for it. The Spaniards called it *pina* because it resembled the pinecone, and the same term soon appeared in the English language: pineapple. The Portuguese coined the word *ananaz* from which the French, German, Italian and Dutch names derived. This fruit, with a firm and fragrant whitish yellow pulp, is used less in the fresh state than in canning or as crystallized fruits.

When eaten fresh as a dessert, the pineapple is delicious sliced and sprinkled with kirsch, which complements its flavor. The pulp can also be scooped out, and, after the hard core has been discarded, mixed with ice cream and stuffed back into the shell, to be frozen until it is to be eaten. If the ice cream is flavored with a sweet white wine it is even better.

The pineapple has over 15% sugar, malic and citric acids, water, and a ferment called bromeline which is very similar to pepsin. In Anglo-Saxon countries, especially in the United States and Canada, pineapples are used as a garnish for roast meats, especially ham. In the regions where the plant grows, a slightly alcoholic, pleasant-tasting wine is obtained by fermentation of the pulp at a temperature below 75°F. This drink is limited to the area of production, as it unfortunately spoils very quickly. The pineapple was also cultivated in hothouses for a certain time in Europe. This method proved unprofitable and was discontinued. Today the pineapple is grown in the Azores and the Canary Isles. Hawaii has extensive acreage in pineapples. Cultivated species are propagated vegetatively using the shoots which arise at the base of the plants. Today many varieties of the original species, *Ananas comosus*, are known. Many differ mostly in the morphology of the fruit. The most common European species is the white pineapple with ovoid fruits, and almost white pulp; it is not the best, having a rather sour taste. The "yellow pineapple," pyramidical fruit with golden flesh, is better tasting than the white; the "sugar loaf pineapple," with very large fruit, has a most delicate flavor. The Antilles pineapple, named after its place of cultivation, has fruit which is olive-colored outside and yellow inside; the fragrance and flavor are fairly close to those of the quince.

Cayenne, Red Spanish, Queen and Pernambuco are cultivars commonly grown in Puerto Rico, Hawaii, Florida and California.

pineapple

Avocado
Papaya
Mango
Litchi

The **Avocado** (*Persea americana* of the *Lauraceae* or laurel family) is originally from Central America and is widespread in Peru, Costa Rica, Guatemala and the southern states of America, where numerous varieties of different color and fragrance are grown. The fruit is shaped like an elongate pear, with a yellowish white pulp tending to green, of a semifirm consistency; in the lower part there is a single large seed. The Israelis seem to have been the first people to bring the avocado across the ocean, thinking, correctly, that the climatic conditions of their country would be suitable for the cultivation of this plant. In a short time their avocado orchards were able to produce the amount needed to supply all the European markets. The chemical composition of the avocado shows that the percentage of water, about 60%, is relatively low compared to the average of other fruits, so consequently there is a higher percentage of other components, increasing the nutritional value of the fruit. Lipids are present in large amounts, 30%. The digestible carbohydrates are only 3 to 10%. As well as protein and mineral salts, there are many vitamins, from A to K, including B_1, essential for normal metabolism, and B_2 which stimulates growth; also vitamin C (antiscorbutic) and pantothenic acid. The avocado is therefore highly nutritious, supplying about 250 calories per $3\frac{1}{2}$ ounces (100 grams) of pulp. It is eaten fresh and, because of the low percentage of sugars, can be used in antipasto and salads. If it is prepared some time before it is to be eaten, the stone should be left in the dish with the pulp, as otherwise it will turn black and look very unappetizing.

The **Papaya** (*Carica papaya*) of the small *Caricaceae* or pawpaw family, is native to the warm, tropical regions of America, India, the Malay Archipelago and Tahiti. Its reputation derives from its fruit, a large berry, almost the size and shape of a melon. The pulp is abundant, soft and orange-yellow in color. The flavor and texture are also similar to the melon's. Papayas are used for antipasto, and as fresh fruit and juice. Because of their digestive enzyme, they are used in meat tenderizers.

The **Mango** comes from the East Indies, Malaya, and southern Florida and California. It vaguely resembles a kidney-shaped peach, tapering at the top, with a juicy and fragrant pulp and a distinctive flavor, something between the apricot and the pineapple. The mango tree, *Mangifera indica* of the *Anacardiaceae* or cashew family, is one of the most productive plants of the tropical regions. Mangoes are normally eaten fresh, but can also be used in sweet chutnies and various jams.

The **Litchi** (*Litchi chinensis*) whose origin is evident from the specific Latin name, is a strange fruit, similar to a large walnut, of $1-1\frac{1}{2}$ inches in diameter, with an involucre covered by a shiny, scaly shell which contains the edible part, composed of a fleshy white mass completely covering the seed. It is grown domestically in the southern states of America.

avocado

section of papaya

papaya

litchi

mango

section of avocado

Passion flower
Actinidia or Chinese gooseberry

The name of the *passiflora* or **Passion flower** is known far and wide, even by those who have never tasted the fruit. The latter name is more common in English-speaking countries and in France (*fleur de la passion*) and Italy (*fiore della passione*). This plant has always aroused some interest, especially the flowers, each part of which has been interpreted, in an imaginative way, as relating to the Passion of Christ. The three styles represent the three nails with which Christ was crucified; the ovary is the sponge soaked in vinegar; the stamens represent the wounds on the hands, feet, and in the side; the crown, which is located above the petals, stands for the crown of thorns, and the petals and sepals indicate the Apostles. Botanically, the genus *Passiflora* includes species typical of warm or warm-temperate regions, found particularly in America. The majority of these species is grown as ornamentals, and a few have a certain nutritional importance for their edible fruit. *Passiflora edulis* is undoubtedly the best among the latter species. It is a climbing perennial, native to Brazil, and widely cultivated in tropical regions. It is also grown today around the Mediterranean. The fruit, which is called Granadilla (Grenadilla) or passion fruit, becomes when ripe, the size of an egg and purple-red in color. It contains a sweet and juicy pulp into which the small seeds are so tightly enclosed that it is difficult to eliminate them when eating the fresh fruit. Through particular processes eliminating the seeds, a juice can be extracted from the fruit, which is bottled and widely used in the countries where it is grown. The fruits are also made into various confections and jellies.

A plant of Chinese origin, *Actinidia sinensis*, usually called **Actinidia** or **Chinese gooseberry**, has only recently, in Italy, aroused interest for its fruits. In other European countries, particularly England and France, it has been known for some time, while California and New Zealand have the largest cultivations. The climate in Italy is favorable for the production of the Actinidia, whose fruits, according to recent studies, are thought to have considerable medicinal properties. The fruit contains protein, iron, calcium, and phosphorus salts, and also a large amount of vitamin C, as much as is found in ten lemons. The fruit ripens at the beginning of winter and can be stored until spring. It may be eaten with the skin which, however, must be rubbed free of the hairs or, better, peeled. The taste is pleasantly sour, but those who do not like such a flavor can improve it with some sugar or a few drops of liqueur.

passion fruit

passion flower

actinidia

Banana
Cherimoya

The most important species of the large group of edible plants belonging to the genus *Musa* can be limited to *M. paradisiaca* and *M. nana*, although almost 30 species are known. The **Banana** tree and its fruits, bananas, have been known since ancient times, even before the beginning of the cultivation of rice. Their place of origin is thought to be in east Asia and Oceania, from where they spread throughout the world. In Africa they were undoubtedly introduced by the Arabs. The Spanish and Portuguese brought this valued plant to America, first to the Antilles, then Santo Domingo, later to the Guianas and Brazil. A flourishing industry has now developed around the banana which is one of the most profitable agricultural resources of many countries situated along the tropical belt. Four South American countries export the largest tonnage of bananas: Honduras, Ecuador, Costa Rica, and Panama. To grow well, the banana needs a constantly warm climate. Some thousands of years ago, before man came to appreciate this plant, it produced almost tasteless fruits with black and bitter seeds. Through cultivation and genetic improvement it has now reached its remarkable flavor and fragrance. The banana is almost as rich as tomatoes and oranges in vitamins B and C, and so has anti-scorbutic qualities. It also contains iron, phosphorus, potassium, and calcium, but it is mostly for its high content (almost 20%) of easily assimilable sugars that it is considered so nutritious. The considerable amount of vitamin A also promotes the secretion of gastric juices, helping the digestion. Bananas can be eaten fresh, or flambéed with brown sugar, brandy or rum, or served with dates. American and Canary bananas are the most abundant, the former being larger, but the latter having more flavor and fragrance.

There is a Hindu legend that the banana was the forbidden fruit in the earthly paradise, and that it was the leaves of this plant with which the first man and woman covered their nakedness. The Indians grow two species of banana which they call Paradise banana and Adam's fig-tree which gives credence to this story.

The **Cherimoya** (*Annona cherimola* of the custard-apple or *Annonaceae*) is a species typical of the Colombian and Peruvian Andes where it grows up to altitudes of 6,000 feet. It is also cultivated largely in the Antilles, Venezuela, and the Guianas. After discarding the outer greenish part, the fruit is eaten raw without sugar. The pulp is digestible and can be eaten by everybody. In its native countries, it is considered one of the most delicate tropical fruits. Its flavor, between the pineapple and the strawberry, is, however, a little unusual for European palates, which may be why it is not very popular in Europe. Also, to develop all its most valued qualities, the fruit must reach perfect ripeness, which can only take place while it is still on the plant, or very soon afterward.

cherimoya

banana

Persimmon or *Kaki*

The **Persimmon** or **Kaki** tree (*Diospyros kaki*) is found in the wild state in some mountainous regions of central and eastern China. Its cultivation is ancient in both China and Japan. The introduction of the persimmon as a fruit tree in the Western World dates back only to the nineteenth century, first in the United States, then France, and finally Italy, as late as 1884. But in less than a century this beautiful autumnal fruit has spread everywhere. Although persimmons become ripe almost at the end of fall, they retain all the characteristics of the most typical summer fruits: sugary, juicy, and colorful. It seems a quirk of nature that, while other plants are disappearing at the approach of winter, the persimmons with their beautiful bright colors can still be seen hanging from the already leafless branches. In some areas, however, the fruit cannot complete the ripening cycle on the plant, so the farmer has to use artificial means to turn the still greenish pulp into its golden perfection. Persimmons have considerable food value, due to their high percentage of glucose and protein. In order to fully appreciate the taste of the fruit, it must be eaten when fully ripe, when all traces of tannic substances have disappeared. It is this that gives the fruit a typically sour taste that, as is often said, sets one's teeth on edge. More for curiosity than practical purposes, as the fruits are bought commercially, and not picked from the plant, they are divided into two groups: those formed by parthenocarpy, that is without being pollinated by the male, and those which form by normal fertilization with the pollen being transported by insects to the female. In the first case the fruits will have no seeds, and, at harvest time will have a consistent pulp with an astringent taste due to the tannic substance in the cells, so they will not be immediately edible. Therefore the fruits have to undergo a process of after ripening (that is, a series of enzymatic reactions which will transform and precipitate the tannic compounds). At the end of this process the fruits will be soft, watery, and sweet, and deep yellow in color. When the fruit forms as a result of pollination it contains from one to eight large seeds; the pulp, even before the harvest, has a good sweet taste and is a deep brown-red color. It is edible even when it has not yet acquired the typical yellow shade which it has when fully ripe. In the groups of the fruits with seeds can be included all the species of persimmon grown in our gardens, that is, those that still ripen on the tree. The presence of seeds is not of concern for common use. In the fruit-growing industry where economic interests are of prime importance, there is a tendency to spread and introduce new varieties of fruits without seeds, obtained by parthenocarpy. This means that because the last stages of maturation take place artificially, the skin does not wrinkle, and the fruit does not lose its attractive appearance. Persimmons are eaten raw or stewed, and are only rarely used in the canning industry. They are commercially cultivated in the southern United States, France, Spain, Italy, and generally around the Mediterranean. They are also known as Japanese medlars, and, more poetically, as "fruit of Jove."

lycopersicum

hatia

ribbed persimmon

fuji

mandarin persimmon

Indian fig or *Prickly pear*
Alkekengi or *Strawberry tomato*

The **Indian fig** (*Opuntia ficus-indica* of the *Cactaceae* or cactus family) has been part of the European flora since around the sixteenth century. The Spanish imported it from Mexico to Europe soon after the discovery of America. It is therefore of American origin, and spread rapidly in the temperate and warm regions of southern Europe and Africa. It is not to be found in the northern regions of Europe and only a few specimens which, in fact, never produce fruits, can be found along the Tyrrhenian coasts. Instead, around the Mediterranean, the Indian fig has become very much part of the countryside, often making a magnificent display. As well as growing wild, the Indian fig was once widely cultivated for its fruits which were considered of great importance as a food. The fruit is about the size of a slightly elongate apple; the color is first green, then, while it ripens, yellow and red. The internal part consists of a very sweet pulp, pale pink or whitish, depending on the different varieties, which enclose many hard seeds. There are also varieties completely without, or with only a few seeds, and fruits of smaller size (Indian fig *ariddari*). To pick and eat Indian figs can literally be a "thorny" problem. For harvesting a stick is used, at the tip of which is attached a tin can with the opening upward. The sharp edge of the can cuts the fruit from the plant and makes it fall inside. Eating the fig is a little more complicated. It is necessary to use a knife and fork. The skin is cut lengthwise so that it separates from the delicious juicy pulp. The seeds are eaten by some people, but others discard them. Little is known about the chemical composition of the Indian fig and its food value. The percentage of carbohydrates, almost all assimilable, is around 10%, but this figure is possibly lower than the actual amount to be found in the ripe fruit soon after harvesting. The mineral salts are few, mostly of the same type as found in other fruits. Indian figs are eaten raw when well ripe but can also be stewed or preserved for domestic use. Some of the varieties more commonly cultivated are: the yellowish Indian fig; the *ficodindia surfarina* of Sicily with very sweet firm pulp; the violet-red Indian or "bloody" fig of small size; the late *bastarduni* Indian fig, large with sweet pulp and excellent for prolonged storage.

The **Alkekengi** (*Physalis pubescens* of the *Solanaceae* or nightshade family) is an unusual plant. The berry is covered with a papery calyx. It is native to Mexico and is related to the tomato, the eggplant, and the pepper. The fruits are agreeable to eat, slightly acid, and vaguely similar to the tomato, although it is not highly regarded. They can be eaten raw or preserved and contain a fair amount of vitamins. They are sometimes called Cape gooseberry, strawberry tomato or winter cherry.

prickly pear

alkekengi

Citrus fruits

Citrus fruits, which are in the *Rutaceae* or rue family, are known to everyone; oranges, tangerines, lemons, grapefruits, limes and citrons. The genus *Citrus* contains woody perennial plants with evergreen leaves of varying size from shrubs, 6 feet high, to small trees of 15–20 feet. They do best in the mild climates of southern Italy, Sicily, Spain, Greece, Brazil, Mexico and, in the United States, Florida and southern California. The fruit of plants of the genus *Citrus* is a special kind of berry called a hesperidium, a term derived from Greek mythology. Traditionally, oranges were identified with the golden apples that grew in the garden of the Hesperides, in actual fact, probably the Canaries. The classification of the citrus is complex, and controversial. It seems right to speak of an "orange type" and a "citron type." There are many species of the same family, *Rutaceae*, including *C. aurantium*, *C. medica*, *C. maxima*, *C. aurantifolia*, and many others.

The sweet orange can be ascribed, according to different authorities, to the following species: *C. aurantium* var. *dulcis*, *C. aurantium* var. *vulgaris*, or *C. sinensis*. Unquestionably there are many synonyms for *C. aurantium* depending on the authority and the time of publication; generally *C. aurantium* refers to the sour or bitter orange that may appear in horticultural literature as *C. vulgaris*, *C. aurantium bigardia*, *C. aurantium vulgaris* or *C. amara*. It was brought from Palestine into Italy by the Crusaders. More resistant to cold than the sweet orange, *C. sinensis* (*C. aurantium* var. *dulcis*), it is often used as a grafting under-stock, or as an ornamental shrub. The fruits are virtually inedible because they are sour and very bitter.

To this same group also belong: the **Chinois** or China orange (*C. myrtifolia* or *C. aurantium* var. *amara*, subvar. *sinensis*); the **Mandarin** or **Tangerine** (*C. reticulata* var. *nobilis*, or *C. nobilis*, or *C. deliciosa*); the **Lime** or Adam's apple (*C. aurantium* var. *limetta*, or *C. aurantifolia*); the **Bergamot** (*C. aurantium* var. *bergamia*, or *C. bergamia*) which has never been found in the wild state, and is therefore presumed to be cultivated; the **Grapefruit** or pomelo (*C. aurantium* var. *grandis* or *C. grandis*, or *C. decumana*, or *C. maxima*). These varieties of grapefruit appear to be only ornamental plants, while the true, edible form would be the variety *uva carpa*.

To the "citron type" corresponds another large Linnaean species, *C. medica*, whose prototype is the citron (*C. medica* or *C. cedra*). This grows around Provence, Nice, near San Remo in Italy, and outside Genoa. The **Lemon** (*C. medica* var. *limon* or *C. limonum*, or *C. medica* var. *acida*) also belongs to this group, as does the pear or sweet lemon (*C. medica* var. *lumia*). A very good summer drink, lemonade, is made from the juice. All these varieties, both orange and citron types, can be considered at the level of species, as can be seen by reading the list of synonyms.

A description of each individual fruit may be more enlightening.

The **Sweet orange** is native to the Far East: India, China (where it is considered to be a wild fruit), and Indochina. Its introduction to the Mediterranean region was relatively late; it probably became known to the Romans around the first century A.D., following the conquest of oriental territories by the Roman Empire. During the expansion of Arab domination the cultivation of the sweet orange became a heritage of the Mediterranean. Vasco da Gama is said to have brought a root to Portugal. According to some authorities the word "orange" derives from the Arabic *narandj*, which comes from the Sanskrit *nagarunga*, meaning "fruit favored by the elephants." The cultivars of the sweet orange are now very numerous. Among them are many important American cultivars, notably Valencia, Washington Navel, Hamlin, Pineapple and Homosassa. Oranges are extensively grown in Florida and California. In Italy they are distinguished commercially as "blondes" and "blood," while in the United States they are classed as normal, blood and navel. Among the former, the most usual is the "common blonde," the "Calabrese" or "oval," the "vanilla," "sweet" or "Maltese." Among the blood oranges grown in Europe the best known are the *tarocco*, the *sanguinello*, and the *moro*. Oranges are commonly used fresh, or as a refreshing drink. They can also be made into a

oval

tarocco

blonde

blood orange

moro

bitter orange

little-known salad: the orange segments are seasoned with oil, vinegar, and pepper and a little curry powder, and served with watercress. Oranges have a high vitamin value, especially vitamin C: 60 mg per $3\frac{1}{2}$ ounces (100 grams) of fruit. The solid residue is 10%; protein less than 1%; sugars are between 7 and 8%; no lipids are present; $3\frac{1}{2}$ ounces (100 grams) of fruit supply 35 calories.

The fruits of the **Bitter orange** have no food interest. But the flowers and leaves are highly prized in the cosmetic industry for essences and perfumes. The rind is used for the extraction of an essential oil for liqueurs such as curaçao.

The **Mandarin** or **Tangerine** (*C. reticulata*), native to southern China (Yunnan) and Laos, is eaten almost exclusively as a fresh fruit, but can also be candied or glazed, or used in the preparation of a delicate liqueur. It is grown in the southern United States (where excellent cultivars include Satsuma, Dancy, Clementine, Kara, Frua, Sweet, and King Orange), and in parts of France. Those of Nice and Algeria are the most prized.

The "temple orange" is a hybrid between mandarin and orange, with large fruits, soft skin, and a pleasing taste. The vitamin value of the tangerine, expressed in vitamin C, is approximately one-third of that of the orange, and the calorific value is also lower: 7–8 calories per $3\frac{1}{2}$ ounces (100 grams) of fruit. The tangerine contains more water than the orange, and the percentage of carbohydrates is distinctly lower.

The **Lime** (*C. aurantifolia*), a small fruit tasting rather like the citron or the lemon, is mostly used candied or for summer drinks. The **Bergamot** is inedible and grown for the essence extracted from the rind, which is the basis for many perfumes. In Calabria, Italy, the bergamot is widely cultivated. Tahiti and Key are two outstanding American cultivars.

Grapefruit grows extensively in the United States, and its cultivation is successfully expanding in many climatically suitable areas, particularly Israel, Greece, Spain and Brazil. The fruit, spherical or globose, can reach up to $5\frac{1}{2}$ inches in diameter. The pulp is juicy with an agreeable bitter taste. It can be eaten fresh, or used in the preparation of an excellent juice. In Europe and America grapefruits are often served at the start of a meal. They are very good when sprinkled thickly with brown sugar and grilled. Excellent cultivars grown in North America are Marsh, Ruby, Duncan, Thompson (pink), and Foster.

The species or variety name of the **Citron**, *Medica*, does not indicate medicinal qualities; it means "coming from Media." The two cultivars that are most known and widespread near the Mediterranean are the Calabria citron with wrinkled peel, and the Florence citron. Diamante, Corsican, and Etron are common American varieties. An essential oil used for liqueurs, perfumes and medicines is obtained by distillation of the rind.

The Mediterranean regions provide the best conditions for growth of the **Lemon**, which is originally from the Far East. In Italy the production of lemons is concentrated in the traditional citrus-growing regions: Sicily, Calabria and Piana di Metaponto. As well as the citron, the lemon is also grown in the Sorrento peninsula and around the northern Italian lakes, especially the Garda, and in the United States extensively in Florida, Texas and California. Among the best known cultivars are the very popular "common," the *monachello* or "little monk," the *spadafora*, and, as a curiosity, the "Turk's Head" with very large fruits, the size of a man's head, having sweet pulp and juice. American cultivars are Eureka, Lisbon, Meyer, and Villa Franca. There are many culinary uses for the lemon, of which both the peel and the juice are used. The high amount of vitamin C, 60 mg per $3\frac{1}{2}$ ounces (100 grams) of fruit, is also a known fact. Less known, perhaps, is that the peel is not only a flavoring and a stimulant of the appetite, but also an antibacterial because of its content in essential oil, so that it is considered as a medicinal plant. Another little-known but highly recommended use, in the opinions of some people, is to rub the teeth and gums with a lemon slice. This has an astringent and hardening action on the gums and a whitening effect on the teeth. Lemons are also used in lemonade, sherbets, ice cream, and to heighten the taste of sea food.

The **Kumquat** (*Citrus japonica* or *Fortunella margarita* in honor of Robert Fortune who introduced it to Europe) has not been found in the wild state; it is said to be native to China, and has been cultivated for a long time in China, Japan, Indochina and Java, while it was only later that it was introduced into the Mediterranean basin, America, and Australia. There is a variety with round fruits (var. *madurensis* or *Limonella madurensis*) called *narum* by the Japanese, and another with oval fruits

citron

lemon

lemon blossom

(var. *margarita* or *Citrus margarita*) called *nagami*. Its rind is very aromatic, sweet and edible, and the fruits are eaten whole, fresh or candied or preserved in alcohol like cucumbers or pickles. It is a perfect garnish for roast duck.

In the "citron type," *C. Medica* (*C. cedra*) is the type species or prototype. Also grouped within this category is the true lemon, *C. limon* (*C. medica acida*, *C. medica limon*) and the pear or sweet lemon, *C. medica limia*. Among other citrus fruits there are the hybrids; temple (sweet orange and mandarin), tangelo (mandarin × grape-fruit: pomelo) and citrange (sweet orange × trifoliate orange, *Poncirus trifoliata*) and lastly the kumquat (*Fortunella Margarite* or *C. japonica*).

The areas of greatest citrus fruit production in the world are California, Florida, the southern states of America in general, some areas of Latin America and South Africa, and all the Mediterranean countries.

A curious aspect of citrus plants is provided by the so-called "freaks," first observed in a Florentine garden in 1640. These are citrus plants whose leaves, flowers, and fruits have characteristics varying between the orange and the lemon: lemons with orange skins or vice versa, alternate segments of orange or of lemon. They are "chimeras" or graft hybrids in which there is a kind of fusion of the tissues of the two species.

grapefruit

clementine

tangerine

kumquat

Italian stone pine
Ginkgo

The **Italian stone pine** (*Pinus pinea*), probably a native of Asia Minor, has been grown around the Mediterranean for a very long time, having been established there because of its climatic needs. Many classical authors have written about this plant: Theocritus, Cato, Virgil, and later, Dante, Boccaccio, and Byron who all speak of the pine woods of Ravenna which, although much diminished throughout the centuries, still remain today one of the greater areas of concentration of pine. In Italy, this tree has a fair economic importance and is extensively cultivated in the peninsula. It is the fruits, rather than the wood, which are the main source of profit, but these fruits do not appear on the plant until their fifteenth year of growth and yield their greatest production only after half a century of life. Pignolia nuts, as the seeds are called in the United States, are provided by the pinecones, and used in the confectionery industry to make various kinds of sweets and cakes. The pignolias are white, fleshy, and resemble almonds in flavor. They can also be eaten raw, or as a garnish for cookies, or in macaroons. In cookery they are known as *pignoli*. They cannot be stored for long because the fats which they contain spoil easily.

The **Ginkgo** (*Ginkgo biloba*) is usually described as a "living fossil," and well deserves this name. It belongs to the order Ginkgoales, plants that existed several hundred million years ago, in the Permian period, and were one of the most typical elements of the forests of that time. Today the composition of those forests is completely changed and of the Ginkgoales group, only *G. biloba* remains. Its common name is, strangely, almost unknown, maidenhair tree. This beautiful plant seems to exist in the wild state only in a limited area of China. It is frequently found in other parts of the Asian continent, however, especially Japan and Korea, mostly around holy Buddhist places, where it grows wild, escaped from cultivation, or else is grown as an ornamental. It became known in Europe only at the beginning of the eighteenth century, when Kaempfer brought it back from Asia where he had traveled extensively. So great had been his surprise at the sight of this hitherto unknown plant, which looked so strange to him, the leaves streaming out like oriental banners, that he could not tear himself away from it for some time. *G. biloba* immediately aroused curiosity and interest in Europe too, and soon spread as an ornamental in parks and gardens everywhere. Today it is found frequently along avenues in cities, mostly because of its great resistance to long droughts or very cold weather. From the aesthetic viewpoint the ginkgo can be considered a plant of extreme beauty and particular charm, but it has relatively limited use for food. Some importance can be attributed to the seeds of the female plant, which are rich in starches and can be eaten cooked or raw. Their use is common in the East especially during wedding ceremonies. In China and Japan ginkgo seeds are sold on the market under the name of *ginan*. An interesting sidelight is that the ginkgo tree has no insect or disease pests of any kind, apparently because it has evolved an immunity, or at least a resistance to them, or, as some believers would think, because it grows on sacred ground.

Italian stone pine

ginkgo

Chestnut

The street vendors with their pushcarts full of roasted, and roasting **Chestnuts** are one of the most nostalgic characteristics of approaching winter in the streets of many American and European cities in late autumn. In the past few decades since World War II they have become less and less numerous. Sadly, this homely tradition is slowly disappearing, but tastes change in the course of time, and the lowly chestnuts are overshadowed by other, more modern, and commercially more profitable, fruits. Also, the cultivation of the chestnut (*Castanea sativa* = European chestnut) is dwindling for other reasons; among them, erosion of the soil, the exploitation of the forests by man, and most important of all, the fungus diseases, primarily chestnut blight and cortical canker, which have been destroying this plant.

Pliny, in his *Natural History* encyclopedia, described eight varieties of chestnut, all with different names. The best ones, it was said, in those times, came from the areas around Taranto and Naples. Pliny maintained that the first chestnuts originated in Sardis, a town of Lydia, previously the residence of Croesus, and he expressed surprise that the Romans ate them only roasted. However, the true place of origin of the chestnut has still not been identified. It is, nevertheless, a Mediterranean plant, extending throughout southern Europe and a few areas in Asia Minor and Algeria.

The known varieties of the chestnut are numerous; the Italian ones number at least three hundred. The American chestnut, *C. dentata*, produces nuts that are richer and sweeter than the European, but it has been almost entirely wiped out by the chestnut blight fungus. Hybrids of the American and Oriental chestnut are the only ones that can be grown and they lack both the size and quality of the true American chestnut. However, for commerce, and also because the knowledge of the systematics of the species is rather scarce, there is a tendency to divide the chestnut into two large groups: marrons and domestic chestnuts. The marrons are heart-shaped, with triangular bases; shiny, reddish-brown shells with darker stripes, sweet and fleshy pulp completely detached from the inside pellicles. The domestic chestnuts which are generally larger, are flattened on one side and have very dark brown shells; the internal skin, or pellicle, is attached to the flesh, which, although less sweet than that of the marron, has a very pleasant flavor.

Until quite recently, there was great interest in this plant as a food source. Chestnuts were considered a staple food, and an inferior flour can be made of them. In Corsica they are made into a kind of polenta, a thick, dry paste which is poured onto a floured cloth, then cut into slices with a thread (as are certain cheeses), and either eaten as they are, or fried or grilled. *Mont Blanc*, by comparison, is a very sophisticated dessert, and can be easily prepared by using a tin of sweetened chestnut purée, whipping it up with brandy or any liqueur, and serving it chilled, in individual dishes with stiffly beaten cream piled on top. It is a tiring and painful process, involving burnt fingers, to make the purée oneself, although the empty can can always be hidden in the trash can and the impression given that the hostess is a cordon-bleu. Unsweetened chestnut purée, also available commercially, is a good accompaniment to turkey and Brussels sprouts. When roasting chestnuts, a small cut should be made on the domed face of the shell, so as to avoid explosive popping. Another use for chestnut flour is as *castagnacci*, thick fritters with a chestnut flour base. Chestnuts can also be made into preserves, particularly that true delicacy, the candied chestnuts known as *marrons glacés*. Chestnuts have undoubtedly a high food value: when fresh they contain somewhat less than 60% water and as much as 37% sugar and starches. The rest is provided by nitrogen compounds, cellulose, ash, lipids and mineral salts. So there is a large amount of carbohydrates, while the protein is present only in traces. Chestnuts can, therefore, partly substitute for bread, although they have a lower nutritive value, but a higher calorific value than other common foods, which explains their wider consumption in the past, especially during periods of famine.

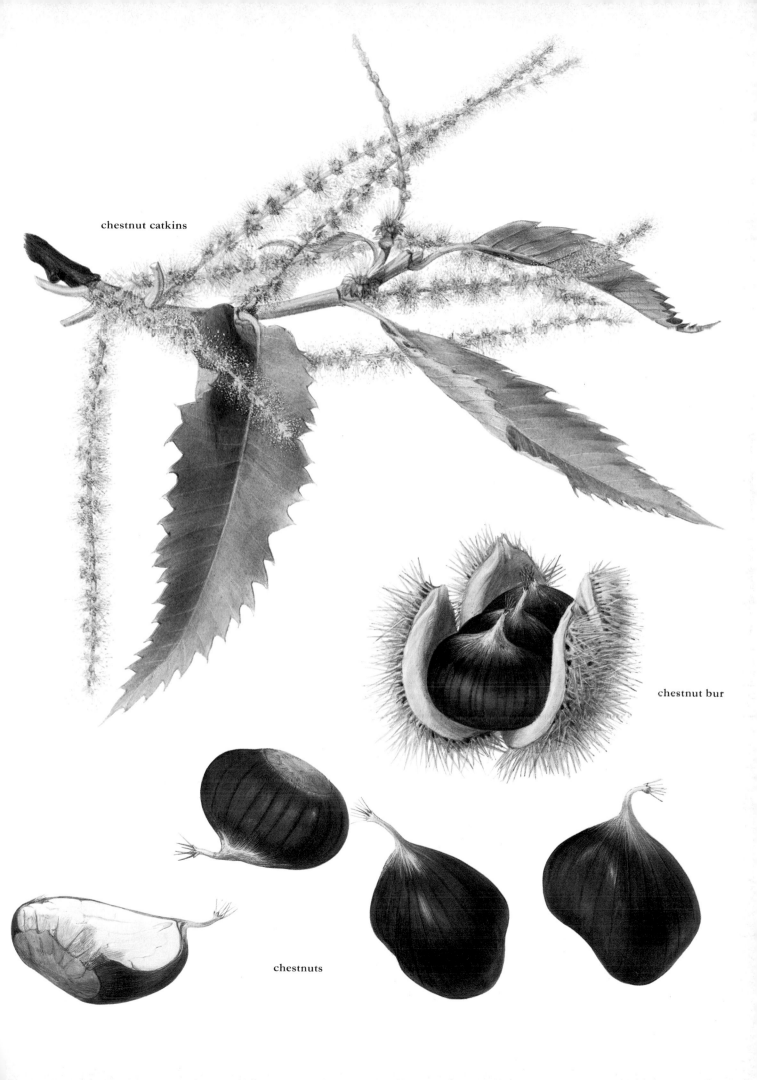

chestnut catkins

chestnut bur

chestnuts

Walnut
Hazelnut or Filbert

Contrary to what has been the case for many "fruits of the earth," little information has been left to us about the **Walnut** by Virgil, or even by Pliny in his encyclopedia of natural history, *Historia Naturalis.* Walnuts are thought to have been used by the Greeks at least four centuries before Christ, and the Romans began cultivation all over Europe. This plant, the most widely known species of the genus *Juglans*, was certainly part of the European flora of those times. Virgil and Pliny speak of *nuces* (nuts), but there is no certainty that they were walnuts. It seems, however, that the common walnut is originally from northern Persia, Armenia, and areas around the Caspian Sea. Although the date of its introduction to Europe is not known, the walnut has become so well adapted in that continent that it now seems native to it. Like all fruit trees that have been cultivated for a long time, the walnut is represented by a considerable number of varieties much prized for their seeds. Among them is the excellent Sorrento with tender and slightly elongate shell, the Saint John, late, of medium size, and the Feltro with a tender shell; all Italian varieties. Walnuts can be consumed fresh shortly after picking from the tree, or dried. The difference lies in a considerable decrease of water, compensated by an increase of nitrogen compounds and lipids, the latter averaging more than 50%. Walnut oil is very good and is sometimes preferred to olive oil, being heavier, sweet, and characteristically aromatic. But if it is not used quickly it turns rancid, loses its fluidity, and thickens into a sort of jelly. The young seeds are used in confectionery. An excellent liqueur, mostly homemade, but also prepared industrially, is obtained from the kernels of the walnuts; it is called *nocino* in Italy, and *brou* in France. It is a good afterdinner liqueur with a helpful digestive action. In the United States the walnut tree has always been the preferred wood for making gunstocks; the supply of the wood was almost exhausted during World War II.

At one time, in the stableyards of all country houses and farms, a walnut tree was to be found. This was to keep flies away from the horses.

There is an old, and certainly untrue, English rhyme: "A woman, a dog and a walnut tree; the more you beat them, the better they be."

Cultivated **Hazelnuts** are called **Filberts** (*Corylus avellana* or *C. maxima*) and this is because they ripen about St. Philbert's Day, August 22. Many fossil remains have been found, proving the cultivation of the filbert to be very old. They are still grown extensively in parts of Italy and Sicily. As with the walnut, there are numerous varieties with different characteristics and uses which can be divided into two large groups: those producing elongate fruits, and those producing round fruits. The latter are more prized and better suited for export. Among the many European varieties are the "gentle round filbert" of Piedmont, round, of medium size and with an agreeable taste; the "Roman filbert" of high yield when shelled, with a good, delicate taste and a very thin shell; and the Saint John from Avellino, very early, large, and highly prized, with a rather elongate shape, a flat base and a not too prominent apex. Filberts are eaten fresh or, more commonly, dried. They are used in confectionery for making particular kinds of chocolate and nougat candies. When subjected to a pressing process, the filberts yield a fair amount of oil, which, although not one of the best from a food point of view, is often used in the preparation of cosmetics and perfumes. Very thin crêpes filled with a cream made of lightly roasted, finely ground hazelnuts, make an unforgettable dessert.

walnut flower

hazelnut

walnut

Almond
Brazil nut
Pecan

The centers of origin of the **Almond** (*Prunus Amygdalus* or *Amygdalus communis* of the *Rosaceae*) were probably some areas of Asian Russia, China and Japan. As a cultivated plant it was known to the Hebrews several centuries before Christ, and is mentioned in the Book of Genesis. The introduction of the tree to the western world is possibly due to the Phoenicians. Later the Greeks brought this plant to Italy, in Magna Graecia, and from there it spread through Spain, Germany, France, and toward the end of the sixteenth century, to South and North America. The almond tree, sometimes associated with the olive and the grape, is grown all over the Mediterranean, from Provence to Algeria, favoring arid and rocky soils. Almond cultures are found mostly in Italy, North Africa, California, southern Sardinia, southern France and Sicily, where it is, with the early almond blossom, a typical part of the January landscape. The almond nut used in commerce is the pit or stone of a peachlike fruit, containing a seed of high calorific value, determined mostly by the abundance of lipids, about 51%. Protein makes up a good 15%. The presence of vitamin B_1 promotes the body's growth and stimulates the appetite. Iron and calcium, the latter often lacking in the normal diet, are also present. Depending on the hardness of the shell and flavor of the seed, two types of almond are distinguished: sweet with soft, semisoft, and hard shells, and bitter, with hard shells. There is not much difference between bitter and sweet almonds: the former are slightly smaller with seeds poorer in lipids and richer in nitrogen compounds. The presence of amygdaline ($2-4\%$) is substantial, and causes the characteristic bitter taste. Almonds, besides being consumed raw, are used in confectionery for the preparation of nougats, candied almonds (i.e. almonds coated with sugar, and traditionally given as presents at baptisms in Catholic countries), macaroons and flour. Over half the almond's weight is oil which is used by the pharmaceutical and perfume industries.

The species of the genus *Bertholletia* characterize the Brazilian flora. They are large trees, well over 100 feet high, and with sizable, leathery leaves, whose large fruits open at maturity to show about 20 kidney-shaped seeds with woody and wrinkled shells, enclosed inside. These seeds are called **Brazil nuts** or Para nuts, and contain a kernel similar to the almond or coconut in taste. The nuts are popular all over the world, and grow mostly in South America, especially in Brazil. In France they are called "American chestnuts." The nut is also the source of an oil which, however, is unsuitable for storage and quickly turns rancid.

The **Pecan** (*Carya illinoensis*) is of North American origin. It is a large tree, 100–120 feet high, belonging to the *Juglandaceae* or walnut family. The fruit, like that of the walnut, is enveloped in a hard and woody husk, which opens when ripe, releasing four nuts with edible, oily kernels of excellent flavor. One of the most famous and irresistible North American desserts is the pecan pie, made with maple syrup. This pie is, unfortunately, almost unknown in Britain, possibly because of the very high price of the nuts.

almond

pecan

Brazil nut

Date

The **Date** is thought of as a highly esteemed food for the African and Middle Eastern populations, and as a dessert for the tables of Western countries. There are people for whom the date represents almost the only available and abundant food; in Persia, Arabia, Egypt, and in general all the countries of North Africa, this fruit is the staple food of the poor. The cultivation of dates goes back to antiquity; records show that they were known to the Chaldeans. Dates are the fruits produced by a particular group of palm trees, the "date palms" which botanically belong to the species *Phoenix dactylifera*, a plant which comes into bearing after the fourth year of life, and which has its greatest production when it is almost eighty years old. After this the production declines, but the palm still serves as a much sought-after shade for the nomadic caravans that cross the desert. The date palm is almost worshiped by the local inhabitants for its fruits and the many other uses that can be made of other parts of the plant. The terminal, upper part of the trunk, where the inflorescence and the new leaf-shoots are borne, provides a juice that, after fermentation, yields a "palm wine," and also a spirit widely consumed by the Arabs, in spite of the restrictions imposed by the Islamic religion which forbids alcohol. The stems and leaves are used for building huts, while the fibers of the leaves are used to manufacture baskets, ropes, hats, mats, and many other everyday objects. The wood of the tree is fairly combustible, and, in some areas, is the only wood product available to make fires. The many varieties of the date palm can be divided in two main groups: hard and soft dates. The latter are much more prized; they are moist and remain so for a long time, even after drying. The best quality is the Deglet Ennour or Sunray, typical of the oases. Dry dates, although less valued, also have good qualities: they are largely grown along the African coasts, and the best varieties, once harvested, are reduced to a paste and exported mostly to the Arab countries where they are widely used as food. They are also grown in South Carolina and Arizona. The date can be considered a concentrate of nutritious and calorific substances: the percentage of sugars makes up 70% of the weight. To prove the high calorific potential, the 300 calories supplied by $3\frac{1}{2}$ ounces (100 grams) of dates corresponds to those of a small steak. In addition, they contain valuable mineral salts and a considerable amount of vitamins A, B, C and D. Unfortunately this fruit is often underrated, perhaps because its goodness is partly lost as a result of the processes necessary for its preservation. In early medicine dates were one of the four fruits renowned for curing throat and chest ailments. The other three were the fig, the raisin and the jujube.

date

Carob
Pistachio
Cashew

It is believed that the **Carob** (*Ceratonia siliqua*) is native to the Orient, probably the Levant. Today it grows spontaneously throughout the Mediterranean, and the varieties growing in Sicily have particularly fleshy fruits, rich in sugar. The varieties cultivated there were probably introduced by the Arabs and have perhaps taken the place of the native forms that disappeared in the course of time, undoubtedly because they were less productive. The carobs are harvested in September by shaking the branches of the tree with long sticks. They are then kept in well ventilated storehouses where they are allowed to dry completely. The fruit is used partly for human consumption, especially in the Mediterranean where the pod is eaten as a form of candy bar by children. It is also used for animal feed. A good yield in alcohol can be obtained by fermentation of the pulp, because of the rich sugar content (up to 50%). The pharmaceutical industry uses carob in the preparation of cough linctus, and a particular syrup, called "carob molasses" which can be made at home. Health-food enthusiasts find the carob a very good substitute for chocolate. The carob is sometimes called "St. John's Bread" as it is thought to be the locusts eaten by John the Baptist in the desert.

The **Pistachio** (*Pistacia vera*) is a plant probably also originating in the Levant, from where it spread through Palestine, Iran, Iraq, and into certain areas of India and Russian Central Asia. The first mention of the pistachio is found in the Bible. It was also known in Persia around the sixth century B.C., and in Greece, according to writings left by Theophrastus and Nicander. The information about the introduction of the pistachio into Europe is controversial. According to Pliny, it is certain that this plant arrived in Rome a few years after the birth of Christ. It was supposedly brought by Vitellius. According to other authorities, it was introduced by the Arabs into Sicily where it is now grown on several thousand acres in the provinces. The pistachio is much valued for its fruits, and even more for the seeds contained in them. Its chemical composition is similar to that of the average dry fruit: low, as is logical, in the percentage of water, hardly 4%; about 17% sugars and cellulose, and of nitrogen compounds; and a considerable content of lipids, up to 54%, which is exploited for the extraction of an oil used mostly in confectionery, and in lesser amounts in the cosmetics industry for its emollient properties. Even greater is the direct use of the shelled pistachio nut, domestically and commercially as flavoring for the preparation of various dishes, sauces, cakes and ice creams with a characteristic flavor, and even in pork curing in Europe.

The **Cashew** (*Anacardium occidentale*) which is commonly called the "pear cashew" can be included among the plants producing dry fruits, although after looking at the pear-shaped body, an enormously overgrown fruit stalk, supporting the cashew nut, it may seem more proper to classify it among the plants producing pulpy fruits. The part constituting the false fruit (cashew apple) is tasty and juicy and, when fully ripe, can be eaten raw, or sliced and sweetened with sugar. The dry fruit called the "nut," which is the true fruit, must be freed from the shell, which contains a very caustic oil, and it can then be eaten either raw or roasted quickly under embers, or broiled. In Brazil the fermented cashew nut fruit produces a kind of wine, which is famous locally, and also a vinegar called *anacard*.

carob

pistachio

cashew nut

Sage
Thyme
Rosemary

Among the most common aromatic and seasoning herbs, some of the best are species all belonging to the *Labiatae* or mint family: sage, thyme, rosemary, peppermint, oregano, calamint, marjoram, basil and balm mint.

As is usually the case for aromatic plants, sage, thyme and rosemary are also considered as medicinal plants. The leaves of **Sage** (*Salvia officinalis*) contain essential oil formed by various components: salviol, salvene, pinene, and borneol (camphol). There are bitter substances and resins, and they are said to have tonic-digestive, antispasmodic, antiseptic, antiperspirant, resolvent, and healing properties, all of which justify the various popular uses of this herb: for example, the custom of rubbing teeth and gums with sage leaves, and of making compresses or simple rubbings of the leaves have been said to have a beneficial action on erythemas (rashes) or eczema. Better known than the pharmaceutical applications are the gastronomic uses of sage in the cooking of certain types of fish, such as trout with butter and sage, as a seasoning for marinated fish or poultry stuffing, and in many other recipes. There are three distinct types of sage in France. In the United States there are only small cultivations of the garden sage and the white sage, so each year large amounts are imported into the States.

Thyme (*Thymus vulgaris*) has pharmacological properties like those of sage. It contains an essential oil, composed of thymol, carvacrol, pinene, borneol, bitter principles and resins, and also is thought to act as a tonic-aromatic, carminative, antiseptic, and antispasmodic. It is excellent in meat stews and casseroles if used with a light hand. Shakespeare mentions it poetically in *A Midsummer Night's Dream*: "I know a bank whereon the wild thyme blows." It will grow very well in small pots on kitchen windowsills, too.

Rosemary (*Rosmarinus officinalis*) is perhaps more often used than either sage or thyme, but still needs to be treated with discretion. In the dialect of some Italian regions, the rosemary is called *rosa marina* (sea rose), certainly not because of any resemblance to the rose, but because rosemary grows preferably in arid areas where rain is very scarce, but where there is a considerable formation of night dew: this phenomenon is typical of even very arid areas, near the sea. This herb is a perennial evergreen, and can grow up to as high as 5 feet. It contains principles similar to those of sage and thyme, essential oil composed of borneol, pinene, and camphene, and bitter principles, tannic acid (tannin) and resins. Because of these components rosemary has some properties of pharmacological interest, and its tonic, stimulant and digestive actions, as well as its flavor account for its widespread use in the kitchen. Rosemary is considered by many gourmets to be the best herb of all for roasts and barbecued meat, and it is also good for boiled meats and sauces. Shakespeare in *Hamlet* has Ophelia say, "There's rosemary, that's for remembrance; pray, love, remember."

thyme

sage

rosemary

Peppermint
Oregano
Calamint
Marjoram

Peppermint (*Mentha piperita*) is one of the best known aromatic herbs, particularly for its importance in the confectionery and spirits industries. It is probably a hybrid between *M. viridis* (gentle or green mint) and *M. aquatica* (water mint). It is a perennial herb with square stems characteristic of the mint family, *Labiatae*. Its opposite leaves are either dark red (black mint) or green (white mint), heart-shaped at the base and oval elongate or lanceolate. The inflorescence is a spike of whorled flowers. Peppermint is grown both in gardens and commercially: for the latter, a cultivar of black mint, called "Italo-mitcham" is preferred. It contains essential oils, especially rich in menthol, and acts as a stimulant of gastric secretions and movements, and is therefore good for the digestion. Besides its use in confectionery and distilling, it is also used to flavor toothpastes and as a component of analgesic and disinfectant remedies. In some countries it is used to season meats, particularly mutton and lamb, and vegetable dishes, while elsewhere, particularly by health-food addicts, it is used only as an infusion for tea. Culpeper recommended boiled peppermint, given to children to "remove the gripes."

Oregano or wild marjoram (*Origanum vulgare*) is a perennial herb with annual aerial shoots, widespread throughout Europe and western Asia, and especially common in Italy where it grows in untilled and grassy fields, woods, clearings, and sunny thickets. However, only the wild marjoram of the southern regions is really fragrant and is therefore much used in cooking. The parts used are the flowering tops that are sold in small, fragrant bunches in many continental markets. Wild marjoram contains essential oils and has aromatic, antiseptic and antispasmodic properties. In cooking, oregano is the typical and indispensible flavoring of the Neapolitan pizza and of meats and sauces rightly called "Italian style" in countries other than Italy. Sprinkled lightly on tomato salad it improves the taste immensely.

Calamint (*Satureja calamintha* or *C. officinalis*) is also a perennial herb with annual shoots. It is widespread around the Mediterranean and in central Europe, and is especially common in Italy, particularly the variety *nepeta*, in arid, sunny fields, on heaths and uplands, etc. The calamint has specialized uses in the kitchen, mostly in the preparation of zucchini, and other "Roman style" vegetables. It is also known by the names of catnip and catmint (both, obviously, irresistible to cats), usually reserved to indicate another species, *Nepeta cataria*. *C. nepeta* is the field balm, also called basil-thyme, a term sometimes used to indicate *Satureja calamintha*.

Marjoram or sweet marjoram (*Origanum majorana* or *M. hortensis*) is also a perennial and suffruticose herb, woody at the base and herbaceous above. It is native to Asia and is frequently grown in gardens, and in pots in kitchens. The herbaceous tops are the parts used. They contain the active principles of the *Labiatae*, essential oils, and have a stimulating and antiseptic action on the body. Sweet marjoram is used to season many dishes from omelets to meat or fish casseroles.

calamint

marjoram

peppermint

oregano

Basil
Balm

Basil (*Ocimum basilicum*), one of the most valued aromatic plants, is native to Africa and other warm areas (perhaps India) in Asia, and has been widely cultivated since ancient times. It possibly came to Europe through the Middle East in comparatively recent times. Boccaccio in the *Decameron* mentions it in the story of Isabella who waters with her tears the pot of basil in which her lover's head is buried. This story is also the subject of a poem by Keats. Basil is an annual herb of variable size, from 3–18 inches high, depending on the cultivars and conditions of growth. It has erect stems, simple or branching, with opposite oval leaves. The flowers, forming large, terminal inflorescences, have white corollas. Commercially, basil is divided into bush basil (or lesser basil) (the variety *minimum*), and greater basil. These two categories include other classifications: the bush group contains the various green bush, green dwarf compact bush, violet bush basil, and violet dwarf compact bush. Greater basil includes the green large, violet large, lettuce-leaved, etc. Like many other *Labiatae*, basil contains essential oils, tannic acid and saponins. Especially because of its content in essential oils, basil, in addition to its uses in cookery, can be used as an infusion thought to have antispasmodic, stimulant, digestive, diuretic and other actions. As a seasoning it is excellent in tomato sauce; tomato and basil seem to have a culinary affinity; and for the preparations of the celebrated *pesto* famous along the coast from Genoa to Provence. *Pesto* is a rather thick sauce made with basil, Romano cheese, and pine or walnuts, salt, olive oil, and sometimes, garlic, all of which are pounded together with a mortar and pestle. *Pesto* is the main condiment in Ligurian cookery for pasta. Gourmets suggest the use of basil for many other dishes, particularly minestrone: it is in fact good with a wide variety of dishes. Used fresh and raw in sandwiches or summer salads, it is a real delicacy.

Balm is often called *cedronella* in Italy and in French country districts, *citronnelle*; but these names could confuse it with herb Louise or lemon verbena which is botanically known as *Lippia citriodora*. It is a perennial herb with annual aerial shoots, found along hedges, in untilled fields and at the edges of woods. *Melissa officinalis* is the botanical Latin name of balm. It contains essential oils and other principles, and is believed to have antispasmodic, sedative, and digestive action. In cookery it can be used to flavor white wines and summer beverages, or in salads, omelets, and pickled or marinated fish.

balm

lettuce-leaved basil

variegated basil

basil with oregano-
shaped leaves

smooth green-leaved basil

Bay or Laurel
Juniper
Rue
Prickly ash

True **Laurel** or **Bay** (*Laurus nobilis* of the *Laureaceae*) is a dioecious plant, that is, with masculine and feminine flower structures on separate plants. The latter are easily recognizable at the time of fruiting as they bear the fruits. Besides being an aromatic plant used in the *bouquet garni* for cooking, bay is a truly medicinal herb, and all parts of the plant are used, including the fruits. The leaves and fruits contain essential oil, bitter principles and tannic acid. The fruits, moreover, also contain an ample amount of lipids, and help to make the laurel oil or butter, which is a component of laurin ointment, used in human and veterinary medicine. The berries are distilled to make a liqueur called Fioravanti. The bay fruits are also employed in sweat-inducing antiflatulent aromatic baths. The laurel is historically an illustrious, symbolic plant. Wreaths to crown heroes and scholars were made with its leaves; the term "laureate" derives from this tradition. In the Middle Ages and even up to the eighteenth century, bay, apart from being a cure-all, also "resisteth witchcraft very potently" according to Culpeper's *The English Physician Enlarged, or the Herbal*, 1653.

The **Juniper** (*Juniperus communis* of the *Cupressaceae*) is also a healing plant. For culinary uses (the flavoring of meats, especially game) and in the spirits industry, for the manufacture of gin, only the berries are needed, while the medicinal action (anticatarrhal, soothing, diuretic) is present in both the berries and the branches. These contain pinene, camphene, borneol, a bitter principle called juniperin, wax and resins. As well as gin, a medicinal wine called Juniper Hippocras is made from the berries.

The importance of **Rue** (*Ruta graveolens* of the *Rutaceae*) is secondary and is practically limited to the flavoring of *grappa*, a brandy typical of northern Italy. In the past however, its reputation as a medicinal plant was very great. The ancients considered it a true panacea; Theophrastus, Dioscorides, Galen, and other great physicians of classical antiquity, used it in many cases to cure poisoning, gout, pimples, dropsy, nose-bleeding, and even hysterics. It was because of its ana-phrodisiac qualities that this plant was grown in the Middle Ages in all monasteries and its use prescribed for monks who wished to preserve their purity. Finally, although there are considerable differences, rue belongs to the same family as the orange, although placed in a different subfamily (*Rutoideae*) than that of the orange (*Aurantioideae*):

Prickly ash (*Zanthoxylum alatum* of the *Rutaceae*) is grown mostly as an orna-mental. However, its small fruits can be used so effectively in cookery as a sub-stitute for pepper that it is popularly known as "false pepper."

bay

prickly ash

juniper

rue

Caper
Nasturtium
Mustard

The **Caper** (*Capparis spinosa* of the *Capparidaceae*) is diffused throughout southern France, Algeria, Turkey, Asia Minor and the Mediterranean region, having as a habitat old walls and cliffs, on which it provides a graceful ornament. It is a perennial plant, more or less woody at the base, bushy, with shoots up to 25–32 inches long that in the northern regions sometimes dry out completely in winter. The leaves are fleshy and shiny, and the flowers are particularly beautiful with four large white petals and numerous long stamens. The ovary is supported by a long peduncle called "gynophore." The fruit is a dry, spongy berry containing numerous blackish, kidney-shaped seeds. Within the vast species *C. spinosa* can be distinguished three varieties: *aculeata* and *inermis*, both completely or almost glabrous, and *sicula*, typical of the southern Mediterranean regions but also grown in the Crimea, the Caucasus, Persia, and Mesopotamia. They are all characterized by the white and tomentose vegetative parts and the presence of thorns. This last variety, besides growing on rocky terrain, is also found on stony and clay-loam soils. The young floral buds, not yet open, the young fruits, as soon as they form, as well as in some areas, the young branches with the tenderest leaves, are the parts of the plant which are used. Preserved or pickled capers are used to garnish hors-d'œuvres, in sauces and stuffings and to flavor meats, like *vitello tonnato*. They contain a bitter and irritant glucoside, having tonic and diuretic properties. The smaller and firmer "nonesuch" capers which grow in France are better than the English variety. They should not be confused, however, with the young seeds of the **Nasturtium** or Indian cress (*Tropaeolum majus*), which can be used as a substitute for capers. This plant belongs to the family *Tropaeolaceae*, close to the *Capparidaceae* family, and is more frequently grown in gardens as a decorative plant than as a food. It was brought to Europe by the Jesuits who traveled across the world converting "heathens." It is sometimes called after them, "Jesuits' cress."

The **Black mustard** (*Brassica nigra* or *Sinapis nigra*) and the white mustard (*B. alba* or *S. alba*) are interesting aromatic and medicinal plants. The black mustard of the *Cruciferae* or mustard family, is common in central and southern Europe, western Asia, and North Africa. It also grows wild in wheat fields and waste places. The Romans brought it to Gaul and it is now extensively cultivated virtually all around the Mediterranean. It is an annual herbaceous plant, from 20–40 inches, or more, simple at the base, branched at the top. The flowers are gathered in a large, loose raceme (panicle). The "drug" (botanically "drug" is the part of the plant used for medicinal purposes) is provided by the seeds, small, about 1 mm in diameter and blackish-red in color. The **White mustard** (of the *Cruciferae*) is a plant scattered all over the Mediterranean area, smaller (about 18–20 inches), found in fields and waste places, either wild or cultivated. Like the black mustard, the "drug" is provided by the seeds, light yellowish in color, about 2 mm in size, with a minutely wrinkled surface. Mustard gives to food a typically pungent taste, and, from a culinary viewpoint, is well known for stimulating the digestion. Mustard is used for preparing sauces and for boiled or roast meats. Some of the French commercial brands such as Dijon and Bordeaux are exported all over the world.

caper branch with buds

nasturtium

black mustard

white mustard

caper fruit

Vanilla
Cinnamon
Licorice

Vanilla (*Vanilla planifolia* of the *Orchidaceae*) derives its name from the Spanish *vaina*, "sheath"; therefore *vainilla*=small sheath, with reference to the thinness of the fruit which is a black capsule. Vanilla is the only genus of the large *Orchidaceae* family to have an economic use. The "drug," which is the part used commercially, is represented by the fruits called "sticks" or, improperly, "pods." The plant is native to Mexico and is grown in several tropical countries: Guiana, Tahiti, Madagascar, Mauritius, the Seychelles, Java, and several South American countries. Commercially there are three kinds of vanilla: "Fine vanilla," "cimarron" or "woody" vanilla, and "vanillon." "Fine" vanilla, which is the most valued, comes from Mexico and is black, smooth and frosted, which accounts for its alternate name, "crystallized vanilla." It is from 8–12 inches long. The "cimarron" (Spanish, meaning "wild") is a woody plant growing in the wild state, with shorter fruits, 5–8 inches, less tapered, more solid, and much less frosted. "Vanillons," or "West Indies vanillons" with long, soft, viscous fruits, rather bitter and with a stronger scent than that of the true vanilla, rarely has a crystallized covering, and derives from another species: *V. pompona*. Vanilla was introduced into Europe by the Spanish after the conquest of Mexico, and from Spain it spread throughout Europe. The minute crystals covering the fruit, which give it its value, are rich in vanillin, which gives stimulant properties to the vanilla, so that it can be used, it is thought, to fight lack of appetite, or lack of tone in the gastrointestinal system. Vanilla is used as flavoring in the confectionery and distilling industries, either as an extract, in powder form, or in its original state. As a medicinal plant it is used mostly as a corrective of bad-tasting medicines.

The scientific name of **Cinnamon** (*Cinnamomum zeylanicum*) derives from the Phoenician, Hebraic and Arabic term *anomon*=fragrant, and with the prefix "kin" means "fragrant plant of China." This name was, in fact, first given to another cinnamon, China cinnamon, cultivated for thousands of years, while the much-prized and only medicinal cinnamon, Ceylon cinnamon did not become known in Europe until the sixteenth century. It comes from the bark of the cinnamon tree and is called *cannella* (thin cane or reed) in Italian, and *cannelle* in French, because the sticks of rolled bark sold commercially resemble pieces of thin reed. The best quality is known as "cannella regina" (queen cinnamon). Wild in Ceylon and in southern India, cinnamon is also cultivated most extensively in Ceylon, and in the Seychelles, Guiana, Jamaica, and Brazil. It contains an essential volatile oil which gives it general stimulant properties and, in particular, digestive functions.

The etymology of *Glycyrrhiza*, the botanical name of **Licorice**, simply derives from the Greek words "glycor" which means sweet, and "rhizos" meaning root: hence, "sweet root." The medicinal qualities of licorice are many and varied. Its emollient and expectorant properties were known to the ancient Egyptians and Indians, and later it was used in Greek and Roman medicine. It is still considered excellent by many people, in cases of catarrh, hoarseness, coughs, and throat infections in general.

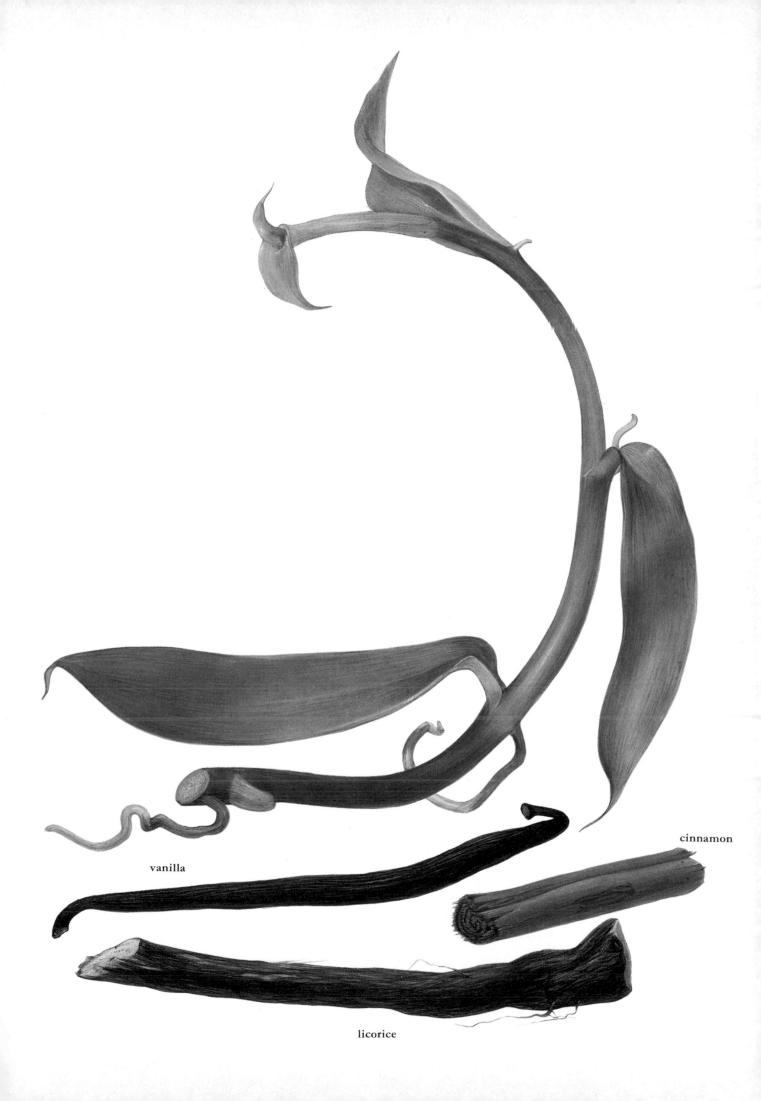

cinnamon

vanilla

licorice

Rhubarb
Nutmeg
Ginger

Rhubarb (*Rheum rhaponticum* or *R. palmatum*) is one of the best-known aromatic plants. It is native to Tibet and northern Asia, and came to Europe around the fourteenth century. Rhubarb is a large, perennial, herbaceous plant with a big, short-branched rhizome, and annual leaves having a thick, cylindrical and fleshy petiole and a large blade. The plants form the first flowers when they are three or four years old and the flower-bearing stalks can easily grow up to 4–5 feet in height. The leaves should not be eaten, being poisonous. The rhizome contains anthraquinones, tannic acid, resinous substances, and its properties are of both pharmacological interest (laxative) and culinary importance. It is the basic ingredient of many aperitifs and aids to digestion. The thick, pink petioles or stems can be eaten either stewed or baked in tarts. Plenty of sugar is needed. It is never eaten raw. It is a popular and fairly inexpensive fruit in European households, but is not often served in restaurants. In Zurich, where it seems to be more appreciated than anywhere else, every small family vegetable garden displays at least one large rhubarb plant. In America the petioles are cooked as a side-dish as well as a dessert, while in France it is chiefly made into jams and compotes.

The reputation and importance of the **Nutmeg** (*Myristica fragrans*) have always been great. The plant providing this fruit is an evergreen tree, 50–60 feet high, native to the Moluccas, but now also cultivated in other tropical regions. The part of the nutmeg used as a spice is provided by the seed. The fruits are harvested when ripe and their fleshy pericarp is discarded; what is left is a large oval seed with a woody involucre and enveloped by a peculiar structure, the aril, which is bright red and divided into narrow ridges. The seeds are freed from the aril and allowed to dry. The aril, reddish-yellow during drying, is sold under the name of mace, and used to flavor curries and meat dishes. When the seeds are perfectly dried, the shell is broken and the seed is extracted. The commercial nutmeg has a whitish coating because the nuts have a cover of milk of lime. Nutmeg has various uses, as a seasoning for a vast range of foods, from meat stuffings and vegetables to desserts. It must be used in small quantities because of its strong aroma and also because in larger doses it could become poisonous. In bygone times it was known as an abortifacient, and one has only to glance through Victorian cookery books giving very big quantities of nutmeg, to understand the enormously high rate of miscarriages at that time.

Ginger (*Zingiber officinalis*) is a sturdy, perennial, herbaceous plant belonging to the *Zingiberaceae*, which originated in Malabar and parts of India, particularly Bengal. It is now grown in many regions with warm climates. It is thought that ginger came to southern Europe from the Orient, just prior to the time of the Romans. From Europe, ginger, through Spanish domination, arrived in the West Indies where its cultivation spread rapidly. In the Middle Ages it was believed to possess miraculous properties, for example, against cholera, but today it is used exclusively in the distilling industry and as a spice. It is, however, still listed in some pharmacopeias. In cooking it is much used in oriental cuisine, especially Indian, and, because of historical connections with the latter country, in English cookery as well. It is sometimes mixed with oranges to make a marmalade with a sharp "bite." As Shakespeare's clown puts it, ". . . ginger shall be hot i' the mouth too." (*Twelfth Night*).

rhubarb

ginger

nutmeg

Saffron
Hop
Clove

Saffron (*Crocus sativus*), originally from Asia Minor, derives, probably through cultivation, from *C. cartwrightianus*, and has been used in the Orient since ancient times. Usually the names of the places of origin influence the scientific nomenclature, but in this case the exact opposite has happened since there is no trace of the Persian term *azupiranu* in the scientific name, but the common name is derived from it. This plant was spread throughout the Mediterranean by the Arabs, and in the rest of southern Europe by the Crusaders. In Europe, Spain, France, Italy, and Austria are the leading producers. Saffron is also grown in Persia, Afghanistan, China, and in Pennsylvania in the United States. The cultivation is easy, but the harvest is burdensome. The "drug" is provided by the dried stamens. If they are mixed with the styles the spice loses its value and is known commercially as "female saffron." The loss of weight of the product is huge: from 176 pounds of flowers the farmer collects only about 2·2 pounds of fresh saffron which, after drying, is reduced to about $2\frac{1}{2}$ ounces. Saffron has a characteristic bitterish-aromatic smell and flavor. It contains a coloring substance and a volatile oil. Besides the pharmacological uses due to its sedative properties, the principal use of saffron is in cooking. It is used to color rice in both oriental and European dishes, especially in risotto and the Mediterranean fish soup, known in France as *bouillabaisse*.

Hop (*Humulus lupulus*) is a very common plant, found wild or cultivated, in Europe, Asia and North America. Its commercial importance is in the making of beer for which the cones of the female plant are used. The hop has an estrogenic action, feminizing and anaphrodisiac, so that, besides serving as a sedative, it is believed by some to be the cause of the disorders (obesity, sterility, hepatic degeneration) afflicting hard beer-drinkers. The hop shoots, that is, the edible shoots of the panicle, are eaten on the Continent as a vegetable. They are boiled in salted water with a little lemon juice, and then served with butter or cream, or added to omelets. In Britain they are used only in brewing, and in the United States they are not to be bought commercially, but are sometimes used as a vegetable in remote country districts.

The aromatic and antiseptic properties of the **Clove** are well known. Cloves are the flowers, in bud, of *Eugenia caryophyllata* of the *Myrtaceae* or myrtle family. In cookery they are used in the preparation of fruits cooked in wine, or in pies (apple, etc.), in the preparation of winter drinks such as mulled wine, and to season meats, especially ham. Cloves are believed to have originated in China and to have been first cultivated by the Dutch in the Moluccas, and to have later spread to Mauritius and the West Indies. Their Italian name *chiodi di garofano* means "carnation's nails." The carnation is, in fact, of a different botanical family, although its common name is "clove pink," ostensibly because of the clovelike fragrance of the flowers.

In olden times cloves were used to make pomanders, which were carried around as a protection against infection. To make these, an orange must be completely stuck all over with cloves, so that no part of the rind shows. It should then be wrapped in tissue paper and left in a warm place to dry out thoroughly. This will take only 2 or 3 weeks in a warm closet, and about five weeks in an ordinary cupboard or drawer. They may then be tied around with narrow ribbons and hung in wardrobes where they diffuse a beautiful spicy scent. They make attractive and inexpensive presents, but pushing in so many cloves makes one's thumb very sore.

saffron

hops

clove

Tea
Coffee
Cocoa

The use of **Tea** (*Camellia* or *Thea sinensis*, fam. *Theaceae*) as a beverage has been known to the Chinese and Japanese since prehistoric times and the southwestern parts of China and northern Indochina are believed to be the places of origin of the tea plant. Tea had a strange and long journey across Asia. In Java, Ceylon, and Formosa, which today have a great interest in its production, tea was introduced only in the mid-nineteenth century. The Dutch made it known throughout Europe during the seventeenth century, and a hundred years later it was brought to the United States. The grades of tea sold commercially are numerous, and, depending on the place of origin, are called Chinese, Japanese, Ceylon tea etc., while their qualities are indicated by indigenous, oriental names such as pekoe, oolong, suchong, and congou. Asians drink mostly "green" tea, obtained by firing immediately after harvesting, without previous fermentation. In Europe and in Anglo-Saxon countries in general, "black" tea is more popular. It comes from partly dried leaves which are allowed to ferment before being toasted. In Russia a particular type of tea is drunk, made of the remains and fragments compressed into tablets. Theine, which is identical to caffein, provides the stimulant properties of tea. Tannin gives it the flavor and aroma. With regard to world consumption, England and Russia occupy first place, importing almost half of all the tea exported from India and China. The Dutch and Americans are also great tea drinkers.

The history of the origin of **Coffee** (*Coffea arabica*) is confused, although Abyssinia is considered to be its native land. An amusing Arab legend, however, relates how a Mullah, or priest, was always falling asleep during his prayers. Overcome by the fear that he was not sufficiently devout, he begged Allah to help him. One day he met a herdsman who told him how his goats gambolled about all night after eating the berries of a certain shrub. The Mullah went to see this shrub, and made himself a strong infusion from the berries. He was awake the whole night, and prayed to his heart's content. This was the coffee shrub.

From Abyssinia coffee arrived in Arabia, Egypt, the Sudan, and Constantinople, and later, through the Venetians, who controlled the Mediterranean during the sixteenth century, it became known throughout Europe. But it is the Dutch who deserve recognition for having fully appreciated the aromatic and stimulant qualities of the new beverage, and for having realized the possibility of its extensive cultivation in their colonies, so coffee was introduced into South and Central America, where it found a better habitat than in its place of origin. Consequently, in a short time Brazil, Colombia, and Mexico had the largest production, and still have today. The many grades of coffee generally take their name from their place of origin. Mocha is the port of Yemen from which mocha (moka) coffee, characterized by relatively small beans and the pronounced aroma, was originally exported. From the Antilles and Central America comes the Puerto Rico with large beans, and the Santo Domingo with medium-size beans. The best grades are from South America which supplies about 80% of the world production. Brazilian coffees hold first place, especially Santos. Coffee infusion, or its active principle, caffeine, excites the nervous centers, especially the brain, and the circulatory functions. In general, coffee is effective against drowsiness. The beans must be prepared with particular care. The grade of the coffee is established by the qualities of the beans which must be homogeneous, whole, dry, and of an agreeable odor, and must retain their color when immersed in water. Coffee cannot be used until it has been roasted at a temperature of 200° C., which causes it to lose almost a fifth of its initial weight and caffeine, increases in size one-third to one-half, and becomes brown because of

tea

coffee fruits

coffee flowers

the sugars and cellulose turning into caramel. Because coffee is of such commercial value, attempts at adulteration are many. The adulteration of raw beans consists in increasing the humidity and color; for roasted beans it consists of oiling, polishing, and the adding of coffee substitutes such as chicory or malt.

Cocoa was introduced into Europe with the discovery of America, but some populations of Central and South America had probably known the plant and its products for centuries. In Mexico the Aztecs used cocoa seeds not only as food, but also as money. The Emperor Montezuma and his courtiers are supposed to have drunk fifty jars a day. The cultivation of the cocoa tree (*Theobroma cacao*) extended rapidly in many areas, but not until around 1820 did the plant appear in Africa. From that time the cocoa tree followed the same pattern as that of the coffee plant: having found favorable conditions of growth, it spread rapidly in the new territories which in less than fifty years surpassed its land of origin in production. The Spaniards used to flavor it with chillies. Today Africa occupies first place. The biggest buyers of cocoa are the countries of central and southern Europe and North America, where there is abundant milk production; a factor of primary importance for the development of the chocolate industry. The best grades of cocoa are Carraco and Marignone, which, when mixed in the right proportions, make an excellent chocolate. Botanically, the cocoa tree is of medium size, similar to the cherry tree. The bark is the color of cinnamon, more or less dark; the wood white, fragile, and very light. The leaves are alternate, lanceolate, bright green, and the flowers, borne in small clusters along the stems and branches, have yellowish or pale pink petals. The fruits, called locally *cabosses*, are shaped like large cucumbers and are dark red speckled with yellow when fully ripe. Each fruit contains many "beans," from twenty-five to forty, ovoid, the size of an olive, fleshy, slightly purple, covered with a thin pellicle, and embedded in a gelatinous pulp. The first chocolate factory in the United States was founded by Dr. James Baker in 1780, and is still in existence today.

cocoa

Taro
Ground nut
Manioc
Arrowroot

The term **Taro** is of Polynesian origin and identifies the *Colocasia esculenta* (fam. *Araceae*) whose globose rhizome, of considerable weight and size, constitutes one of the main foods of the populations of the Spice Islands, and in general of the people living in the tropical areas of Africa and Asia. The taro yields a large amount of starch, and the rhizomes of the sweeter varieties are eaten in the same way as potatoes. In the West Indies the leaves are also eaten, like cabbage.

The **Ground nut** (*Arachis hypogea* fam. *Papilionaceae*) produces a seed, *Apios tuberosa*, which in America is considered to be a form of wild bean. The original *Arachis hypogea* is indigenous to Brazil, but it was from America that its seed came to Europe. Many people thought that it would surpass the potato in popularity. However, the starch obtained from the ground nut was found to be of inferior quality, so the potato continued to reign supreme. This legume, originally of Virginia, is now better known as an ornamental plant for covering walls and fences than as a food.

For Europeans, the potato is the most popular of all plants with edible tubers, so it is difficult to imagine that outside the European continent other plants may be preferred to this species of the *Solanaceae*. Yet in tropical countries the products of **Manioc** and **Arrowroot** are the local staple foods and are commercially very important. They are also tubers or rhizomes, used as vegetables or in the industrial production of starch. There is a picturesque, but false, story that arrowroot is so called because the Indians believed the sap from the rhizomes could cure arrow wounds. In fact the name originates from the American Indian name for all flour-giving roots, *araruta*.

The Manioc or cassava or tapioca belongs to the *Euphorbiaceae* or spurge family. It is native to Equatorial America and Florida, and was already cultivated before Columbus discovered that continent. It was later introduced into Africa and then Asia where today, especially in Indochina and Indonesia, it is extensively cultivated commercially. The tubers of the sweet varieties (*Manihot utilissima*) are eaten as cooked vegetables, as they contain no poison. The sap of the bitter varieties contains hydrocyanic acid. However, in the industrial processes of fermentation and pressing, the poison disappears. These bitter varieties are used to make special starches and flours, the best known of which is tapioca, which is composed of more than 85% carbohydrates, and water, 10–12%; the rest is formed of protein, mineral salts and lipids. Consequently tapioca contains 350 calories per $3\frac{1}{2}$ ounces (100 grams). It is used in soups and puddings and is particularly suitable for children and old or convalescent people, being highly nutritious, and easily digestible.

Arrowroot (*Maranta arundinacea*) is another plant whose rhizomes produce a great amount of starch. It is thought to be native to Brazil and is now widely grown in tropical America and, in smaller measure, in India, Oceania and southern Africa. The industrial product, arrowroot, resembles tapioca in percentile composition: the carbohydrates, the most important compound, can reach up to 87%. Arrowroot too, is easily digestible, being so rich in carbohydrates and poor in nitrogen; it is therefore a good food, although not complete, for infants, the elderly and the sick.

taro

ground nut

Sugarcane
Sugarbeet

Almost two thirds of the world production of sugar is supplied by **Sugarcane** (*Saccharum officinarum*), a native of the Orient, introduced into the Mediterranean basin by the Arabs. It was brought to the American continent in the sixteenth century, and spread rapidly in these regions with suitable climates, an average yearly temperature of $75°$ F. and with precipitations uniformly distributed, totalling about 80 inches per year. The stems of the sugarcane, containing a percentage of sugar of roughly 15% of the total weight, are cut at the base between the tenth and twelfth month of life. This is the time required by the plant to accumulate substantial sugar reserves in its tissues. Most of the sugar produced during the first few months is used by the plant itself for its own growth. After the harvest, the stems or canes are taken to the sugar refineries, having been stripped of the upper part and of the leaves. In the refinery the stems are squeezed to extract the juice (vesou). The fibrous, woody residues (bagasse) of the stems are either used as fuel, or, because of their high percentage of cellulose, to make paper, or composted to form an organic fertilizer. The syrupy, viscous cane juice is then subjected to several boilings to concentrate the sucrose, and to chemical treatment with lime water to eliminate impurities. In the concentrated, clarified solution, sugar crystalizes and is removed from the remaining syrup by centrifugation. The remaining syrup is commonly known as molasses, which is used in food (both animal and human) or distilled to produce rum, alcohol (sometimes called *vin de canne*) and vinegar. The raw crystallized sugar (about 96% sucrose) is further refined by repeated washings and recrystallization, and then delivered to the market.

The area of dissemination of the **Sugar beet** (*Beta vulgaris*) is very different from that of the sugar cane. The latter is characteristic of tropical climates, while the former belongs in the maritime or continental temperate zone. The use of this plant for the extraction of sucrose dates back to the eighteenth century, when the French colonial Empire was on the wane both in India and the Antilles, lands from which the sugar cane was imported. Great impetus was given to the sugar beet's cultivation by the anti-Napoleonic blockade. Today its cultivation is important to both the Euro-Asiatic and the North American economies.

After arriving at the refinery, the beets are washed, cut into strips, and put inside diffusion cells with water at about $175°$ F. The sugar diffuses from the strips into the water, then the pulped strips can be dried for stock feed or chemically treated to yield commercial pectins. Soluble contaminants in the sugar solution are precipitated by chemical treatments and filtered out. The solution is then evaporated to a dense syrup, from which the sugar is crystallized, and then separated from the brown syrup or molasses, by centrifugation. The raw crystallized sugar of the sugar beet has a disagreeable flavor and smell and is used mostly as animal food. When it has been purified it is fermented to make alcohol. Sugar, both from cane and beets, is a product of essential importance for human nutrition although recent dietetic studies have revealed the dangers inherent in an excessive use of it.

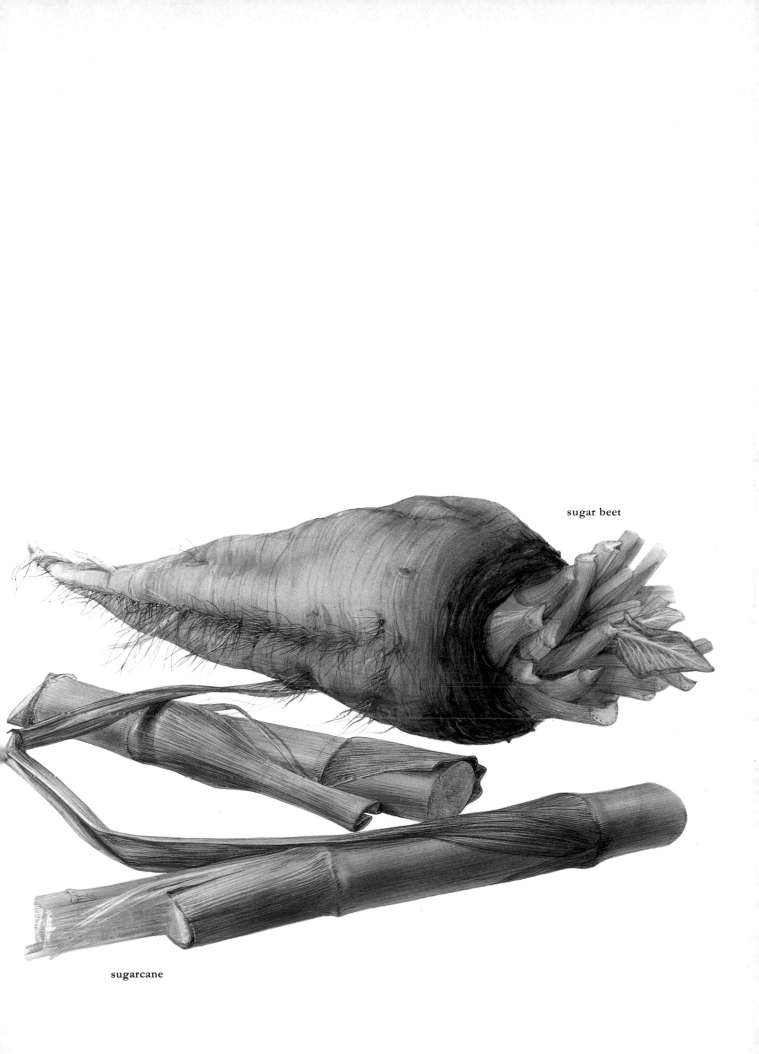

sugar beet

sugarcane

Potato

Among the food plants of great economic interest that the American continent has offered to the Old World (including corn, tomatoes, peppers, and eggplants), the **Potato** (*Solanum tuberosum*), is probably the most important. Its centers of origin can be found in some areas of Peru, Bolivia and Mexico, where it is believed to have been cultivated during the Aztec and Inca civilizations. It was introduced into France and Spain during the second half of the sixteenth century, and in the early years was sometimes grown as an ornamental for its flowers. Sir John Hawkins is thought to have first brought the potato to England in 1563, but it was not until twenty years later, after Sir Francis Drake had reintroduced it to Britain, that its highly nutritious value was recognized and its cultivation taken seriously. Sir Walter Raleigh grew potatoes in Ireland. It was realized that the potato could be very important in human nutrition. Consequently an intensive campaign was begun to spread and increase its cultivation. Sometimes, in periods of scarcity or war, the potato was used as a substitute for wheat and other cereals, which was another reason for further extension. Today it is cultivated in every continent, and the yearly world production is now around 300 million tons, half of which comes from Europe. Russia, Poland, and Germany are in the lead for the quantity and quality of the production. In some countries, like the United States and Britain, the potato is a complementary food, suitable for the preparation of a large variety of excellent dishes (fried, baked, boiled, mashed, dumplings, etc.). But in countries such as those of central and eastern Europe, the potato substitutes, partly or totally, for the starchy food generally included in the daily diet. The dry tuber contains an average of 66% starch, the principal component of its calories; 4% sugars, 9% protein, and about 0.5% potassium, phosphorus and lipids. The potato can provide the human body with such useful elements as copper and iron that are, for example, in minimal percentage in milk, which is considered a complete food. For those who are overweight, the potato could take the place of bread, because as far as calories are concerned, the equivalent of 3–4 ounces of bread corresponds to approximately 1 pound of potatoes. It would be impossible during a meal to eat a quantity of potatoes corresponding in calories to the amount of bread and pasta that the people of some nations normally eat. Because of its low percentage of salts, the potato is often eaten by those suffering from high blood pressure. It also has some vitamins, especially vitamin C and thiamin (B_1), riboflavin (B_2), and pantothenic acid. Besides human nutrition, the tubers of *S. tuberosum* have many other uses: some varieties, rich in water, are grown for forage, others are used for the extraction of starches and the production of alcohol. In Poland a vodka, almost 100% proof, is produced from potatoes. For these secondary uses, the flavor of the tubers is obviously not important.

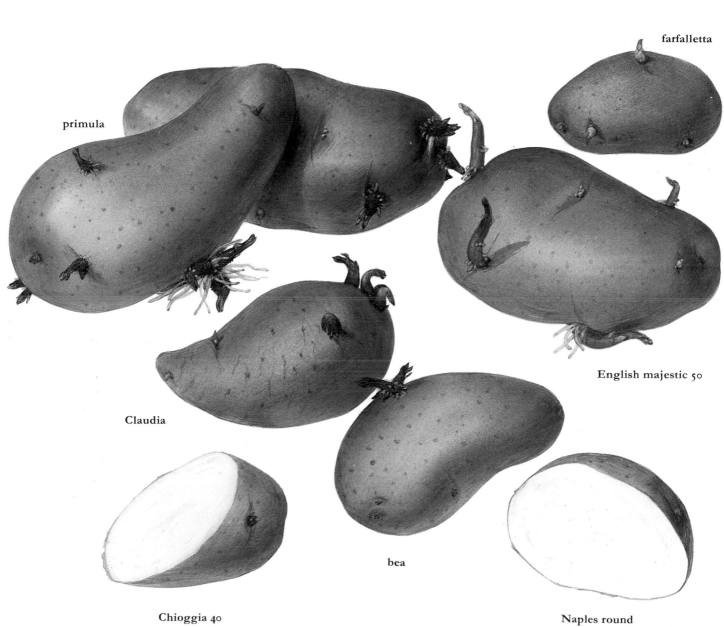

farfalletta

primula

English majestic 50

Claudia

bea

Chioggia 40

Naples round

Sweet potato
Jerusalem artichoke

The origin of the **Sweet potato** (*Ipomea batatas*) causes some confusion. The sweet potato is commonly known in Italy as "American potato," but is not related in any way to the true potato. This name was given to it when Columbus brought it back from America to Europe. However, it cannot be stated definitely that the sweet potato is native to America because some authorities maintain that Asia, where it was extensively cultivated before arriving in Europe, is its true place of origin. Whether American or Asiatic, the sweet potato is a plant of nutritional interest, as it can sometimes substitute for the common potato, with which it shares some properties, such as the high percentage of starch. Although in Europe its use is limited, in some regions of Asia, in particular Indochina, the sweet potato is one of the most important crops from the economic point of view. In the United States it has wide use as a vegetable, cooked, in the same way as yams. It is often featured a lot in Creole cookery, where is it made into cakes and sweet soufflés.

The **Jerusalem artichoke** (*Helianthus tuberosus*) is native to America. It is a close relative of the sunflower, but unlike that plant it is not cultivated for the extraction of oil, but only for its edible tubers. It originated in North America and was brought to France during the seventeenth century. The flavor of the cooked tuber is similar to that of the artichoke; the appearance is that of a knobby potato which, at the moment of harvest, being covered with dirt, vaguely resembles the truffle. The tubers are harvested at the beginning of October and throughout the winter months. This plant spreads rapidly, and the few specimens of one year can multiply enormously in the following one. The use of these tubers in cookery is very varied and they can satisfy many palates. Cleaned, washed and sliced they are very good in the celebrated Piedmontese sauce of anchovies and garlic. They can also be sautéed with parsley, or slowly boiled and then dipped into cold water, drained and fried. They make an excellent accompaniment to meats. The tubers can turn black while boiling, so it is advisable to avoid using aluminium saucepans. The Jerusalem artichoke is rich in nutritive substances, but its consumption is rather limited, and its taste can soon pall. It cannot be considered a competitor for the potato, even though it is as rich in carbohydrates and supplies a large number of calories. Although formed and grown underground and lacking contact with sunlight, this tuber contains a certain amount of vitamins provided by the leaves of the aerial part. Considering the many different ways in which it can be prepared, it is strange that the Jerusalem artichoke does not appear more often on our tables.

white sweet potato

red sweet potato

Jerusalem artichoke

Water chestnut

In the search for food plants which are now obsolete or little known, a prominent place should be given to the **Water chestnut**. This is the fruit of an annual herbaceous plant, *Trapa natans*, belonging to the *Onagraceae* or evening primrose family. It is a water plant, growing anchored to the bottom of lakes or ponds, and sending up to the surface a thin stem which will produce a rosette of floating leaves. The fruit has oddly shaped sharp thorns and is filled with starchy tissues. The typical species is widely dispersed throughout the world, in Europe, western Asia, India, northern and tropical Africa, and northern Italy, and it has become naturalized in North America. Within the species, various forms, supposedly endemic, have been distinguished and must be mentioned for historical documentation; a variety *muzzanensis* of the lake of Muzzano in the Canton Ticino, and a variety *verbanensis*, typical of the lakes Maggiore and Varese but also found in the lakes of Mantua and the valley of the Tartaro. The strange fruits look very unusual and always attract a lot of attention when they are found on the Adriatic beaches after having been carried by the Po into the sea and then washed ashore. In the Tremiti islands the local fishermen make ingenious necklaces out of water chestnuts and sell them to tourists. Under the tough skin, water chestnuts have a sweet and tender pulp, rich in starch, which was greatly in demand in the past. Today its use seems to have become obsolete even in Mantua, which used to be the center of water chestnut cookery. They have an agreeable and delicate flavor, very similar to that of boiled chestnuts. The water chestnut is still celebrated as the main ingredient of a famous risotto, invented by a citizen of Bologna. Brown some shallots in oil and butter, add the rice and let sauté, stirring, for a few minutes. Add some warm meat stock and cook uncovered; when the rice is half done, add thin slices of water chestnut, about 2–3 mm thick. Let the rice cook, adding more stock if necessary. Water chestnuts were, and still are, used in some places, such as the Loire region of France. A *T. bicornis* called *ling kio* is known in China, and a *T. bispinosa* is used in tropical regions, Asia, Ceylon, Africa, and in India where it is called *singhara*. The fruits of *T. bispinosa* are eaten boiled or made into flour used for making confections with sugar and honey. They are served as a vegetable in Chinese restaurants. The water chestnut is another plant connected with the Jesuits, and is sometimes called Jesuits' nut.

water chestnut

Coconut

The coconut palm (*Cocos nucifera* fam. *Palmaceae*) is considered to be "king" of the plants in tropical and subtropical regions by the local inhabitants, because for many of them these plants are their only cash crop and primary source of food. All parts of the plant can be used in various ways. In Sanskrit this palm is called *kalpa vriksha*, which means "tree which gives all that is necessary for living." This is an apt name as the trunk provides excellent wood, the leaves are used by the natives for roofing their huts, and the young terminal buds are eaten under the name of "palm cabbages." The most important products are obtained from the fruit, the **Coconut** (a drupe). Abundant oil is extracted from the endosperm of the fruits; the kernels, freed of the shell and dried, constitute the "copra" which, by pressing, will produce up to 60–65% of an oil that is refined and transformed into a vegetable butter good for human nourishment, especially in vegetarian cookery, and for those who find that ordinary butter has too much cholesterol for their well-being. Today there is a great increase in the demand for coconut oil. At room temperature this oil is solid or semifluid; it is white or slightly yellowish and has a pleasing flavor when it is fresh. As well as its uses in the production of margarine and butter, coconut oil is made into soaps, hair lotions, perfumes, cosmetics, cakes and confectionery. The fruit contains a sweetish liquid, coconut milk, which can substitute for drinking water, while the meat, grated and pressed with a small amount of water, will yield coconut milk. This plant grows in areas with little cloudiness, temperatures not lower than 23° C., and precipitation totalling an average of 80 inches per year. Dietetically, coconuts contain a considerable amount of lipids, around 36%; the percentage of usable protein is 4%, much lower than that of other dry fruits, which range between 9% and 20%. The principal salts are compounds of calcium, sodium, phosphorus, potassium, magnesium, iron and copper, while vitamins are scarce. Coconut "meat" is a good source of energy and easier to digest than other dry fruits.

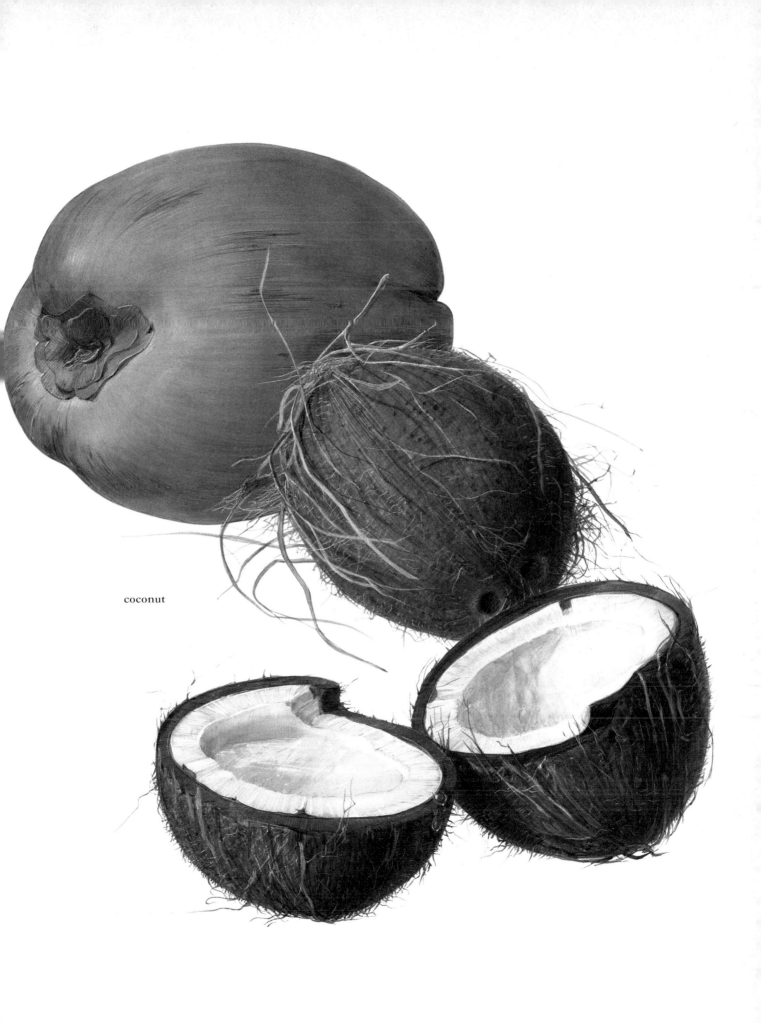

coconut

Olive

The **Olive** (*Olea europaea*) is a plant that throughout history has fascinated people of many races, as shown by the numerous testimonies available. In the Book of Genesis, Moses speaks of this tree that was said to grow on Mount Ararat, and Noah was brought an olive branch by the dove. Records show that the ancient Egyptians cultivated the olive in the seventeenth century B.C. The Jesuits, who appear to have done almost as much for the culinary arts as they did for religion, introduced olives into Mexico and California where they still flourish. Homer, Herodotus, and Virgil all wrote about this tree. Opinions about the origin of *O. europaea* differ, although it is now believed to have come from a region limited by the Caucasus, Iran, and the coasts of Syria and Palestine. From here it penetrated into Egypt, Asia Minor, North Africa, and then Greece, western Europe, and as far as Australia. The beginning of the cultivation of the olive cannot be dated with certainty; but it was undoubtedly known during the Minoan period (3000–1500 B.C.). In Italy, the olive was introduced by the Greeks, first in Magna Graecia, and then later, throughout the peninsula in the regions with mild, not too humid climates and compact, clayey soil. It was, however, only around the seventeenth century that olive oil became part of human nourishment. Before then it was used exclusively in religious rites, as a cosmetic, and for lighting. But since the seventeenth century or slightly earlier, world production of olives has constantly increased. Almost 95% of that production comes from the countries of the Mediterranean basin: each year Spain and Italy compete for the lead. In the Italian peninsula the olive is grown everywhere, with the exception of Piedmont, Valle d'Aosta and Friuli.

The extraction of the oil requires a series of operations. After harvesting, the olives are selected, cleaned, and crushed in special oil mills, where they are reduced to an oily paste. This paste is collected in folded cloths made of reeds, and it is then subjected to pressing. The first pressing produces the "virgin" olive oil, which is the most prized. The residual pulp is subjected to further pressings at higher pressures and yields oil of second and, sometimes, third pressing. The various grades of oil are classified on the basis of the percentage of acidity expressed in oleic acid which goes from a minimum of 1% to a maximum of 4%. In practice the different grades go from "extra virgin olive oil" to "superfine virgin olive oil," to "fine virgin olive oil," to simply "virgin olive oil." Inferior oils are "olive oil" and "husk and olive oil." The best varieties of olive for the extraction of oil are: taggia olive, the Tuscan green coreggiolo, the Campania caiazzana, the Apulia coratina, the caroleo and the mammoles of Calabria. Besides the olives used for the extraction of oil, there are the table olives, and it is the firmness of the fruit which is of primary importance. These olives are pickled, stuffed or preserved in oil, and used for various dishes or snacks. They may be twice as big as the oil olives. Some of the best table varieties are the ascolane, Tuscan cucche, corato olive, nocciolana, and prunara of Sicily.

olive

Peanut
Soybean

The **Peanut** (*Arachis hypogea*) was certainly known to the American Indians long before the arrival of Columbus in the New World. The Portuguese imported this plant into Europe during the sixteenth century. Initially the peanut's cultivation was very limited, almost as a family crop, and the seeds used only as such and not for the extraction of oil. Toward the end of the nineteenth century in France and later in the United States, the peanut was extensively cultivated as an oil producing plant. In a short time the production gradually increased in ratio with the need for ever larger amounts of edible oil. Today China and India are the greatest growers of the raw material, bringing to the market half of the world production. It is important to note that outside the land of origin, particularly in Europe and Oceania, the seeds are used to extract both edible and industrial oil (with the exception of a modest consumption as dry fruit). In India, China, and, above all, Africa, peanuts are part of the daily diet. They are highly nutritious, as shown by the average composition of the dry fruit: 25% nitrogen compounds, about 50% oil, 2–3% cellulose and ash, and only 15% water. Peanuts are often called monkey-nuts and goobers, especially by children. Peanut butter, so popular in the United States, is also manufactured from the nut.

It is believed that the **Soybean** (*Soja hispida*) is native to southwest Africa, but that in very early times it was imported into Asia where its cultivation has become extremely widespread. Today the soybean (of the *Leguminosae*) is probably the most important legume among those cultivated in the Asian countries, for its high nutritive value and the varied industrial ways in which it is used. The largest producer of soybeans is the United States, with two-thirds of the annual world production of about 46 million tons. The soybean plant is rich in lipids and minerals, calcium, potassium, magnesium, and nitrogen compounds. The seeds have a high protein content, among which is one similar to casein, of oil (soybean seeds are one of the major sources of vegetable oils), and of a sugar similar to lactose, as well as other carbohydrates. Soybeans are the cheapest source of vegetable protein, and are important in the daily diet of many Asiatic populations. The seeds provide milk, cheese, flour, bread, oil, and even coffee and cocoa substitutes. Some of these are produced directly, others obtained through processing. Soybeans can also be used to make soups, broths, salads, etc. Soy milk, which is obtained by grinding the seeds previously immersed in water for a day, has a composition similar to cows' milk; it froths when boiling, and in cooling forms a thick cream at the surface. It is lower in fats but richer in protein than cows' milk. Soy flour, besides being suitable for making bread, in spite of some problems in the rising processes, lends itself very well to the preparation of bread-sticks, cookies and pasta. Oil, however, is the main product extracted from the seeds of this legume. It can be used in the manufacture of margarine and soaps. Soybean meal, the protein cake remaining after the extraction of oil, already valued as livestock feed, is likely to become even more important in a world where food proteins are in short supply. It is already often added to meats such as hamburger, or used as a substitute (soyburger). One of its greatest advantages is its freedom from attack by insect pests.

peanut

soybean

Colza
Rapeseed
Sesame

The term **Colza**, one of the many species of the genus *Brassica*, derives from the German *Kohlsaat*, meaning "cabbage seed." This explanation of the common name is the best way to emphasize the part of the plant most used in the food industry. It must be remembered that the plant is good fodder and also grown for pasture in parts of Europe. Colza (*Brassica napus* var. *oleifera*) is probably native to Africa and southern Europe, but is believed to have been known outside its center of origin a few millennia ago, in Russia and China. Information has been available since the seventeenth century when this plant became very important throughout most of Europe as the basis of one of the most important oil seed cultures. Now, even though colza oil is still part of the numerous so-called vegetable oils, its cultivation has decreased. Recent studies now claim that the use of colza oil in cooking may be harmful. It is sometimes used to adulterate mustard seed.

Rapeseed (*Brassica rapa* var. *oleifera*), like colza, with which it is sometimes confused, although known for several centuries, began to be intensively cultivated as an oil-seed plant in central and northern Europe only around the beginning of the eighteenth century. However, with the exception of India and Romania where it is widely cultivated, in other countries where climatic conditions allow it, colza is preferred to rapeseed because of the higher oil content of the seeds.

Sesame (*Sesamum indicum*) is perhaps one of the oldest cultivated plants, known to the Hebrews and ancient Greeks and Egyptians. Famous scholars, such as De Candolle and Watt, made lengthy studies to establish with certainty its true center of origin, and reached the conclusion that this plant was native to tropical Asia. Numerous historical references to sesame were made by Greek and Roman naturalists: Theophrastus in his *History of Plants* gives it a botanical description; Pliny in his *Historia Naturalis* writes that some populations, probably inhabitants of India, had been extracting large quantities of oil from sesame for a long period of time. Sesame seeds contain up to 55% oil. The enormous commercial importance of the sesame is evidenced by the extensive cultivations in Asia or Africa localized in tropical and subtropical areas, where the best sesame seeds are produced. They are known commercially as Indian sesame and African sesame. In the confectionery industry they are used to make *halva*, and added to cakes and cookies. They also produce an oil which is used to make soap and cosmetics.

colza

rapeseed

sesame

Cotton
Sunflower
Ramtil

Herodotus, the great Greek historian, mentioned **Cotton** for the first time in the mid-fifth century B.C., but the highly prized fiber that is still obtained from it today was already known to the ancient Egyptians. Cotton was introduced into Greece by Alexander the Great, and into Sicily and Spain by the Saracens. In the American continent, there is evidence that the Aztecs were growing this plant in South America, but its introduction into North America can be considered relatively recent. Although cotton has been known for several centuries for its fibers, the same cannot be said for it as an oil producing plant. This use dates back only a short time. Today cottonseed oil is sold together with corn and peanut oil and is extracted from the cottonseeds left after the ginning of the cotton fiber. The seeds are freed from the hulls, and the kernels are then crushed, heated, and subjected to high pressure or solvent extraction. The product obtained at the end of this process is a reddish raw oil that must be further refined. The final product, the true cottonseed oil found on the market, is yellow and has a light flavor and color. It is used directly as a cooking oil, in the production of margarines and vegetable shortenings, and in the manufacture of soaps. Compressed cottonseed, known as cotton cake, is used as cattle fodder.

Historic information about the **Sunflower** (*Helianthus annus* fam. *Compositae*) and its place of origin is confused: some authorities believe that it is native to Peru, while others are equally certain that it originated in Mexico and some southern areas of the United States. The sunflower was cultivated in a primitive fashion in America by the Indians who used it as food. In France the tubers are still eaten between November and April, after being cooked like salsify. It was only a century after the discovery of the new continent that this plant was introduced into Europe, first in Spain, later elsewhere, and in particular in southern Russia where its culture has developed enormously. Today in several areas, from Russia to France, the United States to Mexico, China, India, and Australia, the sunflower is considered one of the most important oleiferous plants because its oil can be used for human consumption. Furthermore, sunflower oil is resistant to rancidity, can be used as an extender for more expensive oils and, mixed with other fats, either vegetable or animal, is used in the production of margarines, cooking fats, etc. Sunflower oil, which is extracted from the seeds, is also particularly suitable for the preservation of fish. Its seeds and those of *H. tuberosus* can be toasted for direct consumption and have a pleasant taste similar to that of hazelnuts. In the past, the young petioles of sunflower were eaten grilled and seasoned with oil and salt. The flowers always turn toward the sun, which, as much as for its large vivid yellow petals accounts for its name. Thomas Moore (1779–1852) described the sunflower beautifully: "As the sun-flower turns on her god, when he sets./The same look which she turn'd, when he rose."

On a much smaller and only local scale are the uses of the oil obtained from **Ramtil** (*Guizotia abyssinica* fam. *Compositae*) which is scarcely known outside Ethiopia; the Abyssinians use it with honey and flour to make typical local sweets, but in India it is cultivated for its seeds, from which an oil is obtained.

sunflower

cotton

ramtil

Appendix

p. 16 Wheat is produced by herbaceous plants, generally annual. Recently the Russians have developed some cultivars of wheat, improperly called perennial, that can actually last for two or three years. An important morphological characteristic is the presence of long appendages known as "aristas" or awns. Depending on the presence or absence of the awns, wheats are divided into awned and awnless varieties. The various species of wheat are divided into two natural groups: "naked wheats", such as *Triticum vulgare* (common bread wheat), *T. durum* (durum wheat), *T. turgidum* (poulard wheat), *T. polonicum* (Polish wheat), and "spelt wheats", such as *T. spelta* (spelt), *T. dicoccum* (emmer), and *T. monococcum* (einkorn). More important from a commercial point of view is the division into soft and hard wheats: (fig. 1) spikes of hard wheat: (fig. 2) some spikes of soft wheats.

p. 18 Rye and oats are two well known cereals, sometimes considered as minor cereals.

Rye (*Secale cereale*) (fig. 1) is native to central Asia. It is more resistant to cold than wheat, and, like barley, is well adapted for cultivation in mountain and northern areas, or in sandy soils in the plains, where wheat does not grow. The flour obtained from rye grains is made into bread.

Oats (*Avena sativa*) were cultivated mostly as fodder (and make a valuable horse feed), and in minor measure for human nutrition, mostly used as rolled oats, oat flakes, and oatmeal for cereals: (fig. 2) a panicle of oats, cultivar "Angelica"; (fig. 3) a detail of a naked oat, with the grains coming easily free from lemma and palea; (fig. 4) some isolated grains of oats.

p. 20 The cultivated varieties of **Barley** derive from species native to the Middle East and North Africa; the naked varieties, those in which the grains come easily free from lemma and palea, derive from species native to China.

The cultivated varieties of barley belong to the species *Hordeum vulgare*, family *Gramineae*. They are annual grasses, not very large, at most reaching 3 feet or one meter. The table shows some examples of the three most important forms of barley: "six-rowed" barley, grains placed on six rows (fig. 1); two different cultivars of "two-rowed" barley, with grains placed on two rows (fig. 2) "Sisfor 1797", and "Villa", and (fig. 3) the cultivar "Perga" of a "four-rowed" barley.

Barley is very versatile. The two-rowed varieties are used in the preparation of malt for brewing beer. Other varieties are ground into flour for barley bread, and "pearl barley" is made into soups.

p. 22 **Corn** or **maize** (*Zea mays*) is a plant native to semi-tropical America. It belongs to the family *Gramineae*, subfamily *Maydeae*. Both from a botanical and commercial viewpoint, the various types of corn can be divided into 5 groups (8, according to some botanists), variously considered in relation to their taxonomic ranks (variety, subvariety). These groups are distinguished mainly on the basis of the morphological and commercial characteristics of the kernels. The groups are: *Z. mays* var. *amylacea* (soft corn); whose cultivars have starchy and very soft grains, without corneous endosperm. The mummy corns of Peru, Mexico and southern U.S.A. and some forms still cultivated by American Indians probably belong to this group. The grains of this group can be easily made into flour, even by primitive methods; but commercially they are not much in demand, so their use is minimal and limited to a few localities. *Z. mays*, var. *indurata* (flint corn); the cultivars most used for human nutrition belong to this group; the starchy endosperm is enclosed by the corneous endosperm. Once the endosperm is milled into flour it remains as small granules, not as a pulverulent powdery mass; *Z. mays*, var. *indentata* (dent corn), where the shrinkage in the starchy endosperm at the top of the grain causes the formation of the characteristic dent; these are plants of large size, up to 9–10 feet or 3–4 meters, with high yields and used mostly as livestock feed; the well known corn hybrids, Wisconsin 464, Maygold 49 and Iowa 4316 belong to this group. *Z. mays* var. *rostrata* or *everta* (popcorn); this is a nonhomogeneous group divided into two subgroups; the corns with pointed grains and popping properties belong to these varieties; the grains, when heat is applied, turn inside out into a spongy structure, through the "explosion" of the moisture contained inside them. This group also contains some ornamental corns, with vividly colored grains, such as the so called "strawberry corn", with small, brightly colored ears, shaped as strawberries, and Indian corn often used as a decoration during the fall harvest season in the United States. The cultivars of this variety are more suitable than others for a custom that was once popular with peasant boys: to roast immature ears on embers and then eat the grain. *Z. mays* var. *saccharata* (sweet corn), with wrinkled grains; the green parts and the grains are sweet because they are rich in soluble sugars. In the United States the mature, but still tender grains are used as if they were peas and large quantities are canned for this use. Corn-on-the-cob is a particularly popular use of this corn.

Other groups of lesser importance are the var. *amylosaccharata*, with characteristics intermediate between sweet corn and the others; the var. *ceratina*, with grains maintaining a waxy texture, even when fully ripe; the var. *tunicata* (pod corn) with each kernel enclosed by small bracts (lemma and palea).

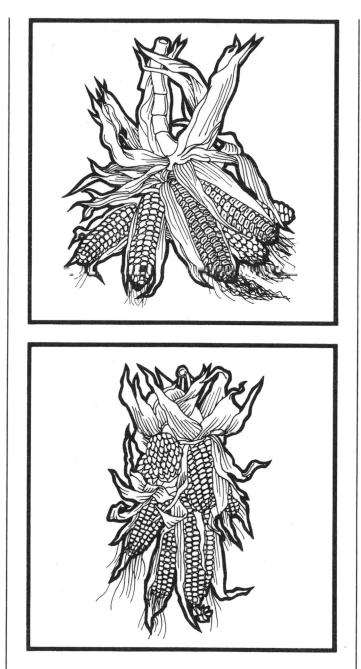

p. 26 Rice (*Oryza sativa*) (fig. 1) is a cereal native to warm climates with at least two centers of origin; eastern Asia and western Africa. After wheat, rice is the most important cereal used for human food. It is an annual plant requiring standing water above the soil for the cultivation of the majority of the commercial varieties.

Many cultivars and varieties are known: among them, the best known and most cultivated in some European countries are the Chinese, common and widely used; the old glories, Maratelli and Vialone; the new and prized Arborio, R.B. and Carnaroli.

Sorghum (*Sorghum vulgare*) (fig. 2) Broomcorn (var. *technicum*), Sudan grass (var. *Sudanensis* etc.), is a cereal probably native to Ethiopia, polymorphic, with numerous varieties and even more numerous cultivars.

p. 28 Branch with leaves, flowers and fruits of **Buckwheat** (*Fagopyrum sagittatum* or *F. esculentum*). Buckwheat is an annual herbaceous plant native to central Asia, and cultivated in alpine valleys and other areas of central and northern Europe and Asia. It belongs to the *Polygonaceae*. The stems are herbaceous, striped with red, and can grow to heights of from 8–20 inches approximately. The leaves are roughly triangular and heart-shaped. The flowers have five petals, white or reddish, green toward the base. The fruits have a characteristic triangular shape; the illustration shows examples with entire margins and winged. Beside *F. esculentum*, another species, *F. tataricum* (Siberian or Tatary buckwheat) is cultivated to some extent, being hardier and more resistant to cold, although less important than the common buckwheat. The flowers of Tatary buckwheat are smaller and more greenish than those of the common variety. The fruits are wrinkled, with tubercles and have toothed edges, instead of smooth with entire or winged margins as in the common form.

p.30 Among the classic examples of the **Kidney bean** (*Phaseolus vulgaris*, fam. *Leguminosae*, subfam. *Papilionaceae*) are: (fig. 1a) the well known Borlotto of Vigevano with stocky seeds brightly striped; there are also several varieties with completely red seeds (fig. 1b); (fig. 2a) Scotch, with pods similar to those of Borlotto but with kidney-shaped seeds; (fig. 3) Cannellino, with white seeds smaller than those of the previous varieties.

p.32 Branch with leaves and pods of **String beans** (green beans) (*Phaseolus vulgaris*) of the cultivar, Yellow ring or Little hook (fig. 1), with pods that are hook-shaped in their lower third. Another well known variety is the Venetian Wonder (fig. 2) with fleshy and flat pods. The cultivars of green beans with cylindrical and green pods are numerous: (fig. 3) green beans or string beans, are simply unripe bean pods.

p.34 Branch with flowers (fig. 1), partially open pod (fig. 2) and various seeds (fig. 3) of the **Scarlet runner bean** (Dutch case-knife bean, flowering bean, or painted lady) (*Phaseolus multiflorus* or *P. coccineus*). As other bean plants, *P. multiflorus* is native to South America; it is a perennial plant, with a tuberous root, but is often cultivated as an annual. It is a strong, large plant, and can reach a height of 10 feet or 3 meters, with beautiful flowers, scarlet in the scarlet runner and white in the Dutch case-knife, that can be used as ornamentals, especially for walls and fences. The pods are large, 2½–6 inches, slightly curved, wrinkled, dark-green when ripe and contain 2–6 large, kidney-shaped seeds of various colors: white or with wine red hues with darker streaks.

Partially open pod and an isolated seed of the **Lima bean** (*P. lunatus*) (fig. 4). Native to South America, this is a climbing plant, annual, of large dimensions 10–12 feet or 3–4 meters. The leaves differ in shape and color (paler, more metallic) from those of the other beans. The flowers are small, greenish-white, in axillary racemes. The pods are short and very flat, with a slightly wrinked surface. The seeds are kidney-shaped, flat, veined and marble-like.

245

p. 36 Leaf, pods and isolated seeds of two of the best known culti-vated forms of the genus *Vigna* (fam. *Leguminosae*). The taxonomy of this genus is controversial. The Italian botanist, Fiori maintains that both forms represented here—**Black-eyed pea** (var. *Melanophtalma*) (fig. 1) and **Asparagus bean** (*Dolichos unguiculata*) (fig. 2)—should be considered as varieties of the species *Vigna unguiculata*. The black-eyed pea which is the most typical variety of this species, is cultivated both for human food (as immature pods or dry seeds) and for forage. This species is also known as *V. sinensis*, **Black-eyed bean** or **Cow pea** of the southern United States.

The immature pods of the **Asparagus bean** or yard long bean (also termed *V. sesquipedalis*) are used as string beans. The pods can reach a length of about 3 feet or 90 cm. Both the black-eyed pea and the yard long bean are herbaceous annuals, and climbing vines, but the latter twines much more than the former and is also much taller; it can easily reach 10 feet or 3 meters in height. Some authorities con-sider these forms as true species, while others ascribe them to the genus *Dolichos* instead of *Vigna*.

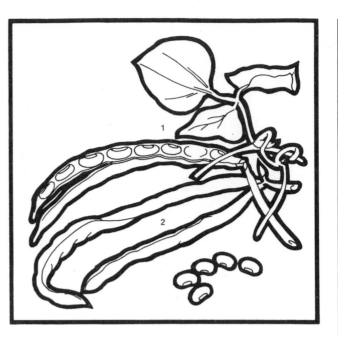

p. 38 Branch of **Lupine** or **Lupin** (fig. 1) with the characteristic palmately compound leaves, hairless on the upper surface, and silky on the lower surface due to whitish hairs, and two pods, upright, turgid and flat. Also illustrated are an open pod (fig. 2) and a single seed (fig. 3). The cultivated lupins are *Lupinus albus* and *L. termis*, the latter considered a variety of *L. albus* by some authorities. Lupins are her-baceous plants between 16–27 inches or 40–60 cm high. They are native to the Mediterranean and have been cultivated since antiquity. The seeds, after soaking for about 3 hours in water to free them of their bitter taste, were cooked and sold in ancient Rome, just as they are today, in some European countries, especially during village festivals. The nutritional properties of lupins are similar to those of other *Leguminosae*.

Broad bean (Windsor bean, horse bean) (*Vicia faba*), another species of the *Leguminosae*, has been known and cultivated for centuries: (fig. 4) Some pods and seeds of the best known European variety, Aguadulce. Broad beans are largely cultivated in the Mediterranean and to a limited extent in the United States where the fresh and raw seeds of the unripe pods are eaten; (very good especially with sharp cheeses) and also the dried seeds, after soaking and cooking.

p.40 **Peas** (fig. 1) are botanically known as *Pisum sativum*, an herbaceous annual plant with weak, hollow stems; the stipules are large, leaf-like and clasping. The leaves are compound, even-pinnate, and terminate in tendrils which are sensitive and clinging.

The pea, derived from a form native to the Mediterranean, very similar, even perhaps identical to several varieties still found in the wild state, has changed a great deal with cultivation. There are dwarf varieties that do not need support, half-dwarf and tall climbing ones. There are varieties with smooth seeds and others with wrinkled seeds, and with green or yellow seeds. With some cultivars only the shelled, dry seeds are used as foods; with others the entire pod is edible (sugar peas or mange-tout). Peas are eaten only after cooking and are used in soups or side dishes. They have good nutritional properties due to their high protein and carbohydrate content.

Chick-peas (*Cicer arietinum*) also have good nutritional properties: (fig. 2) two of the typical hairy pods and some seeds. Chick peas are herbaceous annual plants that have never been found in the wild state; for many centuries they have been cultivated in Mediterranean countries. They belong to the *Leguminosae*.

Another member of the *Leguminosae* is the **Lentil** (*Lens esculenta* in Europe or *L. culinaris* in the United States). (fig. 3) Some of the typical seeds, flat and dish-like. Lentils, just as chick peas, are the seeds of herbaceous annual plants of small size, not found in the wild state, but cultivated since antiquity.

p.42 Two representatives of the chicory group: **Catalonia chicory** (fig. 1) and **Belgian endive** or **Witloof** (fig. 2). The Catalonia (*Cichorium intybus*) is a large plant, cultivated for centuries in southern Italy, and of which the stem and leaves are the edible parts. It has large, runcinate leaves with lobed margins shaped like a pruning knife, or deeply divided, or sometimes entire. The stem is long, tender and hollow.

Witloof is a cultivated product typical of France and Belgium. The market product is the result of forced growth under particular conditions that result in the formation of oval, pointed "hearts" that are tender, crisp and with a typical aromatic taste.

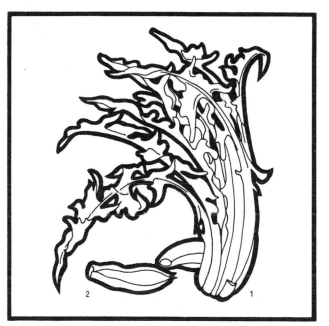

p.44 Three typical representatives of Italian *radicchii* from the Venetian area: **red Verona chicory** (fig. 1), **Castelfranco variegated chicory** (fig. 2), and **red Treviso chicory** (fig. 3). *Radicchio* and chicory are the common commercial names of cultivated varieties derived from the same species, *Cichorium intybus*. *C. intybus* is an herbaceous plant, biennial or perennial, easily found in fields, and widely diffused throughout Europe, temperate Asia and North Africa. It is naturalized in North America and South Africa. *Radicchio* is a classic winter vegetable, suitable mostly for salads.

p.46 (fig. 1) A variety of *Cichorium intybus* known as **Grumolo**, *ceriolo* or broad-leaved chicory. It has small dark green leaves, and a characteristic central "eye"; it is consumed from fall to spring.

The other figures show specimens of two varieties of *C. endivia* (**Endive**) (fig. 2), a plant thought to be native to India. Some botanists distinguish two varieties within this species: *crispa*, to which they ascribe, under the name of endive, the forms with curly and indented leaves, and *latifolia*, to which is ascribed the **Escarole** (fig. 3), with entire leaves. Escarole and endive are produced during the summer, fall and winter and are used in salads. The escarole grown during the summer has hard, tough leaves and is better used as a cooked vegetable.

248

p.48 **Wild chicory** (*Cichorium intybus*) (fig. 1), often found in uncultivated grassy places. At this vegetative stage it is difficult to distinguish the different members of the *Compositae* family; many of them, when young, are good in salads. With the common name of **Bitter chicory root** (*Tragopogon porrifolius*) are often indicated the roots of plants of both genus *Cichorium* and *Tragopogon*. More popular as a food are the roots of the **Black salsify** (*Scorzonera hispanica*) (fig. 3) growing wild in the fields of central and southern Europe, and West Asia; often cultivated and used both as a cooked vegetable and as a relish.

p.50 **Lettuces** are perhaps the best known salad vegetables. Common lettuces are sometimes considered a true species (*Lactuca sativa*) and, others, as varieties of the wild species *L. scariola*. They belong to the *Compositae*.

Cultivated lettuces are divided into two groups: head lettuces (var. *capitata*), (figs. 1 and 2) with many different cultivars, and Cos or Romaine lettuces (var. *longifolia*), (fig. 3). Some wild lettuces are also edible, for example, *L. perennis* and a few others.

p.52 Young plant of **Corn salad** or lamb's lettuce (*Valerianella olitoria*) (fig. 1), of the *Valerianaceae*, in the characteristic rosette stage, which is the best time for consumption. It is a small herbaceous, annual plant, often cultivated, and also found during the spring in meadows and uncultivated fields, and sometimes on mountains in southern Italy. *V. olitoria* grows in Europe, the Middle East and North Africa and has been imported into the United States.

Young stem of **Water speedwell** (*Veronica anagallis-aquatica*) (fig. 2) also known as water pimpernel. Sometimes called "fat grass", it is of doubtful use. In some European regions it is known as "watercress", which creates some confusion since the true watercress is the *Nasturtium officinale* (*v.* p. 251). *V. anagallis—aquatica* is an aquatic plant, quite common in brooks with clear and cold water. It is also found throughout the Northern Hemisphere including North America. It belongs to the *Scrophulariaceae* or figwort family. Basal rosette of *Cardamine amara* (fam. *Cruciferae*) (fig. 3) **Bitter cress**, an aquatic, perennial herb. This plant has many forms, with numerous varieties found in several areas in Europe. It is also found in the Middle East and Central Asia.

p.54 Basal rosette of **Plantain** (*Plantago coronopus*) (fig. 1), known commonly as Capuchin's beard. It is usually found in sandy or moist places, especially along the shores. This is a polymorphic species and is quite common in Europe, western and central Asia, North Africa, Australia, and occasionally in the United States.

Flowering branch of the **Judas tree** (*Cercis siliquastrum*) (fig. 2). It is sometimes found in arid, warm woods in Europe, the Balkan states, Asia Minor, the Crimea, Syria and Iran. It is often cultivated in gardens, and sometimes used as a shade-giving tree on roads. The Judas tree belongs to the *Leguminosae*.

Young, unripe fruits (samara) of **English elm** (*Ulmus campestris*) (fig. 3). This tree is common in woods and sometimes hedges, in Europe, temperate Asia and North Africa. The English elm is often grown along the sides of roads.

p.56 Characteristic deeply incised leaves of the basal rosette of **Dandelion** (*Taraxacum officinale*) (fig. 1). This plant belongs to the *Compositae*; it is a polymorphic species found practically everywhere, either native or volunteer. It is very common in fields, meadows, untilled soils, sometimes on old destroyed walls, and along roadbanks. Basal rosette of **Garden burnet** (*Poterium sanguisorba* or *Sanguisorba minor*) (fig. 2), a perennial herb, very common in Europe in grassy places, and sometimes on crags, ruins and waste places. It is a cosmopolitan plant and belongs to the *Rosaceae*.

p. 58 Plant in bloom of **Borage** (*Borrago officinalis*) (fig. 1), of the *Boraginaceae*. Borage is an annual herb, with numerous bristly hairs. The flower-bearing stem (scape) emerges from the rosette of basal leaves; it is hollow and the height is variable from 3 to 20 inches. The flowers are beautiful, with a star shaped corolla with 5 petals, generally blue, rarely white or pinkish. The flowers are formed from April throughout the summer.

Young cyme, in the initial stage of flowering, of **Watercress** (*Nasturtium officinale*) (fig. 2), an aquatic perennial plant, native to Europe and central north Asia, but today naturalized almost all over the world. It prefers the clean flowing waters of springs and brooks. Watercress flowers during the spring and produces small white flowers. It belongs to the *Cruciferae* or mustard family.

Root and young shoots of **Wall rocket** (*Diplotaxis muralis*, var. *tenuifolia*) (fig. 3). It is a perennial herb, sometimes woody at the base, with numerous leaves on the stem. The flowers are yellow and formed from February to October, sometimes even later. It is spread throughout Europe, Asia and North Africa, and is usually found in arid and stony cultivated fields, also in untilled fields, and in waste places. It has a characteristic aromatic smell when rubbed, very similar to that of the rocket.

Flowering branch of **Sea rocket** (*Cakile maritima*) (fig. 4), an annual fleshy herb, characteristic of the seashores. It flowers from March to October and the flowers are pinkish or purplish. It is diffused throughout Europe, western Asia, North Africa, Australia and the United States, and is common along the seashores of the Mediterranean.

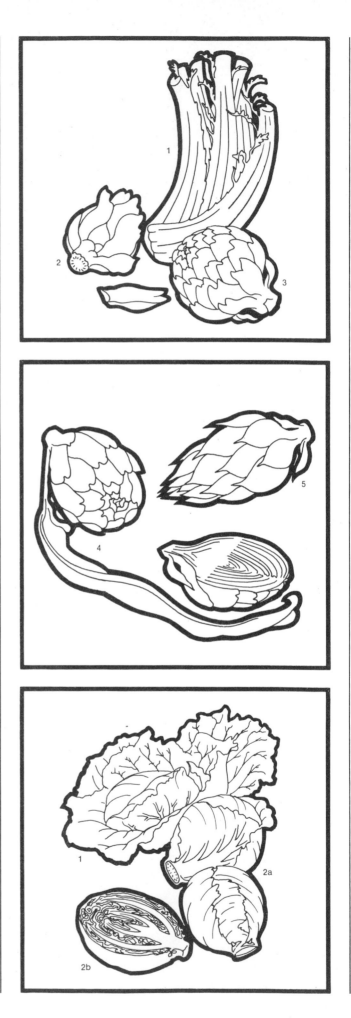

p. 60 **Cardoons** and **Artichokes**, in spite of their different aspects, are very close relatives and can be considered as two different varieties of the same species, *Cynara cardunculus*. The edible part of the cardoon (*C. cardunculus* var. *altilis*) (fig. 1) is formed by the basal part of the large leafy petioles. The leaves form a large rosette. Various blanching techniques are used to make the leaves tender and edible, since they are otherwise tough and stringy.

The edible parts of the **Artichoke** (*C. cardunculus*, var. *scolymus*) are the unripe heads, that is, their inflorescences, of which the tips of the bracts or scales, commonly and improperly called leaves, are eaten. The central part is formed by the receptacle bearing the numerous flowers, and the upper fleshy part of the stem. Sometimes, as for the cardoons, the young shoots formed at the base can also be used. The illustrations show four of the best known cultivars: Tuscany violet (fig. 2) with purple heads shaped as a truncated cone; the Roman (fig. 3) with very large, thick and globe-shaped heads, of a dark green color; the thick artichoke (fig. 4), with a longitudinal section showing the insertion of the scales and the flower-bearing head, and the thorny (fig. 5) with scales terminating in sharp thorns.

p. 64 Some typical cabbages in the best condition for eating, when the head is still tight. Cabbages belong to the species *Brassica oleracea* of the *Cruciferae*; the number of varieties within this species is immense; the best known among them are the var. *sabauda* or *bullata* (**Savoy cabbage**) (fig. 1) with bullate and curly leaves; and the var. *capitata* with very tight heads, and smooth leaves, of which two cultivars are shown, one with green leaves (fig. 2a) and the other with purple-red leaves, known as **Red cabbage** (fig. 2b).

p. 66 Other typical varieties of *Brassica oleoracea*. (fig. 1) typical unripe inflorescence of **Broccoli** (var. *cauliflora*) at the best time for eating. The floral pedicles are less condensed than in the cauliflower and form a head not globe-shaped, but spread out and slightly flattened, like an umbrella. The sprouting broccoli belong to the var. *Italica*. **Brussels sprouts** (fig. 2) (*B. oleracea*, var. *gemmifera*). The sprouts are axillary buds formed along the stem at the base of the leaves which are scarce and scattered. A plant of Brussels sprouts can reach a height of 3 feet, and produce about 30 sprouts.

p. 68 An example of a "non-heading cabbage", the **Black cabbage** (*Brassica oleracea* var. *acephala*) (fig. 1). **Collards** and **Kales** belong to the same variety. Young specimen of *B. campestris* (fig. 2) (navet, wild turnip), showing the terminal leaves and young inflorescences (collectively **Turnip tops**) (*v.* p. 254.) **Sea kale** (*Crambe maritima*) (fig. 3) is a plant belonging to the *Cruciferae*, quite common along the seashore. It is very popular in Atlantic countries.

p. 70 Typical head of **Cauliflower** (var. *botrytis* of *Brassica oleracea*). The edible part is provided by the unripe hypertrophic inflorescence (head or "curd") forming a large mass, generally globular, but sometimes shaped like a child's top or a snail shell (see example in figure); a cultivar from the Marche region in Italy, locally known as "little snail".

p.72 Three different species belonging to the *Cruciferae* (all in the same initial stage of growth, the rosette stage): **Corn rocket** (*Bunias erucago*) (fig. 1), **Hairy bitter cress** (*Cardamine hirsuta*) (fig. 2) and **Shepherd's purse** (*Capsella bursa-pastoris*) (fig. 3); the leaves of these three plants are runcinate, that is, deeply incised with the lobes turning backwards in the shape of a pruning knife. The examples of *Cardamine* and *Capsella* also show the flower-bearing stems.

Also belonging to the *Cruciferae* is **Horseradish** (*Armoracia lapathifolia*) (fig. 4); the edible part is the root that can grow to 15–18 inches with a diameter of 1–1¼ inches. In the upper part, the rhizomatose portion, can be seen numerous buds. The cut surface of the root is white, with a radial structure in the cortical zone and wood in the center. The group of small winter leaves is short and deeply incised. The leaves produced in spring and summer are large, up to 10 inches in length, and have entire margins.

p.74 These plants of the mustard family (*Cruciferae*) show a characteristic enlargement or tuberization of the hypocotylar axis; the tuberized part is edible. (fig. 1) A flat form of **Turnip** (*Brassica campestris*); (fig. 2) a **Wild radish**, also called jointed or white charlock (*Raphanus raphanistrum*) and (fig. 3) **Radishes** (*R. sativus*). The upper leaves and young flowers (turnip tops, *v.* p. 253) are also used as vegetables. Other varieties of *B. campestris* with oil-rich seeds are described together with oil-producing plants (*v.* p. 294).

Both wild and garden radishes are considered by some botanists to be different varieties of the species *R. raphanistrum*; others believe the garden radish a true species (*R. sativus* or *R. radicula*) and the wild radish a variety (*nigra*) of the above. However, the taxonomy of the *Cruciferae* in general and of the genus *Brassica* in particular, is somewhat confused and confusing.

Commercially the radish is distinguished by long, medium and globose roots.

The list of species in the genus *Brassica* below may perhaps be of help to the reader.

Brassica oleracea, var. *fruticosa* and var. *acephala* = Kale, collards

            var. *gemmifera* = Brussels sprouts
            var. *capitata*   = Cabbage
            var. *italica*   = Sprouting broccoli
            var. *botrytis*   = Cauliflower
Brassica caulorapa   = Kohlrabi
Brassica napus (*B. campestris* var. *napus*) = Rape
            var. *oleifera*   = Colza
Brassica napobrassica   = Swede (*Britain*)
                           Rutabaga (*U.S.*)
Brassica pekinensis   = Pe-Tsai or Chinese
                           Cabbage
Brassica rapa (*B. campestris* var. *rapa*) = Turnip
            var. *oleifera*   = Rapeseed

p.76 **Chard** (*Beta vulgaris* var. *cicla*) is also known under various names; leaf beet, Sicilian beet, sea kale beet, spinach beet, Chilian beet, Roman kale, Swiss chard. It has characteristics practically identical to those of the sugar beet (*v.* p. 291), but with a smaller, less fleshy branched root. The leaves are very large (fig. 1) and with a thick main rib. Beet is a biennial plant, but is cultivated as an annual. It requires loose, fresh soils well tilled and fertilized, and can withstand the coldest weather.

Spinach (*Spinacia oleracea*) is an herbaceous plant with a branched flower stem and leaves clustered to form a rosette. The leaves (fig. 2) are large, arrow-shaped, sometimes curly and bullate, smooth, pliable, rounded at the margins, of a dark green color. There are several varieties divided into two types: prickly-seeded group (seeds with three sharp points) and the round-seeded group. The environmental requirements of the two groups are quite different.

The **Field poppy** (also red or corn poppy, *Papaver rhoeas*) is an annual plant with a taproot and leaves either toothed or deeply incised (pinnatifid) (fig. 3) with the teeth terminating in a hair. To the same genus belongs *Papaver somniferum* (opium or garden poppy) (*v.* p. 288, var. *hortense*).

The **Common saltwort** (*Salsola Kali*) belongs to the genus *Salsola*, found all over the world (fig. 4). It is an annual plant found on sea beaches, and other saline places with elongate, narrow and cylindrical, awl-shaped leaves.

p.78 **Goosefoot**, also known as **Good King Henry** (*Chenopodium bonus-henricus* of the *Chenopodiaceae*) (fig. 1) is a plant native to Europe, found in Italy, in the Alps and in the Appennines. There are about fifteen other species of the same genus with differing common names such as pigweed, allgood, etc. The stem is erect, sulcate (grooved) with few branches; the lower leaves have long petioles and are triangular to arrow-shaped; the upper leaves are small and much reduced. In some cases goosefoot is used as a rather poor substitute for spinach.

Purslane (*Portulaca oleracea* of the *Portulacaceae*) (fig. 2) is a small plant 4–6 inches in height, with ascending or branched stems; the leaves are fleshy, obovate and without petiole. It is common along road banks and beside cultivated fields, but is also grown as a pot-herb, especially in France and central Europe; the leaves of the cultivated plants are greenish-yellow and larger than those of the wild plants.

The name **New Zealand spinach** or New Zealand ice-plant given to *Tetragonia expansa* (fig. 2) of the *Aizoaceae* or carpet-weed family, derives from the morphology of the leathery, four-angled fruit. It is a plant with ascendent or prostrate stems, and fleshy, short-petioled triangular or rhomboidal leaves. It is native to Australia and New Zealand and is cultivated as a substitute for spinach.

p.80 Beetroot (*Beta vulgaris*, var. *rapa*, form *rubra*) is derived from the only wild species, from which, throughout the centuries, have originated the forage beets, characterized by large roots, the sugar beet, important for its sugar content, and the foliage beets (*v.* p. 255). The beetroot's edible part is the root, variously shaped, (fig. 1) more or less flattened, frequently red, with a series of paler concentric rings on the inside. The basal leaves (fig. 2) have long petioles, and are oval shaped, rather large and reddish green. It forms flowers in the second year of growth, but the roots are harvested at the end of the first year. This plant does not have strict climatic requirements and adapts easily to different conditions. It should be grown in loose and fresh soil, either a sandy or a calcareous loam. In soils with too much clay the flesh of the root turns dry, and in very wet soils it becomes tasteless.

p.82 The **Onion** (*Allium cepa*) belongs to the genus *Allium* of the lily family. It is a biennial herb that dies during its second year after flowering, although, sometimes, small bulbs are formed at the base of the old one, and the plant behaves as a perennial. The leaves are pruinose, cylindrical and hollow. The bulbs are formed by bulb scales originating from and surrounding the short stem. The diagram shows some of the characteristic forms: the Florence long (fig. 1), with an elongate bulb, to be eaten during the summer, as the bulb does not keep well. A red onion (fig. 2); a white onion (fig. 3), an early variety with a delicate flavor, unsuitable for winter use because of its poor storage qualities; the classic Milan Coppery (fig. 4) with a top-shaped bulb, excellent for winter use; the Borrettane small onion, with a short, flat bulb (fig. 5).

p.84 Typical bulbs of **Garlic** (*Allium sativum*, of the lily family) (fig. 1), known commonly as "heads". Garlic is an herbaceous plant with flat leaves that rarely flower, but reproduces vegetatively from the cloves of the compound bulb which is formed by many small bulbs; the cloves. Each planted clove forms a new garlic head. Garlic originated in central Asia and is used as a seasoning in every Mediterranean country. Commercially, three types are distinguished; white or common garlic, with the outer scales silvery-white; pink garlic, with rose-tinged scales, and red garlic with wine-red scales.

The **Shallot** also belongs to the same family and genus (*A. ascalonicum* or *A. cepa*), (fig. 2) with awl-shaped, hollow leaves. It is more similar to the onion than to garlic, with long and pointed bulbs, with entire scales of a beautiful copperish-yellow color. The bulbs are sometimes attached together at the base. It has never been found in the wild state and its place of origin is uncertain. It is also known as eschallot.

256

p.86 The **Leek** (fig. 1) is commonly considered to be the species *Allium ampeloprasum*, widely spread in arid places, on cliffs and old walls in the Mediterranean basin. The straight species is not found growing wild, unless escaped from cultivation. The leek belongs to the lily family and is a biennial, herbaceous plant with a simple, not very developed bulb. It forms flowers during the second year of growth. The leaves are long in layers, forming a sheath around the stem and the cluster of roots at the base of the bulb.

The **Grape hyacinth** (fig. 2) (*Muscari atlanticum*), very popular especially around the Mediterranean, also belongs to the family *Liliaceae* and is widely spread in the meadows and cultivated fields of central-south Europe, western Asia and North Africa. The bulb is compact and swollen. The inflorescence is a raceme with the top flowers more showy than the others, but sterile; they do not produce either seeds or fruits; their function is possibly only that of attracting insects acting as pollen vectors from one plant to another.

p.88 **Asparagus** (*Asparagus officinalis*) in its most sought after and common variety, is a member of the *Liliaceae*, native to the Mediterranean, spreading to central Europe and to central-east Asia. In the wild state it is found in fertile and sandy soils, near rivers and the sea, and can be found in similar areas in the United States where it was introduced in the seventeenth century. The asparagus has an underground stem growing horizontally and producing in the spring shoots that are very tender and fleshy (turions); those to be used as food should be cut at this stage, while still young. If not cut, the shoots start lignifying and will grow to heights of 3–5 feet and form leaf-like structures. On asparagus the structures commonly called leaves are not real leaves, but leaf-like branches called cladophylls, flowers, and fruits.

A good substitute for the common asparagus is the *Asparagus acutifolius* (fig. 2), that is sometimes preferred, being more aromatic. *A. acutifolius* is a wild species found in arid and sunny places, characterized by cladophylls terminating in a thorn. It is widely diffused around the Mediterranean.

Hop (*Humulus lupulus* of the *Urticaceae* or nettle family) is a common, well known plant, diffused throughout Europe in the native state, and also largely cultivated because of its importance in brewing beer (*v.* p. 289). Its apical shoots (fig. 3) shown in this figure because of a similarity with asparagus tips, also have a culinary use similar to that of asparagus tips.

The **Butcher's broom** (box holly, knee holly, shepherd's myrtle) (*Ruscus aculeatus* of the lily family) is a shrub commonly found in the woods around the Mediterranean and in central-south and western Europe. It is often cultivated for ornamental purposes. It has characteristic red berries, and produces turions with a bitter-aromatic taste.

p. 90 The **Tomato** (*Lycopersicum esculentum* or *Solanum lycopersicum*) belongs to the family of the *Solanaceae* or potato family. It is an annual herbaceous plant, sometimes quite large, and can grow to a height of 6 feet, with stems profusely branching and drooping, so that they have to be supported with stakes, wires, or poles. The edible parts of the plants are their characteristic large berries. In the diagram are some of the most typical forms: (fig. 1) fruits of the cultivar Principe Borghese, especially suited for preservation until winter; (fig. 2) a smooth tomato, yellow even when fully ripe, long lasting after picking and suitable for winter preservation, but also good for immediate eating; (fig. 3) a specimen of pear-shaped tomato, sometimes considered as a true variety, var. *pyriformis*, or even a true species, *Lycopersicum pyriforme*, or *Solanum pomiferum*, called San Marzano, especially suited for the preparation of tomato paste or for canning as peeled tomatoes; (fig. 4) a smooth tomato for salads; (fig. 5) another well known tomato, used in the preparation of salads, the beef-heart cultivar, with a firm and sweet flesh, and pale color, much less used now than in the past.

p. 92 The *Solanum Melongena* var. *esculentum*, is called **Eggplant** in the United States and **Aubergine** in Britain. Its fruit is a fleshy berry, of variable dimensions, often quite large; the base of the fruit is covered by a green and spinose calyx.

Commercially, the different varieties are classified on the basis of the color (white or purple) and shape (thick and short, or elongate) of the fruit. Among the purple elongated varieties the most well known are early long purple, also called Naples early purple, intensively cultivated (fig. 1) and another new variety (fig. 2), dark purple, long and with a characteristic swelling in the lower third of the fruit. Among the white, short varieties (fig. 3) that can be either smooth or costate, the best known are the smooth white oval, and the costate New York giant. Two of the most popular purple, thick varieties (fig. 4) that are characteristically costate, are Black Beauty and New York black giant. There are also intermediate forms, white with purple hues. The blue-purple flowers of eggplants (fig. 5) are very beautiful.

p. 94 The **Pepper** plant (*Capsicum annuum*) is cultivated as an annual herb, but in warm countries, can behave as a perennial. It originated in South America and belongs to the *Solanaceae* (potato or nightshade family). The figures show some of the best known, classical varieties of sweet peppers that may be stuffed or used in salads: the square (fig. 1), the beef-heart or top (fig. 2), and the bull's horn or Spanish (fig. 3). Characteristically the calyx does not entirely cover the base of the fruit, whose walls are thick and fleshy; the seeds, white, flattened, kidney-shaped, and numerous, are inserted on the swelling at the base of the fruit. Peppers are low in calories; some people may find them indigestible but the fruits are rich in vitamin A, and, to a lesser degree, B_2, C, and E.

p.96 The **Hot peppers** (Tabasco, red, Cayenne) are characterized by smaller fruits than those of the sweet peppers and by their very hot taste. The hot peppers are considered to be either varieties of the special *Capsicum annuum*, or, according to some authorities, as true species (such as the *C. cerasiforme* found mostly in southern Italy), or varieties of *C. frutescens*, a perennial shrubby plant, originally from South America.

The principal characteristic of the hot peppers is their burning taste, due to the presence of capsaicin, a pungent alkaloid. This substance gives the pepper certain medicinal properties, and it stimulates the gastric juices which is one of the main reasons for its use in seasoning food.

Cayenne peppers (fig. 1) also belong to this group. They have oblong-acute and thin fruits, which, some botanists claim, is the perennial species *C. frutescens*. Other varieties of hot peppers cultivated in Hungary are commercially processed as *paprika*. Also shown in the diagram are cherry peppers (fig. 2); hot peppers (fig. 3); a form intermediate between sweet and hot peppers (fig. 4) and a specimen of the common long red cultivar (fig. 5).

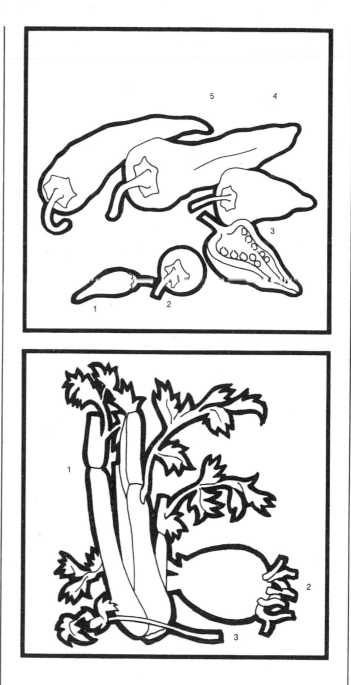

p.98 **Celery** (*Apium graveolens*) is an herbaceous plant belonging to the *Umbelliferae* or carrot family; it has a spindle-shaped root, branched and whitish; the stalks are sulcate, cylindrical and reddish at the base, angular and greenish above (fig. 1). The lower leaves have long, deeply incised petioles; the upper leaves have shorter and even more deeply incised petioles. The small flowers, clustered in umbel inflorescences, have greenish-white petals. In some northern Mediterranean countries celery is found in the wild state in salty marshes; it is cultivated everywhere for its many uses in cooking. There are several varieties, among which is the **Celeriac** (var. *rapaceum*) with a swollen and fleshy tuberose root (fig. 2) resembling a turnip, and very good to eat.

Another species belonging to the *Umbelliferae* and of common use in the kitchen is **Parsley** (*Petroselinum crispum*). It has a white fusiform root and cylindrical, striate and branched stems; the lower leaves with narrow segments; the upper ones entire or trifoliate with entire segments. The flowers, forming an umbel inflorescence, have white petals with the tips curved inwardly. The entire plant is of a beautiful bright green color and has a pleasant smell. Parsley is found in the wild state in southern Europe, Algeria and the Lebanon; it can be found growing wild in many other areas, from the sea to the foot of mountains. The wild species is widely cultivated as a seasoning and for use as a garnish.

p. 100 Many of the aromatic plants belonging to the *Umbelliferae* (carrot or parsley family) are used in distilling gin or whisky, or to season bread, cakes, cheeses, etc. Some of the best known are listed below.

    Coriander (*Coriandrum sativum*) (fig. 1) originated in the eastern section of the Mediterranean, and can be found there either wild or cultivated. This plant is 2–4 feet in height, with compound leaves, the lower ones large and lobed, the upper ones long, divided into narrow, pointed segments. The flowers, clustered in an umbel inflorescence, are either white or pinkish. The fruits are often candied in a sugar solution and sold as sugar plums.

    The **Garden poppy** (*Papaver rhoeas*) (figs. 2a–2b), cultivated as an ornamental plant, is a herb with deeply incised median leaves, wrapped around the stem; the flowers are large with colors varying from purple to red, or pink to white. The fruit is globose or ovoidal, with numerous pores through which the mature seeds come out when the plant moves in the wind.

    Caraway (*Carum carvi*) (fig. 3) is originally from Europe, north and western Asia and is also quite common in the Italian Alps and the North Apennines. This plant is 15–20 inches high, with a tap root, and stem profusely branched from the base up; the leaves are alternate and divided into narrow, pointed segments; the flowers are white or pinkish white.

    Cumin (*Cuminum cyminum*) (fig. 4) is a plant native to Central Asia, and widely cultivated in Europe. Cumin is a small plant, about 8 inches high, branching profusely from the base up, with leaves deeply cut into narrow, pointed lobes. The flowers, clustered in umbel inflorescences, have white or purple red corollas. **Dill** (*Anethum graveolens*) (fig. 5), native to Asia, but cultivated and wild in Europe also, is slightly over 20 inches high, with a smooth stem, very thin, extremely subdivided leaves and small yellow flowers.

p. 102 **Wild** and **Sweet fennel** are both plants of the carrot family typical of the flora of most temperate regions. One grows wild in arid places along the sea and in fields; the other is cultivated in several different varieties.

    Wild fennel (*Foeniculum officinale*) (fig. 1) has an erect, branched, lightly striate stem, with large basal leaves divided into numerous filiform segments; the yellow flowers form large umbels. The fruits of this plant have a characteristic aroma. Sweet fennel (var. *dulce*) (fig. 2) is generally similar to the wild fennel, with one important difference: the basal portions of the leaves are enormously swollen, white and fleshy and form a compact structure. Among the various cultivated varieties which are largely exported throughout Europe are Sicilian large fennel and Bologna large fennel. Sweet fennel is also called finocchio or Florence fennel in the United States.

    Star Anise originated in China, Japan and Formosa (Taiwan). Botanically it is known as *Illicium anisatum*, (fig. 3). It is a shrubby plant belonging to the magnolia family, with alternate, simple leaves, and solitary flowers with a variable number of petals and sepals. The name star anise, which is the common name for badiane, is derived from the star-shaped fruit, formed by eight parts, each containing one seed. The star anise, especially in China, is highly valued for its therapeutic properties; in the Western world it is used mainly as a spice.

p.104 The root of the **Carrot** (*Daucus carota* of the *Umbelliferae*) is of the greatest importance for cultivation and consumption (fig. 1a). It is elongate, fleshy and deeply buried in the soil. In the root can be distinguished two regions; the outer one, cortical, tender, deeply colored, varying from orange to yellow or red; sometimes to white; and the inner part or heart, tough and woody (fig. 1b). The aerial part of the plant consists of an erect, striate, hairy-hispid stem; the lower leaves are deeply incised, the others are linear. The flowers are small, clustered in multirayed umbels; the fruits (achenes) are formed by two greenish seeds with aromatic essential oils. The carrot is probably originally from the temperate regions of Europe and western Asia. Having been widely grown for several centuries as an edible plant, the carrot was once known only in the wild state and used as a medicinal plant. It does not have strict climatic requirements; the preferred soils are sandy or calcareous loams, fresh, rich in nutrients, deep, and without large pebbles that could cause splitting and forking of the roots. Numerous varieties are known, distinguishable for the shape and color of the roots.

    Sea fennel (*Crithmum maritimum* of the *Umbelliferae*) (fig. 2) is a plant that grows near seashores in the wild state, around the coasts of the Mediterranean and the Atlantic, where it can be found in large quantities on sands and rocks, especially where the soil is impregnated with salt. The stems of the sea fennel are 8–20 inches high; the leaves are fleshy, compound, with many rigid and acute leaflets. It is also cultivated as an horticultural plant to be used in salads.

p.106 Fruit (fig. 1a) and longitudinal section (fig. 1b) of a fruit of **Cushaw squash** (Canada crookneck or crookneck squash) (*Cucurbita moschata*), an herbaceous, annual plant with long, vine-like stems, probably native to southern Asia. The fruits are large, fleshy berries, known as *pepo*, the typical fruit of the *Cucurbitaceae* or gourd family. The "neck" is full and fleshy; the spongy pulp full of seed is limited to the upper part of the fruit.

    The round and flattened fruit of another cultivar of *C. moschata* (fig. 2); this cultivar is one of the least known and corresponds to the **Yokohama squash**.

    The **Chayote** (*Sechium edule*) (fig. 3), another species of the *Cucurbitaceae*. This herbaceous plant with very long, vine-like runners is probably originally from Mexico and Central America and has later spread throughout most of the tropical countries. It was introduced into Algeria about 1850, and from there came to Europe. A typical characteristic of *Sechium* is that the fruit contains only one seed that begins to germinate while still inside the fruit.

p. 108 Another variety of squash that, in spite of its morphological characteristics, can still be ascribed to *Cucurbita moschata* is the **Naples stuffed**, (figs. 1–2) which is very popular in southern Italy. These squashes have full and fleshy necks, and the seeds and spongy tissue surrounding them are found only in the cavity of the swollen upper part of the fruits. They can easily reach a length of 3 feet and a weight of 5–8 pounds. The pulp is very tender, especially compared to that of the sea squash, and is a beautiful deep orange color.

Fruit of **Club-shaped** or **Bottle gourd** or cocozzelle (*Lagenaria vulgaris*) (fig. 3) another plant belonging to the *Cucurbitaceae*. The species of the genus *Lagenaria* are herbaceous plants, with well developed vegetative parts and white flowers; the fruits are of several different shapes with a woody texture; in the past, after being hollowed out, they were used as containers or floats.

Two specimens of **Pumpkin** (*Cucurbita pepo*) (figs. 4–5). Zucchini that are generally used when still unripe also belong to this species. The fruits shown in the diagram are ripe specimens, with good keeping qualities, suitable for winter use. Fig. 4 shows the **winter Crookneck squash**. Fig. 5 belongs to the var. *melopepo* and is known as **Custard** or **Scallop gourd**, and is often used as an ornament.

p. 110 It is easy to confuse pumpkins (*Cucurbita pepo*) with squashes (*Cucurbita maxima*) and some of the large fruits taking prizes at pumpkin fairs are often really squashes. An important difference which distinguishes pumpkins from squashes is the contour of the fruit stalk: angular and polygonal in pumpkins, and thick, soft and round in squashes.

Fruits of two specimens of **Pumpkins** (*C. pepo*), suitable for winter consumption, and shown in a fully ripe stage: the **Crook-neck pumpkin** (fig. 1), and a form very similar to the **Brazilian pumpkin** (fig. 2). The fruit shown in fig. 3 is the **American pumpkin** (*C. foetidissima*). Fig. 4 illustrates **Ohio squash**, also shown on the next page. Fig. 5 shows some similarity with the "mammoth" or **"Whale" squashes**, so called because the fruits sometimes grow to 3 feet and can weigh 10–15 pounds. These cultivars with large fruits are not suitable for human use and are mostly used as livestock feed.

p. 112 The other specimens shown in this diagram belong to *Cucurbita maxima* (**Squash**). *C. maxima* is an annual herbaceous plant with long, vine-like stems producing fruits of very large dimension. The leaves are stiff, with rounded, not very prominent lobes. Fig. 6 is a specimen of **Sea** or **Chioggia squash**, with a rugose rind, of various colors, but usually grayish-green or bronze, with very firm, brightly colored flesh. According to the botanist, Naudin, **Turban squashes** (figs. 8 and 9) can be ascribed to this family. (Some authorities consider it a true species, *C. turbaniformis*.) Turban squashes are colorful, for example bright red at the base and lemon-yellow at the apex, and can be used for ornamental purposes, especially the small ones. Fig. 7 shows another species of the **Ohio squash**, which is popular in the United States. Sometimes similar specimens are called Portugal squash.

262

p. 114 **Zucchini** are a variety of *Cucurbita pepo*, believed to have originated in South Africa. The diagram shows the true zucchini, that is, those species whose fruits are used when still unripe and are known commercially as Italian zucchini.

Figs. 1a and 1b show fruits, whole and in cross section, of a new, high-yield cultivar, Ambassador, suitable for forced culture to obtain an early market product. The cultivar Green round (figs. 2a–2b) is another early variety, also suitable for forced culture in cold frames. Fig. 2a shows a ripe fruit and fig. 2b an unripe one still showing the corolla with joined petals of a bright golden-yellow color.

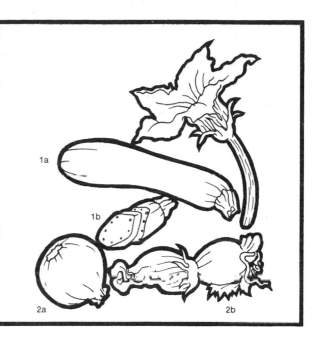

p. 116 Whole fruit, stalk with flowers and cut fruit of **Cucumber** (*Cucumis sativus*), which belongs to the *Cucurbitaceae*, and originates from India or warm Asiatic regions.

The edible part is the unripe fruit that, as in other *Cucurbitaceae*, is a large berry called a *pepo*. The nutrient value of the cucumber is modest, as the water content of the fruit is very high, about 95%.

p.118 The common name of "Sponge mushrooms" indicates numerous edible species mostly belonging to the genus *Morchella*, such as the **Morel** (*Morchella vulgaris* or *M. esculenta*) (fig. 1), and also to other genera such as **Mitrophora** (*Mitrophora hybrida*) (fig. 2), and **Verpa** (*Verpa bohemica*) (fig. 3). The morels are soil-growing mushrooms, mostly found in the spring, April–May, characterized by a spongy, honeycombed cap and by a hollow, fragile stalk with a waxy texture. Morels belong to the *Ascomycetes*, as do truffles.

The **White truffle** (*Choiromyces meandriformis*) (fig. 4) produces underground receptacles, of globoidal shape, more or less irregular, sometimes lobate, with a smooth surface, yellow or brownish in color. The size can vary from that of a walnut to that of a potato. In section the flesh, firm and soapy in texture, shows thin whitish veins that form a support structure for the entire receptacle.

The **Black truffle** (*Pachyphloeus melanoxanthus*) (fig. 5) has been so named because of the color of its receptacle and spores; the microscopic structures used for vegetative reproduction, contained inside the receptacle. The receptacles are either globose or kidney-shaped, often gibbous or lobate. The surface is covered by polygonal warts, more or less protruding. The flesh, in section, appears reddish or brownish with branching white veins.

The **Red truffle** (fig. 6) is less well known commercially than either of the other two. Botanically, it is known as *Melanogaster variegatus*.

p.120 The receptacle of **Caesar's mushroom** (*Amanita caesarea*) (fig. 1) shows different shapes depending upon the stage of development. In the initial stages the mushroom is completely wrapped inside a membranous structure, the universal veil, and looks almost like an egg. Later the veil breaks up and part of it forms the volva, a structure surrounding the base of the stalk or stipe; the volva is white, membranous and irregularly lobed. The stalk is 4–6 inches high, yellowish, first compact then hollow, with a ring (annulum) in the upper part. The ring is membranous, striate and yellowish. The cap or pileus, first convex, then flat, is 3–6 inches in diameter, orange-colored with an easily detachable smooth pellicle. The residues of the veil are seldom found on the surface of the cap; these residues simulate the presence of warts. The flesh is firm, with a pleasant odor and taste.

The **Field, Meadow** or **Button mushroom** (*Agaris* or *Psalliota campestris*) (fig. 2) is similar, and characterized by a cap, first globose, then expanded and flattened; by a stout and firm stalk, cylindrical and full, and somewhat swollen at the base. The gills are always colored, from pinkish to brown depending on the ripeness of the receptacle. The flesh is tender with a pleasant smell and taste. The wild species are found in woods, fields and vegetable gardens. The receptacles are formed from May to September or October. These mushrooms are practically cosmopolitan.

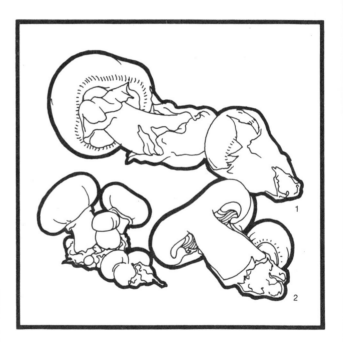

p. 122 The **Parasol mushroom** (*Lepiota procera*) (fig. 1) is one of the most common and best known mushrooms, even though it is rarely fully appreciated. It produces big receptacles, that in ripe specimens can reach to 12 inches, and in the initial stages of development look like drumsticks. Later the cap expands and the receptacle becomes the typical umbrella shape. Small scales are present on the cap's upper surface, which shows a typical swelling in the center, known as *umbo*. The stalk is hollow and bulbous at the base; the ring, found on the upper third of the stalk, is multi-layered with a lacerated margin.

The receptacles of the **Chanterelle** (*Cantharellus tubaeformis*) (fig. 2) are trumpet-shaped. The cap of this mushroom is 1–2½ inches in diameter, shaped like a funnel, hollow in the center, somewhat hairy and with undulate margins; the gills are decurrent, that is, prolonged down the stalk, and branched; the stem, stalk or stipe, is 1¼–3 inches in height, cylindrical and hollow, tapering at the base.

The receptacles of the **Horn of plenty** (*Craterellus cornucopioides*) (fig. 3), also known as "trumpet of the dead" are shaped like funnels or cups, similar to those of the chanterelle. However, the hymenium (the fertile structure on the lower surface of the cap, forming the spores) is different, being smooth and not covering gills or pores. The texture is fleshy-membranous, and the stalk hollow and tapered at the base. There is neither a ring nor a volva.

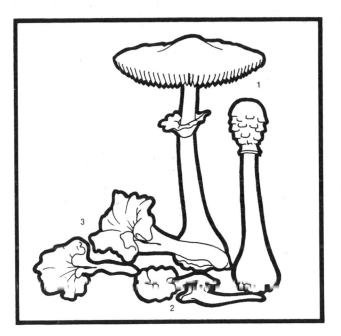

p. 124 The common names of **Boletus** or **Ceps** indicate two similar species: *Boletus edulis* (edible boletus) and *Ceps boletes* (fig. 1), easily confused with each other. In these mushrooms, the cap is hemispherical first, and then flattened, or even with an upturned margin. Their color is variable depending on the season, the weather, and other environmental factors, from light brown to whitish. In *Ceps boletes*, the color of the cap should be darker. The hymenium or fertile structure producing the spores, does not form gills, but is arranged in tubules or pores. The stalk is squat and bulbous in the younger specimens, and more elongated, but still thick in the ripe ones. The surface is reticulated. There is neither a ring nor a volva.

. The **Oyster mushroom** (*Pleurotus ostreatus*) (fig. 2) produces characteristic aggregations of receptacles, sometimes very numerous, with a structure like that of roof-tiles, each element partially covering the one beneath. The entire aggregate can reach large dimensions. It grows on trees or rotting tree stumps. The cap is eccentric to the stalk, with a variable color from hazel- to cinereous-brown to bluish. The gills are white and longly decurrent on the white stalk. The flesh is also white and tenacious, but with a pleasant scent and an aromatic taste. The **Girolle** (*Cantharellus cibarius*) (fig. 3) is characterized by small receptacles, only 1¼–3 inches; the cap is convex initially and becomes funnel-shaped in ripe specimens, with an irregularly shaped margin. The color is golden- or orange-yellow. The gills are longly decurrent on the stalk which is short, the same color as the cap, and tapered at the base.

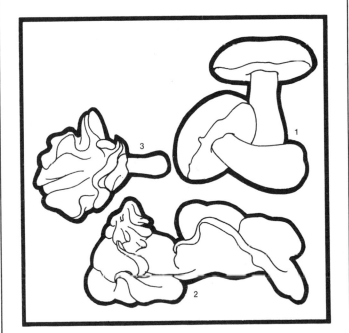

p.126 The **Apple** tree (*Malus communis*), originally from central Asia and the Caucasus, is the most widely cultivated tree of the rose family. Morphologically, the apple tree is 30–35 feet tall, with a trunk covered by a scaly ash-brown bark, profusely branching with strong branches forming a round-flattened head. The twigs are reddish-brown, glabrous or lightly pubescent, bright, dotted with lenticels of a lighter color. The leaves are petiolate, oval, often pointed at the tip, round or truncate at the base, with finely toothed margins, deep green on the upper surface; the lower surface is lightly hairy, pale-green or whitish. The flowers appear between the end of February and April, depending upon the climate and the area; the petals are white on the outer surface and pink, more or less deep on the inner face. The fruit of the apple tree is botanically known as a *pome*, and commonly as an apple. The apples have a globoidal shape, elongate or slightly depressed (figs. 1 to 10), yellow, green or red skin, with crisp or floury, sweet, slightly tart, and aromatic flesh. The small, dark seeds are enclosed inside cavities with parchment-like walls (fig. 3b). The apple tree does not like soils that are exceedingly moist, compact calcareous, or sandy, but prefers those that are deep and fresh, but not wet. It does not have strict climatic requirements and is very resistant to drought and hot or freezing weather; but for its best growth it prefers fresh and humid climates, which is the main reason why the largest apple crops are obtained in countries with temperate or cold climates. Apples are used for human consumption. Some varieties with particular characteristics are used for the extraction of a juice that, following fermentation, yields an alcoholic drink known as hard cider or applejack, drunk mostly in France, Germany and the United States. In Normandy a type of brandy, called Calvados, is distilled from apples. The figures show specimens of the following cultivars: Delicious (fig. 2), of American origin, introduced into Europe between the two world wars. The surface is markedly costate-like, the skin is yellow spotted with red, and the pulp is very fragrant. Several mutations have been obtained from this cultivar, among which is the Starkcrimson Delicious (fig. 1).

Golden Delicious (figs. 3a–3b), medium-sized fruits, yellow when ripe, with firm flesh and a pleasant, aromatic taste.

Rose of Caldaro (fig. 4), slightly depressed, yellow with bright red areas; sweet pulp, slightly tart and fine-textured.

Jonathan (fig. 5), of American origin, with smooth and coriaceous skin, greenish-yellow, deep red on the side directly exposed to the sun, and with a yellowish, firm, juicy, pleasantly tart pulp.

Calvilla (fig. 7), medium-large fruits, conical with irregular surface, similar to that of the quince; skin waxy yellow with carmine red hues; pulp yellowish-white, fragrant and juicy.

Abundance (fig. 8), widely cultivated in parts of Italy; medium-large fruits, smooth skin variegated with wine-red color; pulp yellowish-white, fragrant and juicy.

Rennet (fig. 10), slightly depressed, irregular shape; skin often rough and marbled yellow; pulp yellowish-white, fragrant, sweet and slightly tart. Cultivated largely in France.

Other good cultivars are Stayman (fig. 9) and Granny Smith (fig. 6).

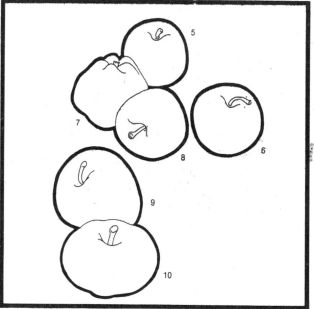

The species of the genus *Pyrus* known today number about thirty. They are all originally from Europe, Asia and North Africa. The most important species is the **Pear** tree, *Pyrus communis*, a robust plant with grayish and rough bark, oblong-ovate leaves, entire or toothed, and white flowers with numerous stamens. From this species, throughout the world, were derived the various cultivars, numbering thousands, producing a variety of fruits, **Pears**, differing in size, shape, color, texture, consistency, taste, and time of ripening.

The Argentine William and Butter William (figs. 1 and 7) have been known since the beginning of the nineteenth century. They were in fact, discovered in 1770 by Mr. Williams, a London horticulturist. The fruits had been formed on a plant grown from seed. They are medium-large, ovate, or sometimes elongated and top-shaped, with a woody peduncle implanted obliquely. The skin is smooth, yellowish, red-spotted and slightly oily. The flesh is whitish, juicy, sweet, aromatic and melting. They ripen in August, in the period between the second and the third weeks.

The Comice (fig. 2) first appeared in France in 1849; the fruits are large and the fruit stalk is implanted vertically; the skin is a yellowish light-green with rust-colored spots. It ripens during October through the first days of November. The flesh is fragrant and sweet, sometimes granular toward the center of the fruit.

Kaiser (fig. 3) is rusty-colored and rough skinned; flesh yellowish-white, sometimes granular because of the presence of sandy cells; the fruits are rather large with a woody peduncle. It ripens between October and November.

The cultivar Abbé or Abate (fig. 4) was discovered in France by the Abbé Fétel, in the nineteenth century; the fruits are large, more or less elongate; the peduncle is rusty-colored, partly fleshy at the base and obliquely inserted; the skin is rather thin, pale yellowish-green; the flesh is whitish, melting, juicy, sweet and aromatic. It ripens in early fall.

The fruits of Passa crassana (fig. 5) come into full ripening during the winter. They are of medium to large size; generally larger in width than in length; the skin is tough, yellowish with rusty stains around the insertion of the peduncle; the flesh is white, slightly granular, sweet and fragrant.

Early Butter Morettini (fig. 6) is a recently developed cultivar of Italian origin; the fruits are medium sized with obliquely inserted peduncles; the skin is smooth, yellowish light green, but red in the parts directly exposed to the sun; the flesh is whitish and firm, juicy and sweet. It ripens in late July.

Max Red Bartlett (fig. 8) is of American origin. The "Butter Hardy" (fig. 9) is of French origin; the peduncle is woody, swollen at the top and inserted obliquely; the fruits ripen during the last days of summer; the skin is green, or reddish in the parts directly exposed to the sun; the flesh is greenish-white and with a sweet-acid flavor.

Those presented above are only a few of the thousands of cultivars available commercially. By selecting the cultivars best suited for local climatic conditions, and because of the easy availability of cultivars with different ripening seasons, it is possible to enjoy this fruit at its best almost throughout the year.

p.134 The **Quince** or Cydon apple (*Cydonia oblonga*) is a plant of the rose family, native to western Asia. It is a shrub or small tree, 12–20 feet in height at the most, with a contorted trunk, ovate, entire leaves, cottony on the lower surface. The flowers are white or light pink, large and terminal on short leafy branchlets. The fruits (fig. 1) have a tomentose-floccose yellowish surface; they are very fragrant, with rather coriaceous flesh, and a slightly acid, pungent taste. Quinces, even at the end of October, when fully ripe, are practically inedible raw; but are very good after cooking or as preserves. Botanically, quinces are closely related to pears and apples. They can be easily distinguished for the different size and shape of the trees, the larger and hairy leaves, and for the fine and resistent hair covering on the surface of the fruit. This tree finds suitable environmental conditions throughout the Mediterranean, but can be found in other countries with a temperate climate such as Romania, Bulgaria and Yugoslavia.

The **Loquat** or **Japanese medlar** (*Eriobotrya japonica*), is another species belonging to the *Rosaceae* and, as indicated by its specific name, originated in East Asia. It is a small tree; the leaves are large, short-petioled, lanceolate, rather coriaceous, lustrous and glabrous above, tomentose underneath. The flowers are clustered in inflorescences and are yellowish, small, and pleasantly fragrant. The flowers appear between August and September; the fruits, ripening in March, are clustered in small groups, globoid in shape, orange-yellow, rather watery, with a sweeitsh and agreeable acid flavor, and contain one to ten large seeds. Agricultural selection has been used to reduce the number of the seeds to improve the market value of the fruits. The loquat prefers temperate-warm or maritime climates, and it can also grow in regions with subfreezing winter temperatures, but the formation of fruits is either scarce or none at all.

p.136 The **Service tree** (*Sorbus domestica*) often confused with the European mountain-ash (*S. aucuparia*) is long-lived, and can reach to 65 feet high. It has dark-brown bark exfoliating into small scales, with many branches forming a large round head. The leaves are compound, formed by 13 to 21 leaflets, ovate-elongate, acute, and serrate; the fruits (fig. 1) are ovoidal or pyriform, generally yellow, and red only on the side directly exposed to the sun. The service tree is found wild in woods in Europe, and is also sparsely cultivated for its fruits.

Among the numerous species and thousands of cultivated varieties of the genus *Rosa*, are the **Wild roses**; climbing rose, meadow rose, prickly rose, Arkansas rose, Wood's rose, swamp rose, glossy rose, pasture rose, dog rose or wild briar and sweetbriar, that not only contribute so much, with their flowers, to the beauty of the countryside, but also produce delicate fruits (fig. 2). Despite its scientific Latin name, the **Medlar** (*Mespilus germanica*) is not of German origin, but probably native to oriental countries, possibly western Asia. It is a small tree, with a twisted trunk, sometimes only brush-like. The branches are often thorny and covered by soft hair in their juvenile stages. The lanceolate or elliptical leaves have short petioles. The flowers are borne singly, white, rather large and appear in May. The fruits, top-shaped (fig. 3), attain their full size in the fall. The medlar is found sporadically in woods, along the borders of mountain thickets, and is sparsely cultivated, mostly in Europe, for its fruits.

A typical Mediterranean plant, quite common in the wild state, is a *Crataegus* known as **Azarole** (*C. àzarolus*), a close relative of the hawthorn (white or May thorn) (*C. oxyacantha*). The genus *Crataegus* belongs to the rose family. When cultivated, the azarole is a small tree; the young branches are velvety-tomentose; the leaves are pubescent, deeply 3–5 lobed, with the lobes nearly entire or incised at the apex, 1–3 toothed. The fruit looks like a small, fleshy apple, yellowish or red, containing one or two stones, which are the transformed carpels, of bony consistency, containing one, or rarely, two seeds. It flowers in May and the edible fruits ripen in early fall.

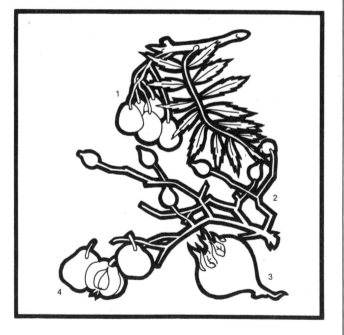

p. 138 Watermelons, typical of warm and temperate countries, are the fruits of *Citrullus vulgaris*, an herbaceous plant of the *Cucurbitaceae* (gourd or cucumber family). The large fruits, ascribable to the great, polymorphic group of berries, are called *pepo*, a term specifically indicating the fruits of the *Cucurbitaceae*. Among the large number of cultivated forms, are three characteristic cultivars that can be considered as emblematic of this species: Sugar Baby (fig. 1), spherical, 6–10 pounds, with dark-green and pruinose skin (rind), and deep-red flesh; Miyako (fig. 2), also spherical, larger than the Sugar Baby, with a variegated rind on a pale-green background; Charleston Gray (fig. 3), oblong fruit, large dimensions (19–24 inches long, 9–12 inches diameter), and large weights (up to 40 pounds), skin uniformly variegated and flesh of strawberry-red color.

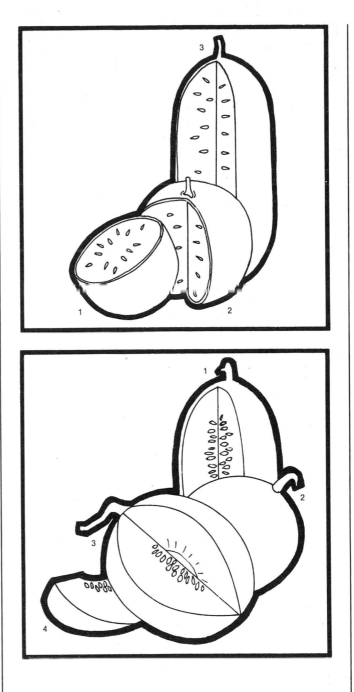

p. 140 Melons (also muskmelon or cantaloupe, from the castle of Cantalupo, in Italy, where it was first grown in Europe) are of the same family as the watermelon, and the same genus as the cucumber. They are not grown in the United States. Botanically melons are ascribed to *Cucumis melo*, a species within which several botanists including Fiori, distinguish at least five varieties: var. *agrestis*, the wild or spontaneous plant, with small, plum size, inedible fruits; var. *scandens* or *reticulatus* (**Netted melon**) (fig. 1), with more or less netted rinds, sometimes almost smooth; var. *cantalupensis* (**Cantaloupe** or Rock melon) (fig. 2), with rind deeply furrowed or grooved, warty and rough; var. *inodorus* (**Winter melon**) (figs. 3 and 4), rind smooth and relatively thin, late ripening, flesh white and sweet; var. *flexuosus* (Snake melon) (not illustrated), with very long, almost cylindrical fruits, rarely cultivated. The large number of cultivated forms can be divided into two groups (some authorities distinguish up to ten groups): the netted or reticulated melons, and the cantaloupe or warty melons. Winter melons are also called Neapolitan or Spanish melons and are known in Spain as *melon amarillo oro* and *melon tendral tardio*. The species include honeydew and casaba.

p.142 The numerous varieties of **Plums** that have been obtained through years of cultivation derive from at least ten different species and their hybrids. It is therefore difficult to describe the general characteristics of so many varieties. However, considering their area of origin, they could be subdivided into three groups: the Euroasiatic species, fundamentally derived from *Prunus domestica*, the Sino-Japanese species and the American species.

The varieties of the species *P. domestica*, surpass those of any other species of plums, both for quality and in number. *P. domestica*, as well as many other fruit trees, belongs to the *Rosaceae* or rose family; it is a tree, of variable height, between 16–35 feet with a contorted trunk and a rather rough, dark bark, longitudinally cracked. The leaves are ovate to oblong, somewhat hairy on the lower surface, and dentate (toothed). The flowers appear either at the same time, or before the leaves, and have 5 petals and numerous stamens. The fruits differ in shape and color, depending upon the variety; their flesh is tender and yellowish, acid-sweet and very fragrant, and contains only one stone (the hard structure enclosing the seeds), free or adhering to the flesh, more or less elongated or pointed.

Plum trees adapt easily to various types of soils, provided there is no standing water; climatically they are quite resistant to cold. However, sudden freezing weather during the flowering season can cause enormous damage, therefore one of the aims of selection is to obtain cultivars with higher resistance to meteorological calamities typical in springtime in temperate areas. A short list of cultivars, selected from among the thousands that are known, is given below:

The mirabelle or rustic (fig. 1): this plum is the nearest relative of the original forms; it is often used as stock on which to graft other varieties.

Florentia (fig. 2): medium sized fruits, spheroidal to heart-shaped; skin red, pruinose; flesh yellow with red veins, very juicy, sweet, slightly acid; ripens during the first days of July.

Saint Peter (fig. 3): rustic plums, ripening in early summer; flesh at first firm and crunchy; softer and very aromatic when fully ripe.

Ruth Gastetter (fig. 4): variety with medium size fruits, dark red and pruinose skin; flesh greenish-yellow, firm, juicy, acid-sweet, aromatic; tree strong and very productive, plums ripening during the second half of June.

Shiro (fig. 5): also known as "gold drops"; fruits medium to large, rather thin skin, yellow, a little pruinose; flesh yellow, translucent, very juicy, sweet, but slightly acidulous near the stone; ripening during the first half of July.

Saint Clare (fig. 6): American variety; skin dark purple and pruinose, flesh firm.

Reine Claude (fig. 7): variety with almost spherical plums, green in color, and dirty creamy yellow when fully ripe; flesh greenish, very firm.

Santa Rosa (fig. 8): large spherical plums; skin of dark-red color, with many lenticels and slightly pruinose; flesh pinky-yellow, pleasantly fragrant, acidulous; ripens about the middle of July.

Burbank (fig. 9): a variety of American origin; plums medium-sized, spheroidal, with a dark-red thin and slightly pruinose skin; the flesh is yellow, juicy, very aromatic, sweet and firm; ripens about the end of July.

Sugar (fig. 10): very sweet plums, particularly good for drying.

Stanley (fig. 11): variety similar to Saint Clare; exceptional for the productivity and beauty of the plums that are excellent when dried; plums medium to large, asymmetrical and ovate; the skin is thin, dark purple, and pruinose; the flesh is greenish yellow, tender, rather juicy and sweet; ripens about the end of August.

The numerous varieties of fruits commonly known as **Cherries** can be divided into two groups. The first is that of the "sweet" cherries, derived from *Prunus avium*; the second group is that of the "sour" (pie, Morello) cherries, derived from *P. cerasus*.

The sweet cherry (*P. avium* of the rose family) is a tree that at full development can reach 35–45 feet in height; the trunk is straight, covered by a red-brown or blackish bark, usually rough, not smooth, transversely striated. Branches and twigs are covered by smooth, light brown to gray bark. The leaves are rather large, oblong-ovate, with serrate margin (fig. 1); the flowers have white petals and form small clusters of one to six flowers. The fruits, cherries, are pendant, globular, globular-depressed or heart-shaped (fig. 1), yellow, pale red or dark red; the flesh is almost the same color and sweet; the stone is rounded, smooth and semi-adherent to the flesh. Cherries are probably native to a region between the Caspian Sea and Anatolia where they grow wild. The tree is typical of temperate or temperate-cold climates, and can grow further north than the plum tree. It does not like very hot summers and prefers climates without sudden great changes in temperature. It needs good soil, which should be light, sandy, gravelly or even stony loams, rich in humus and not too dry. Among the thousand or so varieties and cultivars of sweet cherries are the following:

Japanese yellow cherries (fig. 1).

Rainbow Stripe (fig. 2): flesh crisp and crackling, late ripening, light colored.

Vignola I (fig. 3): large, flesh firm, sweet, resistent, highly valued for export.

Vignola Black (fig. 4): blackish fruit, flesh juicy, sweet and pleasant.

Starking Hardy Giant (fig. 5), with firm, crackling flesh.

Early Marchiana (fig. 6): cultivar obtained in the Apennines, with watery and aromatic flesh.

Early Bourlat (fig. 7): firm, crackling flesh, pleasant flavor and resistent.

The sour cherry (*Prunus cerasus*) is a smaller tree than the sweet variety, seldom reaching to more than 18–22 feet. The tree head is expanded or roundish; the bark is brown-red, spotted and, in time, comes off in transversal strips. The leaves are smaller than those of the sweet cherry, smooth, glabrous and glossy. The fruits are light or dark red, globular or globular-depressed. The several cultivars obtained within this species have been divided in two groups, the Morello cherries, dark or light in color, with a very sour flavor (figs. 1, 2, 4), and the Amarelles, with large, lightly colored fruits slightly less acid than the Morello. Fig. 3 shows a specimen of wild cherry.

The sour cherry is probably also native to Asia, and can be found further north and in colder climates than the sweet cherry. The sour cherry grows well on almost any soil, but prefers those that are dry and well drained.

p.150 The **Peach** (*Prunus persica vulgaris*) belongs to the *Rosaceae* or rose family. The tree has a straight or slightly twisted trunk covered by reddish-gray to blackish bark; its height varies from 10–25 feet; the diameter is seldom more than 15–20 inches. The branches spread out and are covered by dark-red or grayish bark. The leaves are oblong-lanceolate, alternate; the upper epidermis is green, smooth, dull or glossy; the lower epidermis is grayish-green, sometimes slightly pubescent. The peach flowers with a pleasant and delicate scent, are borne singly or in small clusters of 2–3 individuals; the corolla is light pink; the size depends upon the variety. The fruit is a drupe, of spheroidal shape, with a longitudinal groove; the pedicel is attached to the fruit at the bottom of a rather deep cavity. Depending on the variety, the fruits are different shades of yellow, green, orange, or red; the flesh, also of different colors and textures in different varieties, is fragrant and sweet; the stone is hard and deeply pitted.

The peach prefers light, fresh and deep soils, even sandy if moist, and without too much limestone. It can adapt to a large variety of climatic conditions and, in Europe, suitable conditions for cultivation are found from northern France down to the African coasts.

Peach varieties are very many, at least 5,000. The causes for this great number are the widespread cultivation practiced for many centuries and the high frequency of formation of hybrids, either natural, or cultivated.

Hale (fig. 1) is one of the best known American varieties. The tree is not large, but is highly productive and sets fruits early. They are big, regular, round, with two symmetrical halves, and only slightly downy. The skin is orange-yellow, with red hues and carmine spots. The flesh is yellow, red around the stone, firm and juicy.

Lugo Beautiful (fig. 2), originally of Romagna, Italy, is one of the best known varieties on the Continent.

Loadel (figs. 3 and 4) is a Californian variety, with medium sized fruits, orange-yellow with red hues; the flesh is orange-yellow, firm and sweet; this is one of the varieties suitable for canning.

Glohaven (fig. 5) was introduced in the late fifties or sixties; the fruits are large and uniform, with a deep yellow skin tinged with bright red; the flesh is very firm and pale yellow. This is another variety highly prized by the canning industry.

p.152 A particular group of peaches is that of the **Nectarines** (*Prunus persica* var. *nectarina*). Their fruits are quite different from those of the common peaches; their skin is smooth, they are smaller, and the flesh is firmer, but less juicy. Prominent among nectarine varieties is the Armking, introduced recently by the United States (fig. 1), ripening about the end of June, and the Blanca del Jalon or Jalon White (fig. 2).

The **Apricot** (*Armeniaca vulgaris*) is a tree, 13–25 feet in height, often with a twisted trunk, covered by dark-reddish bark often longitudinally fissured. The branches are darkish to darkish red; the leaves are rather leathery, shiny, round-ovate, heart-shaped at the base and closely serrate. The flowers appear in March, before the leaves, and are pale pink turning to white. The fruits are either globoid or oblong with a lateral groove; the skin is mostly yellow, slightly tinged with red, especially on the side directly exposed to the sun. The stone contains a seed of bitter to sweetish flavor. Today apricots are intensively cultivated in the United States, the Mediterranean and Australia.

Among the various cultivars, the best known and most intensively cultivated on the Continent are the Caninos (fig. 3), ripening in June, the Nugget (fig. 4), ripening at the end of July, reddish yellow on the side directly exposed to the sun, and the Imola Royal (fig. 5). The latter is a highly productive variety, the fruits are large, oval, orange-yellow tinged with red, with a firm, sweet, fragrant flesh.

p.154 Raspberries (European raspberry, *Rubus idaeus*, and the red raspberry of the United States, var. *strigosus*), are common on mountains and in subalpine woods in Europe and the United States, and are also intensively and widely cultivated in many countries. The raspberry is a small shrub, slightly more than 3 feet in height, with erect or arched stems or canes bearing small prickles (fig. 2). The young branches of *R. idaeus* are covered by a downy pubescence and their bark is yellowish-gray. The old branches appear glabrous and their bark is dark-gray. The compound leaves are formed by 3 to 7 leaflets, ovate and serrate, with a green upper surface. The flowers are mostly solitary or in small clusters, with a corolla of pink-white petals. The fruits, deep red, have an exquisite flavor and a sweet scent. The many different varieties of cultivated raspberries can be divided in two categories: to the first belong the raspberries that form fruits twice a year, in June on the branches of the previous year, and in September at the end of the new branches. The second category includes the cultivars that form fruits only once a year, in June, on the branches of the previous year.

Blackberries are the fruits of *Rubus fruticosus*, another plant of the *Rosaceae*, a close relative of the raspberry, but with palmately compound leaves formed by 3 to 5 leaflets (fig. 1), almost evergreen. The blackberry withstands long periods of drought better than the raspberry, but is less resistant than the latter to intense cold. The fruits are formed on branches of the previous year, that later dry out and are substituted by new suckers.

p.156 The species of the genus *Ribes* of the *Saxifragaceae* or gooseberry, currant and saxifrage family are over a hundred. Many of these species have edible fruits; others are cultivated as ornamental plants. Gooseberries and currants grow in the temperate regions of Europe, North Africa, north and central Asia, North and South America and along the Andes.

Both the **Red** and **White currant** (*R. rubrum*) (figs. 1 and 3) are shrubs with large leaves, heart-shaped at the base, with 3 to 5 dentate lobes; the flowers are in axillary racemes; the fruits are red berries with an acid flavor; the berries of the cultivated varieties may be of different colors, yellowish or white.

The **Black currant** (*R. nigrum*) (fig. 2) can be distinguished from the red, for the aromatic scent of all its parts and for its black berries which have a sweetish taste. Both the red and black currants were unknown in Europe before the Middle Ages, when their cultivation began for their edible fruits.

The **Gooseberry** (*R. grossularia*) is a small shrub, with spinescent branches ascending or reclining; the leaves are almost rounded with 5 lobes; the flowers are greenish or reddish; the tart, round fruits may be red, yellow, green or white, and hairy or smooth depending on the variety. The gooseberry is very resistant to cold weather and prefers cold northern climates and shady places. It does not have particular soil requirements, although it prefers light calcareous soils, rich in humus. The most popular American variety is *R. hirtellum*. Figs. 4 and 5 illustrate the white and the red varieties.

p. 158 The genus *Fragaria* (strawberry), that includes the European **wild** or **wood Strawberry**, belongs to the *Rosaceae* or rose family, and includes numerous species and varieties originally from Europe, Asia and America. The varieties cultivated now are derived from the original species and their hybrids. The most important species scattered over the temperate areas of Europe, Asia and America are *F. vesca* (wild strawberry), *F. alpina semperflorens* (Alpine strawberry), *F. collina* (hill or pine strawberry), *F. chiloensis* (Chilian strawberry), native to Chile; and *F. virginiana* (scarlet Virginia strawberry), native to the United States and Canada. The large-fruited cultivated varieties are hybrids of the two American species. *F. vesca* or wild strawberry, (fig. 1) is a rhizomatose plant, with long, thin stolons or runners, from which, at ground level, arise leaves and flowers. The compound leaves are formed by three oval leaflets, deeply dentate, light green on the upper surface, whitish and slightly hairy on the lower one. From the center of the leaf cluster arises an unbranched stem, thin and bristly, terminating with 4–6 or more white flowers. According to botanical nomenclature, the strawberry is a false or accessory fruit, since most of it is formed by a swelling of the receptacle; the true fruits are the achenes, improperly called seeds, on the surface of the fleshy part. Achenes are one-seeded fruits. The strawberry plant grows wild in woods and other un-cultivated places, especially in mountainous areas. The cultivated fruits have a fragrant, porous and light flesh, not very watery. Some of the best known cultivars are listed below:

Belrubi (fig. 2) produces large, ribbed fruits with firm and deeply colored flesh, and can be frozen with good results.

Pocahontas (fig. 3), of American origin, produces very large fruits with a firm and juicy flesh, deep pink in color; the fruits travel well and can be used either fresh or frozen.

Gorella (fig. 4) is a Dutch variety; the fruits are rather large, with deep pink, sweet rather aromatic and not very juicy flesh. This cultivar is very resistant to cold and droughts and can be frozen with excellent results.

Queen or Regina (fig. 5) is a German strawberry; the flesh is firm, juicy, pale pink or whitish, lightly aromatic; it does not have good keeping qualities.

Rossella or scarlet (fig. 6) produces medium-sized, kidney-shaped fruits; the flesh is firm, juicy, tart and pleasantly aromatic.

The genus *Vitis* (**Grapes**) belongs to the *Vitaceae* or vine family, and is widely diffused throughout the northern hemisphere, especially North America. In the seventeenth century Lord Baltimore introduced the *Vitis vinifera* into the United States but it did not thrive.

The common grape (*V. vinifera*) has twisted trunks, covered by a bark exfoliating longitudinally. The long flexible stems, the vines, bear coiling support organs called tendrils, opposite the leaves, which are about as long as they are wide, palmate and heart-shaped at the base. The flowers are small, lightly scented and clustered in large, pendant bunches. The fruits are berries attached to a grape-stalk, clustering into bunches of roughly cylindrical, conical, or pyramidal shape. The skin of the berries is either white or dark, and pruinose; the flesh is juicy, rich in soluble sugars, and almost always containing seeds (grape-stones). The common grapevine (Old-world grape) does not grow well on moist, compact soils, rich in organic humus. Climatically, grapes require warm weather and clear, sunny days. Other species of the genus *Vitis* are listed below.

(fig. 1) Cornicella, an Italian grape with small, slightly curved berries.

(fig. 2) Muscatel, which originated in Malaga, and is used mostly to produce a strong, sweet wine.

(fig. 3) Typical table or dessert grapes of European origin.

(fig. 4) An American variety largely cultivated in California.

V. aestivalis (Summer grape), found mostly in the center and eastern regions of the United States; the grape bunches are elongated and the berries are small.

V. rotundifolia (Southern Fox grape), originally of the central and eastern regions of North America, with short sparse bunches of large berries. The cultivation of grapes has always been spread over a very wide area. Intensive cross-breeding has produced a large number of cultivars that, depending upon their use have been divided into two main groups: that of the table or dessert grapes and that of the wine grapes. The best known varieties of the table grapes cultivated in western Europe are listed below.

July or Saint Anne: large bunches with yellowish and ovoidal berries, ripening about the end of July.

Golden Chasselas: roundish, medium-sized berries, skin amber-yellow or rose-yellow; flesh medium sweet, very pleasant; ripening during the second half of July.

Baresana with long bunches, and amber-colored berries, fleshy, not very sweet, but very pleasant; ripening in August.

Bicane, with thin bunches, ovoidal and sweet berries, ripening during the first half of August.

Grape Queen; the bunches are cylindrical, rather long; the grapes have a resistant amber skin and a sweet, crisp flesh; ripening between the first days of August and the beginning of September, depending upon the regions.

The *Terracina* Muscatel, with large and thick bunches; the grapes are roundish, their skin resistant and the flesh aromatic and very sweet; it ripens during the second half of August.

Gros Vert, with pyramidal bunches, roundish, slightly elongated grapes with a hard, yellow skin; the flesh is soft and slightly acidulous.

Some of the cultivated varieties are used essentially as dried grapes; they are known as Sultanas, a seedless variety originally from Anatolia; Corinth or Zanta currants and raisins; the variety of grapes used for the preparation of the raisins is also used in the preparation of a sweet and aromatic *passito* wine, whose largest center of production is the Mediterranean island of Pantelleria.

Three of the numerous varieties of wine grapes are: Sangiovese (fig. 5), with large, oval, purplish-black grapes used for the production of an excellent table wine; Trebbiano d'Empoli (fig. 6) with amber-yellow grapes, and Labrusco or Northern Fox grape (fig. 7) with blue-black thick-skinned grapes, used for the production of a dark colored wine, slightly sour and with a low alcoholic content. The leaves are covered by a rusty tomentum. The berries have a scent slightly similar to that of raspberries.

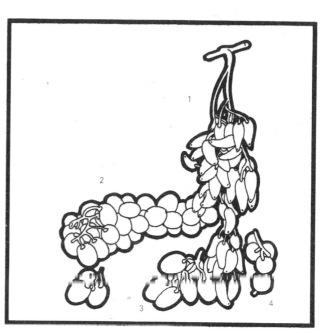

p.164 The cornelian cherry or **Cornel** (*Cornus mas* of the *Cornaceae* or dogwood family) (fig. 1) is either a shrub or a small tree, about 10–18 feet high. It is a slow-growing, long-lived plant; the trunk is usually twisted with a brownish-gray bark; the branches are greenish, tinged with red on the sides directly exposed to the sun, and bearing opposite, oval leaves, appearing at the beginning of spring. The yellow flowers cover the branches almost completely and are formed before the leaves; the fruits are about the size of an olive, red, with a pleasantly flavored flesh, slightly tart, and ripen during late summer. The Cornelian cherry is a close relative of the flowering dogwood (*C. florida*). The wood is often used for golfclub heads.

The **Strawberry tree** (*Arbutus unedo* of the *Ericaceae* or heath family) (fig. 2) is an evergreen shrub or small tree, native to the Mediterranean, at most 18–22 feet tall, but often smaller, covered by a smooth bark peeling in thin red plates. The leaves are leathery (coriaceous), glossy, oblong-lanceolate and last on the tree for one or two years. The flowers are rose-white. The fruit is a globose berry, warty and tuberculate, amaranthine or cochineal red, with yellow flesh of sweetish flavor, sometimes faintly aromatic, ripening in late summer.

The **Jujube tree** (*Zizyphus jujuba* of the *Rhamnaceae* or buckthorn family) (fig. 3) is a shrub or a small tree with large, contorted branches, having a dark-red bark; the leaves are simple, short-petioled, thorny, smooth, glossy and rather coriaceous. The flowers are axillary, in groups of 1 to 3, small and white. The fruits are the size of an olive, edible and sweet, green during development and rust-colored when fully ripe, containing a single, large, pointed stone.

The **Whortleberry**, also called blueberry or bilberry (*Vaccinium myrtillus* of the *Ericaceae* or heath family, not the commonly known American form) (fig. 4) is a low-growing shrub, no more than 2–3 feet in height, with erect, stiff stems and slender branches bearing small, ovate or oblong, short-petioled leaves with serrated margins, dark green above and light green below. The flowers, appearing at the end of the spring, are white or greenish and grouped two by two. The berries, ripening in August, are black or dark blue and globose, about the size of a pea or slightly larger, covered by a thin patina of bloom, edible and very pleasantly flavored.

p.166 The **Fig** (*Ficus carica* of the *Moraceae* or mulberry family) can be a large shrub or a small tree; the trunk is covered by a smooth, ash-colored bark; the large branches are dark; the leaves are alternate, large, with 2–7 rounded lobes, pubescent, scabrous and coriaceous. All the parts of this plant are rich in an irritant milky juice. The inflorescences are characteristic: the small flowers are born inside a closed pyriform receptacle or syconium, communicating to the outside through a little opening, protected by small scales, that opens only when the fruit is ripe. The syconium is actually a false fruit; the true fruits are the thousands of little grains inside it.

There are two forms of *F. carica*, the wild one (*F. carica* var. *sylvestris*), known as caprifig, and the cultivated one, the common fig, of which several different varieties are known. The diagram illustrates the black fig (fig. 2) and the white fig (fig. 3). Fig. 1 shows a fig of the first crop, called brebas.

The fig is easily adapted to almost any soil, but its productivity seems higher when planted on rich, deep, well-drained and fresh soils. It is not particularly resistent to very cold winters. Its needs are similar to those of the grape, but it does much better in the olive tree areas, and is at its best in the orange and lemon regions.

p.168 The **Pomegranate**, also known as Carthaginian apple (*Punica granatum*), belongs to the family of the *Punicaceae*, which has only one genus, *Punica*. The pomegranate is a shrub or a small, profusely branched tree, at most 16 feet tall; the trunk is erect and covered by reddish bark which later becomes gray; the branches are stiff and spiny; the leaves, opposite or almost opposite, sometimes in small cluster, are lanceolate and bright green. The flowers are large, bright red (fig. 1), borne solitary or in small groups, 2–3, toward the end of the branchlets, and appear at the end of the spring or the beginning of the summer. The morphology of the fruit is peculiar; it is a spherical berry, the size of an orange and often larger, with a smooth coriaceous skin, ranging in color from yellowish to a purple reddish (fig. 2). The inside (fig. 3) is divided by septa into small irregular cells, containing many polyhedral seeds, whose outside is a gelatinous flesh, while the inside is woody. There are several varieties of cultivated pomegranates, some cultivated for their fruits, others exclusively as ornamentals for the beauty of their flowers and glossy, dark-green leaves.

With the general name of **Mulberry** different species are ▓▓▓▓▓▓▓▓▓▓▓▓▓▓▓▓▓▓▓▓▓▓▓▓▓▓▓▓▓▓▓▓▓▓▓▓ white mulberry (fig. 4), *M. nigra*, the black mulberry (fig. 5), and *M. rubra* (red mulberry) (not illustrated). The first two, but especially the white mulberry, were once cultivated much more intensively than now, for the rearing of silkworms. The white mulberry, so called for its white fruits, introduced into Europe from China after the twelfth century, was grown only for silkworm culture, while the black mulberry was cultivated more for its edible fruits. The latter is smaller, slower to grow, and forms leaves later in the spring than the other two species. The leaves are oval, pointed, entire or lobate, rather coriaceous, rough, irregularly dentate or serrate, and slightly hairy on the lower surface. The fruit (improperly called a berry), actually a group of many fruits, hence a multiple fruit, an infructescence, is black, glossy, with a sweet-tart flavor, and very juicy. Generally the black mulberry is more resistent to cold climates and can grow at higher altitudes than the white mulberry.

p.170 The **Pineapple** (*Ananas comosus*) is a monocotyledonous plant belonging to the *Bromeliaceae* or pineapple family. The stem is short and fleshy and bears a rosette of stiff, grooved, pointed, and serrate leaves, from which, 2–3 years after planting, emerges an inflorescence of sessile flowers, each one at the axil of a purple bract. As the single flowers start their transformation into fruits, these fuse together and join with the bracts to form the succulent and fleshy pineapple fruit (botanically a multiple fruit; in this particular case an infructescence). The stem continues to grow above the fruit and forms a crown of leaves.

Originally from tropical America, the pineapple is intensively cultivated today in Mexico, the Antilles, and especially Hawaii, which is the largest producer of pineapples, and whose economy relies heavily on its cultivation. The pineapple is a plant with rather strict climatic requirements, for humidity, temperature and light; it does not like high humidity.

p. 172 The **Avocado** (*Persea americana* of the *Lauraceae* or laurel family) probably originated in Mexico. The first avocados were sold in Europe only since the beginning of the twentieth century. They were the object of suspicion at first, because of their unfamiliar appearance and flavor, but are now one of the most popular ways of beginning a meal in very many countries. It is always eaten uncooked, usually *à la vinaigrette*, or filled with prawns and mayonnaise. The tree is about 45–50 feet in height with a large head and big, coriaceous, persistent leaves. The fruits (fig. 1a) are pyriform, green, purplish or brown, depending upon the variety, with a soft, buttery flesh, and a rich, pleasantly nutty flavor. Inside the fruit is a large seed (fig. 1b) containing a milky juice. The nutritional properties of the avocado have been the main reason for the spread of its cultivation outside Mexico, especially in the United States (Florida, Texas, California) where it has become a crop of great economic importance. To fully appreciate the avocado, it must be selected at the right stage of ripening, when the flesh yields lightly under the pressure of the fingers, but has not yet become too soft or mushy.

The **Papaya** or melon tree (*Carica papaya* of the *Caricaceae*) is a large evergreen plant, about 20 feet high, crowned by large, deeply lobed leaves. The fruit is a large berry (fig. 2a), from 4–20 inches in diameter, with an average weight of 2 pounds (but sometimes much more), with a yellowish rind, deep yellow to salmon colored flesh, and a large central cavity (fig. 2b), containing numerous seeds. The papaya is originally from Mexico and Central America, and is now widely cultivated in all tropical countries where it has become economically almost as important as the banana.

The **Mango** (*Mangifera indica* of the *Anacardiaceae* or cashew family) is a species of Malayan origin. It is a very large, evergreen tree, up to 115–120 feet in height, with a rough bark and oblong-lanceolate, pointed, dark green leaves. The fruit (figs. 3a and 3b) is a kidney-shaped drupe, of sizes varying from those of a peach to 2–4 pounds. The skin is rather thin, but leathery, colored red or yellow; the flesh has a pleasant flavor and extremely variable characteristics, depending upon the particular varieties.

The **Litchi** or Chinese plum is the fruit of *Litchi chinensis*, a small tree with compound leaves formed by 3–4 pairs of lanceolate and leathery leaflets, glossy on the upper surface. The skin of the fruit is covered by red tubercules (fig. 4). The flesh is sweet, acidulous and white. The litchi is used in large quantities in East Asia, and is canned for export.

p.174 The genus *Passiflora* (**Passion flower**) includes about 250 species, most of them native to America. These plants are mostly herbaceous or woody vines, climbing by tendrils inserted on the branches or at the axil of the leaves. One of the most interesting species is *P. edulis*, with large, deeply 3-lobed leaves and white flowers with purplish hues and of peculiar shape (fig. 1b). The flowers are solitary, with sepals and petals almost equally long, under which are inserted three shorter bracts. Inside the corolla is a showy double crown of colored fringes, blackish at the base, surrounding the 5 stamens and the 3 styles. *P. edulis* produces a many-seeded berry-like fruit, juicy and of an unusual, but pleasant flavor, known as granadilla. The fruits of *P. incarnata* are known as Maypops. Fig. 1a illustrates *P. Coerulea*.

The **Actinidia** or **Chinese gooseberry** (*Actinidia sinensis*) (fig. 2), a plant native to East Asia, particularly China, belongs to the *Actinidiaceae*, which includes about 40 species, some of which were imported to Europe during the nineteenth century to be used as ornamental plants. *A. sinensis* is a small tree that can reach 18–25 feet in height, hairy in the young parts, with pubescent, velvety, roundish, dark-green leaves, and white flowers that are tinged with brown-yellow appearing toward the end of the spring. The fruits, covered by a light down, are about the size of a walnut and have a pleasant flavor, like that of the currant. Since World War II they have appeared on sale in Europe and America.

p.176 The genus *Musa*, the **Banana**, includes about 70 species, among which those most important for the production of edible fruits are *M. paradisiaca* (cooking banana, Adam's fig), with large fruits, unsuitable for eating without first being cooked; *M. sapientium* (common banana), with small to medium size fruits, eaten raw, and *M. nana*, whose fruits are the best known in Europe under the name of Canary bananas. The stem or trunk of the banana tree is not a real stem, being composed entirely of tightly wrapped large leaf bases or sheaths, one upon another, tile-like. At the top, about 10–15 feet high, is an open crown of leaves. These are large; they can reach to 9–10 feet in length and 20 inches in width. The blades of these leaves are not very strong so they can easily break between the secondary veins. The inflorescence emerges from the center of the crown of leaves; the flowers are yellowish wrapped by purplish-reddish bracts; the fleshy fruits (fig. 1) can be greenish, yellow or purplish. Because of the high nutritive value of their fruits, bananas are widely and intensively cultivated; they require high average temperatures and prefer loose, fresh and deep soils, rich not only in organic compounds, but also in mineral salts, especially potassium.

The **Cherimoya** (*Annona cherimola*) is a close relative of both the custard-apple (*A. reticulata*) and the sugar-apple (*A. squamosa*). The species of the genus *Annona* are tropical and subtropical woody plants cultivated for their fleshy fruits and for ornament. The cherimoya is a small tree, roughly 15–20 feet in height, with velvety leaves of a beautiful shade of green. The flowers are green outside, white inside, and pleasantly fragrant. The fruits, often rather large, vary in shape and appearance: oval, spherical, conical, or cordiform (heart-shaped). The skin is greenish and the surface can be smooth, or resemble putty marked by fingerprints, or sculptured (fig. 2). The weight of the fruits can vary from about 3 ounces to 2 pounds or more.

279

p.178 The **Persimmon** or **Kaki** (*Diospyros kaki*) is a fruit tree whose diffusion in Europe is constantly expanding, because of the excellent results obtained by cultivation. The genus *Diospyros*, of the *Ebenaceae* or ebony family, includes more than 200 species, many of which produce edible fruits. Some species (*D. ebenum*, *D. melanoxylon* and *D. ebenaster*, commonly known as ebony trees) provide excellent wood for furniture making. The species of the genus *Diospyros* grow throughout the temperate, subtropical and tropical areas of the world. The persimmon originates specifically in China and Japan. It is a tree, 30–40 feet high, with a trunk covered by a dark bark finely cracked. The leaves are large, entire, lightly acuminate, dark shiny green above, paler with evident veins beneath. The flowers have a four-lobed calyx, which remains attached to the mature fruits, and a whitish corolla; the stamens vary in number from 8 to 16. The fruit is a berry with a smooth skin ranging in color from reddish to orange-yellow, depending on the variety; the flesh is sweet and soft when ripe; the seeds are flat, slightly elongate, and blackish; some of the varieties are seedless. The number of cultivated varieties known in Japan is about one thousand; but even in those countries where the persimmon has been known only recently, the number of varieties is large and constantly increasing.

The best known among the well established varieties, are the following: lycopersicum (fig. 5), with very large, round, golden-red fruits, and the ribbed persimmons (fig. 4), with medium-size, regular, orange-yellow fruits, with creases on the surface. Hatia (fig. 1), mandarin persimmon (fig. 2) and fuji (fig. 3) are three new varieties. The persimmon does not need special soil; it can produce satisfactory growth on dry, sandy or limestone soils, but prefers and grows better on clay-loam soils, fresh and deep.

p.180 The **Indian fig** or **Prickly pear** (*Opuntia ficus-indica* of the *Cactaceae* or cactus family), is a plant of very variable size, 3–12 feet, sometimes prostrate, sometimes erect, tree-like. The stem and branches are composed of flattened and fleshy joints, bearing more or less elevated aeroles covered with wool and small spines. The flowers are sparse, with numerous beautiful golden-yellow petals. The fruit (fig. 1a) is a large, edible, meaty, juicy, oval berry, covered by bristles, and containing many seeds (fig. 1b). Originally confined to the United States, the Indian fig has now spread along the shores of the Mediterranean, and can be found up to altitudes of about 1,500 feet. It is highly resistant to long droughts and high temperatures, and is not a very demanding plant; it can grow on rocks or old walls, if they are not cool and wet. As well as growing wild in many parts of the world (sometimes as a weed), the Indian fig is also cultivated for its edible fruits.

The **Alkekengi** (*Physalis pubescens*), a plant of the potato family (*Solanaceae*) native to Peru, is the species of the genus *Physalis* most widely cultivated and sometimes confused with the wild alkekengi (*P. alchechengi* or *alkekengi*). The fruits of both plants are edible, but that of the latter is less popular. The alkekengi is a low growing plant, no more than 3 feet in height, with pubescent leaves, heart-shaped and entire, slightly viscous. The fruits are small berries, about the size of a cherry (fig. 2a), of orange-yellow color, enclosed by the rather large and vesicular calyx. The complex calyx-fruit (fig. 2b) resembles a Chinese lantern. English names of *P. pubescens*: strawberry tomato, dwarf Cape gooseberry, husk tomato, ground cherry; English names of *P. alkekengi*: strawberry tomato, winter cherry, bladder cherry, Chinese lantern plant.

p. 182 Oranges (*Citrus aurantium* var. *dulcis*, or *C. aurantium*, var. *sinensis*, or *C. sinensis*); the varieties represented here are: oval (fig. 1), Tarocco (figs. 2a and 2b), blonde (fig. 3), Sanguinello (fig. 4), blood orange (fig. 5), and bitter orange (fig. 6.).

Oranges and other citrus fruits (of the *Rutaceae*, subfam. *Aurantioideae*) are a special type of berry, called a hesperidium. The peel is easily separable from the edible part of the fruit and is made of two parts, the *flavedo*, corresponding to the epicarp and the *albedo* corresponding to the mesocarp. The flavedo or outer portion of the peel, is smooth or rough, of orange color and with many minute cavities containing essential oils. The albedo or inner portion of the peel, is white and spongy, closely adhering to the outer portion. In the albedo the mesocarp is probably represented only by the membranous wall of the segments; their fleshy part is formed of many large fusiform cells, visible to the naked eye, and interpreted as transformed hairs. The segments contain the seeds. There are some seedless varieties.

The bitter orange (*C. aurantium*, var. *bigaradia*), (shown with the rind peeled in a continuous ribbon) is too acid and bitter to be eaten as a fresh fruit. It is used to make marmalade. The rind is also acid and bitter and is used in making liqueurs (curaçao) and a number of medicinal preparations. It can also be candied. The orange blossom yields the perfume, oil of Neroli.

p. 184 Whole and cut fruits of **Citron** (figs. 1a and 1b), the typical form of *Citrus medica*, called by some botanists, *C. cedra*. This is a large fruit, generally oval-shaped, with smooth or bumpy rind, very thick, due to the thickening of the albedo. The pulp is rather reduced.

Whole and cut fruits of **Lemon** (*C. medica*, var. *limon*, or *C. limonum*, or *C. limonia*) (figs. 2a and 2b). Lemons have a rather thin peel, smooth or rough depending upon the variety, and abundant pulp of acidulous flavor, almost always pleasant. The flowers are white, tinged with red, or purplish in the lower part. In fig. 3 some flowers are shown still in bud form; one is blooming and another shows only the ovary, already on its way to a fruit. The flowers of all the citrus fruits are very fragrant.

p. 186 Whole and cut fruits of **Grapefruit** (*Citrus paradisi*) (figs. 1a and 1b). The taxonomy of the grapefruit is confused; depending on various botanists, it has been classified as *C. maxima*, *C. decumana*, and *C. grandis*; it has also been considered a variety of *C. aurantium*, and classified as *C. aurantium*, var. *grandis*. Other authorities believe that the above species and varieties are those relative to the ornamental grapefruit, while the edible fruits are produced by the variety *uva carpa*.

Whole and cut fruits of a hybrid between orange and tangerine (figs. 2a and 2b), the **Clementine**.

Whole and peeled fruits of **Tangerine** (*C. reticulata*) (figs. 3a and 3b). The peel of the tangerine is easily separable from the edible part of the fruit.

Fruits of **Kumquat** (*C. japonica*) (fig. 4), a globose fruit.

p. 188 The **Italian stone pine** (*Pinus pinea*) together with the olive, is the most characteristic tree of the Mediterranean landscape. It is a beautiful tree easily recognizable for its shape and fruits. When it reaches its growth peak, its shape is like a large umbrella (from this derives its French name, *Pin parasoll),* the trunk is branchless in the lower 3/4, and the branches at the top spread out widely like a green dome. The cones (fig. 1), solitary or in couples, about 6 inches long, are composed of scales bearing two nut-like seeds or pinyons, each; the seeds have a rather dark, tough shell; the kernel is white, rich in starch and aromatic resin oils, and covered by a membranous light brown pellicle. *P. pinea* is widely spread along the Mediterranean shores; it prefers temperate-warm climates and forms woods in areas where the winter temperature remains always above freezing.

The **Ginkgo** or **Maidenhair tree** (*G. biloba*) (fig. 2), like *P. pinea*, belongs to the great division of the *Gymnospermae*, even though the morphology of the leaves is quite different. The Ginkgo is a large tree of Asiatic origin, sometimes reaching about 140–160 feet in height, and profusely branched. The leaves are fan-shaped, cuneiform at the base. Unlike other Gymnosperms, the leaves have bifurcate veins diverging from the petiole and without cross-connection. The margin of the leaf is more or less deeply notched at the tip so that the leaf blade is divided in two lobes; this is the origin of the Latin name for the species. *G. biloba* is a dioecious plant (staminate and pistillate flowers on different plants). The male and the female trees can be distinguished by the general shape: the female have almost horizontal branches and deeply incised leaves; branches of the male trees make a sharper angle with the trunk and the leaves are not so deeply lobed. Fig. 2 shows the ripe fruits and seeds.

p. 190 The **Chestnut** (*Castanea sativa* of the *Fagaceae* or beech family) is a tree with a cylindrical, straight trunk, profusely branched, with a spreading, but thick head; the leaves are oblong-lanceolate and dentate. The flowers are clustered in pendulous catkins (fig. 1) of yellowish color, practically covering the entire tree and giving it a characteristic aspect. The edible part, the commercial chestnut (fig. 2), is the seed which is covered by a thin membrane of astringent flavor and by a coriaceous, inedible shell. One to three chestnuts are enclosed inside a globose, very prickly bur that opens when dry (fig. 3).

Chestnuts are the most common trees to be seen in Mediterranean woods and forests, in Spain, southern France, Italy, the Balkan peninsula, and sometimes in Asia Minor, Hungary and Algeria. It is found in hill and mountain woods up to a certain height. Outside these areas, or others with similar climatic conditions, the chestnut is occasionally cultivated, but the fruits may not reach maturity. The American chestnut (*C. dentata*) is hardier than the European species (*C. sativa*). The chestnut grows best in well drained soils, sandy loam and clay loams, even rocky, but dislikes limestone and wet soils. It requires mild, temperate climates, with open and ventilated exposures, possibly on sunny slopes, and does not like very cold winters, frosts and too high altitudes. It forms new leaves at the beginning of April, the flowers in June, the fruits in October and November, and the leaves fall immediately after the ripening of the fruits.

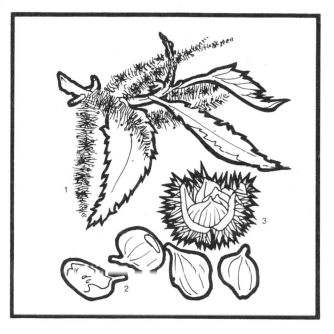

p. 192 The **Walnut** (*Juglans regia*) belongs to the *Juglandaceae* or walnut family, and is a tree typical of mild and temperate climates. It is long-lived, and can thrive for as long as 200 years. It can reach 60 or more feet in height and has a large, spreading head. The trunk is often as much as 3–4 feet in diameter, and is covered by a smooth grayish bark that becomes darker and cracked after the first few decades. The leaves are large, compound, with 5–9 leaflets, oval, entire and with an aromatic fragrance. The fruit, commonly called a nut, is actually a globose drupe. The outer part of the drupe, green in the unripe fruits, is a thick husk (shuck) (fig. 1a); the inner woody and resistant shell is formed by two valves and encloses the edible kernel (fig. 1b), which is covered by a thin, yellowish pellicle. Fig. 3 shows the flowers.

The **Hazelnut** (*Corylus avellana*), together with the white and black hornbeams (*Carpinus betulus* and *Ostrya carpinifolia*), belongs to the *Corylaceae*. Hazelnut trees are diffused in areas with temperate and relatively moist climates; this species is found mostly as a shrub, or as a small tree, 6–15 feet, with a spreading head, and short-petioled, more or less acuminate leaves. The fruits, called hazelnuts, are elongated or globose (fig. 2), with an outer hard, woody shell, and contain a single seed, rich in oil, as much as 65% of the seed's weight.

p.194 The **Almond** (*Prunus amygdalus* of the *Rosaceae* or rose family) is a peach-like tree, that can reach 30 feet in height, with a regularly shaped trunk, covered by a smooth, ash-colored bark in the young plants, darker and cracked later. The leaves are lanceolate, serrulate, with a shining upper surface. The pink flowers are solitary or in small clusters and appear before the leaves; the corolla is formed by 5 white or rosy petals. In the ripe fruit, the outer rind splits and the stone (fig. 1a) becomes free. The hard, woody shell (endocarp) encloses 1 or rarely 2 white seeds (shelled almonds of commerce), covered by a thin rather coriaceous, brick-colored pellicle (fig. 1b). Almonds originated in Asia, and are cultivated today in areas with temperate-warm climates, dry during the flowering period and without fog or frosts during the spring. It does not require special soils, but does grow best in those that are deep, dry, well-drained and rich in limestone.

The numerous cultivated varieties are classified on the basis of the bitter or sweet flavor of the seed, and the shape and consistency (more or less hard) of the shell.

The **Brazil-nut** (*Bertholletia excelsa* of the *Myrtaceae*) (fig. 2) and the **Pecan** (*Carya illinoensis* of the *Juglandaceae*) (fig. 3), both plants of American origin, produce fruits whose seeds (commercially called nuts) have a very pleasant flavor, similar to that of the almond and the walnut respectively.

p.196 The **Date palm** (*Phoenix dactylifera*) belongs to the *Palmaceae* or palm family, and is one of the most characteristic plants of tropical climates. Besides being extensively cultivated for its edible fruits, it still grows wild in some limited, desert areas of Arabia, western Asia, Libya and the Sahara. The date palm has a cylindrical stem, rather elastic, with a diameter of about $1\frac{1}{2}$ feet and a height ranging from 30–75 feet. Along the entire length of the trunk can be seen the remains of the large petioles, persistent on the plant even after the fall of the leaves. The leaves are very large, up to 18 feet long, and have a stiff axis bearing elongated, lanceolate segments very close to one another. The position of the leaves on the plant changes depending on the temperature and moisture content of the air. When the weather is hot and dry, the leaves orient themselves to expose the minimum surface to the sun's rays, and change their orientation in different meteorological conditions. The flowers are clustered in inflorescences of a general brownish-yellow color. The fruits (dates) are fleshy, very sweet berries containing one very hard seed.

The **Carob** (*Ceratonia siliqua* of the *Leguminosae* or pea family), is a species growing naturally along the Mediterranean coasts. It is a handsome evergreen tree, 25–30 feet high, with a large diameter trunk, and long-lived. The leaves are compound, formed by 2 to 5 pairs of leaflets from round to oval, shortly petioled, entire, shining of a deeper shade of green on the upper surface. The fruit (fig. 1) is a dark-brown pod, flattened, 4–8 inches long, $\frac{3}{4}$–$2\frac{1}{2}$ inches wide, ribbed, coriaceous outside, fleshy and sweet inside, containing 4 to 12 brown and very hard seeds. The carob grows well in climates that suit oranges and other citrus plants, and does not like hot, humid weather. It is well adapted to calcareous soils, well drained and fresh, but can also do well on gravelly and rocky terrains, and is quite resistant to drought and salty air.

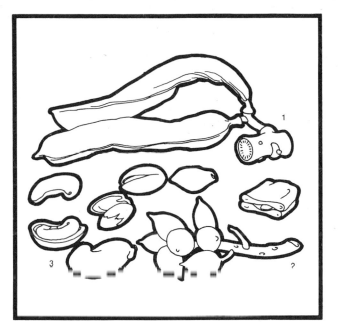

The **Pistachio** (*Pistacia vera* of the *Anacardiaceae* or sumac and cashew family) is a medium size tree, 10–15 feet tall, erect, with a trunk covered by a grayish bark. The leaves are compound, formed by 3 to 5 leaflets, rather coriaceous, velvety when young, glabrous later, of oval shape and with entire margin. The fruit, the pistachio nut, is an oblong drupe (fig. 2), covered by a yellowish-green shell tinged with pink, enclosing a small nut (the seed) of sweet and aromatic taste. The pistachio is a plant typical of Mediterranean climates, although in Italy it is found only in Sicily. It requires dry and warm-temperate climates and well-drained, light, deep soils.

The **Cashew** (*Anacardium occidentale*), also of the *Anacardiaceae*, is of Brazilian origin, and is now cultivated in all American tropical countries and some areas of North America. The cashew is a tree, 30–36 feet high, with simple, coriaceous, oval leaves, and rosy-white flowers, pleasantly fragrant. Its most characteristic aspect is its fruits, borne on fleshy peduncles that become swollen, taking on the appearance of pears. These false fruits, yellow to red in color, sweetish-sour, lightly refreshing and edible, are known commercially as cashew-apples. The true fruit, of smaller dimensions, is found at the base of the cashew-apple and is kidney-shaped (fig. 3); the outer part is very hard; the kernel inside is oily and edible when roasted, and is sold as the cashew nut; the shell of the nut is exceedingly acrid and irritant.

p. 200 Terminal spiked inflorescence of **Sage** (*Salvia officinalis* of the *Labiatae* or mint family) (fig. 1), with small whorls of 3–4 flowers at the axil of bracts. The corollas are purplish-blue (rarely whitish). The petioled leaves are oval-lanceolate, wrinkled, more or less grayish on both surfaces and particularly on the lower one. The stem is tetragonal (quadrangular). Sage is native to southern Europe and is widely cultivated domestically for its leaves that are mostly used to flavor meat.

    Thyme (*Thymus vulgaris* of the *Labiatae*) (fig. 2), is a small shrub, natural in the western Mediterranean countries. It is found growing wild on the hills facing the Tyrrhenian Sea and is widely cultivated in kitchen gardens everywhere.

    Two twigs of **Rosemary** (*Rosmarinus officinalis* also of the *Labiatae*) (fig. 3), a shrub common in gravelly and dry places, especially along the Mediterranean shores. In the interior, it is often cultivated in kitchen gardens from which, under favorable climatic conditions, it sometimes escapes and spreads into the countryside.

p. 202 Flowering top of **Peppermint** (*Mentha piperita* of the *Labiatae*) (fig. 1). Peppermint is probably a hybrid between *M. viridis* and *M. aquatica*, but has been known and cultivated for several centuries. The entire plant can be used. Its typical fragrance is due to an essential oil, mainly constituted by menthane and menthol.

    Flowering tip of **Oregano** (*Origanum vulgare* of the *Labiatae*) (fig. 2). Oregano (sometimes known as wild marjoram) is native to Europe and western Asia and is found everywhere, especially in the south, in wood clearings, amongst bushes and in warm, sunny fields.

    Fig. 3 shows young shoots of **Calamint** (also known as basil-thyme) (*Satureja calamintha* or *Calamintha officinalis*), a small evergreen herb of central-south Europe and other circum-mediterranean regions, usually found in dry and sunny fields. It is a close relative of the savory (*S. hortensis*). Young shoots of **Marjoram** (*Origanum majorana* or *M. hortensis*, the true marjoram) (fig. 4), a plant of Asiatic origin, often grown in kitchen gardens. Both calamint and majoram contain essential oils and have antiseptic and stimulant properties.

286

p.204 Some of the best known forms of **Basil**: two types with smooth leaves, one green (fig. 1), the other variegated (fig. 2), one called lettuce-leaved basil (fig. 3), and the small and very fragrant fine green basil with oregano-shaped leaves (fig. 4). Basil belongs to the *Labiatae* and the species *Ocimus basilicum*, a polymorphic species, due to cross-breeding and selection during centuries of cultivation. It is an annual herb originally from the warm regions of Asia and Africa and is often cultivated. It is one of the best known, most used aromatic plants and acts as a eupeptic and digestive.

Young shoots of **Balm** (also known as lemon balm and bee balm) (*Melissa officinalis*) (fig. 5) of the *Labiatae* or mint family. It thrives under warm conditions and is common on roadbanks, in woods, copses and untilled fields.

p.206 Fruiting branch of **Laurel** (bay) (*Laurus nobilis*) (fig. 1) of the *Lauraceae* or laurel family, an evergreen shrub or small tree, thought to be originally of Asia Minor, now widely cultivated. In Europe, either cultivated, wild, or escaped from cultivation, it grows along the Mediterranean shores and islands, and on the hills surrounding the northern Italian lakes.

Twig of common **Juniper** (*Juniperus communis*) (fig. 2). Juniper is a gymnosperm ascribed either to the *Cupressaceae* (cypress family) or the *Pinaceae* (pine family). It is widely spread throughout the Northern Hemisphere. In Europe it is quite common in woods, especially those that are thin and sunny, from the Mediterranean shores to the mountains. The fruits are used for flavoring gin, and are improperly called berries. They are actually cones, like those of other conifers, although they differ slightly in shape. These berry-like globose cones are rich in essential oils and resins.

Branch with flowers of **Rue** (*Ruta graveolens*) (fig. 3) of the *Rutaceae* or rue family. Rue is a shrubby plant, woody at the base, up to 3 feet in height, growing wild in southern Europe, in rocky and sunny places. It is widely cultivated in southern Europe, and is an old medicinal plant with a strong aromatic odor.

Fruits and branches of **Prickly ash** (*Zanthoxylum alatum*) (figs. 4a and 4b) of the *Rutaceae*, originally of North America. It is sometimes cultivated in gardens as an ornamental plant. The seeds, known as false pepper, have an acrid and strong flavor.

p. 208 Branch with flowers, leaves and buds (fig. 1a) and a fruit (fig. 1b) of the **Caper** (*Capparis spinosa*) of the *Capparidaceae* (caper family), which is diffused throughout the Mediterranean and shows a characteristic habitat, growing on old walls and on cliffs. The parts of the plant commonly used are the flower buds and the young, unripe fruits, with stimulant, aromatic and appetitive properties.

The young flower buds of **Nasturtium** (also known as Indian cress) (*Tropaeolum majus*) are used in the same ways as capers; the peppery-tasting leaves are sometimes used like cress, in salads. Nasturtium is a herb mostly cultivated as an ornamental.

Spike with fruits and seeds of **Black mustard** (*Brassica nigra*) (fig. 3a), and seeds of **White mustard** (*B. alba*) (fig. 3b). Mustards belong to the *Cruciferae* or mustard family. The seeds of black mustard show a reticulum (net) of very fine crests or ridges; those on the seeds of white mustard are less marked. Mustards are cultivated for their seeds containing glycosides (sinigrin in black mustard and sinalbin in white mustard) that releases the familiar essence of pungent flavor under the action of the enzyme myrosinase, also contained within the seeds.

p. 210 **Vanilla** (*Vanilla planifolia*) (fig. 1) belongs to the *Orchidaceae* (orchid family) and is native to Mexico and Central America. It has fleshy, parallel-veined leaves and characteristic, whitish, adventitious roots, which have a spongy-like appearance, being covered by the velamen, a sleeve of tissue used by the plant to soak up water running over it or that in the air. The fruit representing the commercial product, is at the base of the stem, and is a black pod-like capsule, formed by three carpels enclosing a single cavity, 6 to 8 inches long. It is covered by a crystalline efflorescence, *givre*, and contains a large number of very tiny seeds immersed in a blackish pulp. The fragrance of the fruit is strong, characteristic and pleasant.

A stick of **Cinnamon** (fig. 2) in the typical form sold commercially. Cinnamon sticks are made of sections of bark that upon drying are rolled into the tubelike, concentric layer structure of the marketable product. The bark is furnished by *Cinnamomum zeylanicum*, a small tree of the *Lauraceae* (laurel family), native to Ceylon. Cinnamon has stimulant properties and is considered one of the true medicinal plants.

Stolon of **Licorice** (*Glycyrrhiza glabra* of the *Leguminosae*) (fig. 3). The drug or part of the plant used for medicinal purposes, is either the root or the long stolons (runners) running horizontally below the surface of the ground at a shallow depth (*radix glycyrrhizae* of the pharmacopoeia). Licorice is a perennial herb with stems growing up to about 3 feet. It is common in southern Europe and western Asia. It is very abundant in Europe, especially Italy, sometimes to the extent of being considered as a weed, in sandy places near the sea. Licorice is used as a medicinal plant (as an emollient and expectorant) and in the liqueur and candy industries. The black licorice sticks are made from the concentrated juice extracted from the roots.

p.212 Plant of **Rhubarb** (fig. 1) in an early stage of growth, shortly after sprouting. The rhubarb (*Rheum rhaponticum*) is a tall perennial herb native to the regions of Tibet. The rhizome is the part of the plant used for medicinal purposes; it contains anthraquinone derivatives and other active substances, conferring bitter eupeptic, cholagogue and purgative properties to the rhubarb.

Two seeds, one whole and one in transverse section, of the **Nutmeg** (fig. 2), (*Myristica fragrans* of the *Myristicaceae*) which is a medium size evergreen tree native to the Moluccas or Spice Islands, now cultivated in many tropical countries. The commercial nutmeg is the seed, spherical or oval, $\frac{3}{4}-1\frac{1}{4}$ inches long and wide, marked by grooves. The transversal section of the seed shows the characteristic marbled or ruminated aspect of the nutritive tissues (endosperm) due to the presence of darker veins formed by a second type of storage tissue known as perisperm.

A dried rhizome of **Ginger** (*Zingiber officinalis*) (fig. 3), a perennial herb probably originally from Asia and now cultivated in most tropical countries. The dried rhizome is used as an aromatic and a stimulant, domestically and in the distilling industry.

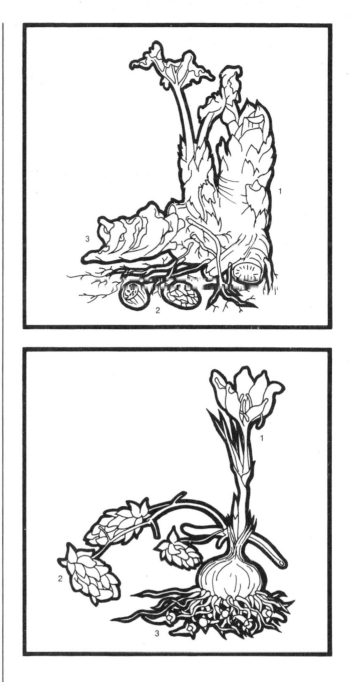

p.214 **Saffron** (*Crocus sativus*) (fig. 1), of the *Iridaceae* (iris family), is a perennial herb, native to Asia Minor and Persia, both widely cultivated and wild (probably escaped from cultivation) in Mediterranean countries. This plant is characterized by a solid bulb or corm, from which the leaves sprout at the beginning of September; they are narrow, channeled, dark green and with a whitish sheath around the base. When the plant flowers, in October, the leaves are about 2–3 inches long and continue to grow to a length of 8–10 inches; they dry out at the beginning of the summer. Each plant produces only one flower (rarely more than one, never many) with a perianth (the external envelope of flowers when not differentiated into calyx and corolla; the segments of the perianth are called tepals) formed by 6 violaceous sepals (the inner smaller than the outer ones) fused at the base into a long, thin tube; the stamens are three and the style is divided into three enlarged stigmas. The ovary is inferior and practically underground, at the level of the corm. (In a flower the ovary is said to be inferior when all the other floral parts are born above it.) The cultivated plants are sterile and do not produce seeds.

Pistillate inflorescence of common **Hop** (*Humulus lupulus*) (fig. 2), a perennial herb belonging to the *Urticaceae* (nettle family) according to some botanists, or to the *Moraceae* (mulberry family) according to others. The hop is widely diffused throughout the Northern Hemisphere and is common along roadsides, in thickets, untilled fields and on riverbanks. The ripe pistillate inflorescences are called hops, these are formed by numerous flowers arranged in pairs under large overlapping bracts borne on an axis with a zigzag pattern, the whole making a cone-like catkin. The bracts and other parts of the inflorescence are sprinkled with yellow resinous glands imparting the bitter and aromatic flavors to the hops. They are used for making beer.

Cloves (fig. 3) are the dried flower buds of *Eugenia caryophyllata* (clove tree), belonging to the family of the *Myrtaceae* (myrtle family). They have some interesting pharmacological properties and are used in odontology for their anesthetic and antiseptic action. The clove tree is cultivated in many tropical countries, the most important production center being Zanzibar.

p.216 **Tea** is cultivated on a large scale in tropical and monsoon areas with temperatures between 50°–96°F and uniform rains totalling about 120 inches a year. Tea (*Thea sinensis* or *Camellia sinensins*) (fig. 1), of the camellia or tea family (*Theaceae*) is a tree that can grow to a height of 30 feet in the wild state, but in cultivation is kept to an average height of 6–7 feet to facilitate the harvesting of the leaves, which are alternate, dark-green, elliptical-lanceolate, and with a finely incised margin (serrate). The aromatic drink is prepared with the leaves. The black and green teas that are marketed are the results of different treatments of the leaves after harvesting, and are not derived from different varieties. Black tea is the result of long fermentation of the leaves, followed by roasting; fermentation of the leaves for green tea, is short or none at all, and the roasting is done at a lower temperature than for black tea.

Like coffee, tea has a stimulating action on the nervous system, due to the same alkaloid, caffein (once improperly called theine); tea leaves are used also for the industrial extraction of caffeine.

Cultivated **Coffee** (*Coffea arabica* of the *Rubiaceae* or madder family) is an evergreen shrub, 6–10 feet in height, with short-petioled, shining leaves, about 2½–5 inches long. The flowers are white and fragrant (fig. 2a), similar to gardenias and coffee flowers that also belong to the same family. The fruit is a two-seeded berry, first green, then red, finally reddish. The coffee beans of commerce are the seeds (fig. 2b), convex on the dorsal side and flat on the ventral one. The caffeine content of coffee beans can reach 2–3% in some varieties; aroma and flavor are due to an essential oil, caffeol. The presence of the stimulant caffeine gives coffee its economical importance.

Coffee is grown between the 35° north and south parallels; within these limits it can be cultivated from sea level to an altitude of 4,500–5,000 feet provided climatic conditions stay at an average temperature of 60°–85°F., with no sudden temperature changes, and rains totalling at least 60 inches a year.

p.218 The **Cocoa** tree (*Theobroma cacao*), whose seeds are the source of cocoa powder and chocolate, belongs to the *Sterculiaceae*, a family of tropical and subtropical plants. It is a small tree typical of tropical regions with warm and wet climates with mean annual temperatures around 78°F. and rains totalling about 90 inches a year. The leaves are pinnately-veined, the flowers white, and the large fruits (10–12 inches long and 3–4 inches in diameter) contain from 25 to 40 seeds in regular rows. The flowers and fruits are formed on the trunk and larger branches. The seeds, once freed of the fruit pulp and dried, are roasted and then ground to obtain cocoa powder.

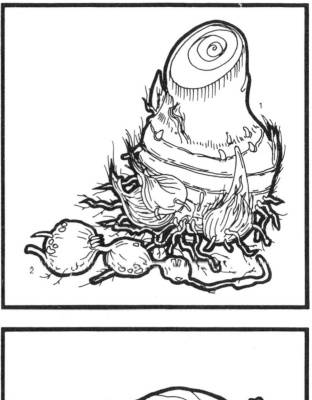

p. 220 The genus *Colocasia* of the *Araceae* or arum family, originated in the tropical regions of Asia and includes approximately six species, among which *C. antiquorum* is known in the West as a beautiful ornamental plant. Of more importance is *C. esculenta* (**Taro**) (fig. 1) that, in the Pacific Islands where it originated, is widely cultivated for its large leaves, used as a vegetable, and the tuberized, starchy roots, from which the Hawaiian *poi* is made. Taro leaves are very large; the flowers small, clustered in an inflorescence called spadix (a spike with a fleshy axis) protected by a spathe (a large bract enclosing an inflorescence).

The **Ground nut** (*Apios tuberosa*), of the *Leguminosae* or pea family, originally of North America, has spread to other parts of the world and can be found in many European countries. It is a twining herb with compound, trifoliate leaves, and small, fragrant, dark-purple flowers. The part of the plant of economical importance is the subterranean tubers formed on the roots; these once represented a valued food source for American Indians. The meal obtained by grinding the tubers was once used to make cakes, but has now been replaced by species with higher yields. It is also known as Dakota potato, wild bean, and American groundnut.

p. 222 The **Sugarcane** (*Saccharum officinarum*) (fig. 1), and another dozen species of the same genus, belong to the *Gramineae* or grass family. Sugarcane has a stout subterranean rhizome and cylindrical stalks from 9–18 feet in height, and 1–3 inches in diameter. Intensive cultivation over a long period has resulted in the production of several varieties, differing in the color of the stalk and the sugar content. The extreme limits of the geographical distribution of the sugarcane are 37° latitude North and 30° latitude South. It grows best on rich, moist, well-drained soils. Although a typical tropical plant, with particular care, sugarcane can be cultivated in subtropical or desert regions.

The **Sugar beet** (fig. 2), garden beet and leaf beet (Swiss chard) used domestically, and the forage beet, all belong to the same species, *Beta vulgaris* of the *Chenopodiaceae* or goosefoot family, and are all different forms of the variety *rapa*. Among them, the most widely and intensively cultivated, and of great economic importance is the sugar beet (*B. vulgaris*, var. *rapa*). Large quantities of sucrose (the commercial sugar) are extracted by special processes from the roots of the sugar beet. Sucrose is one of the fundamental substances for the energy balance in man. The sugar beet is a plant with large roots and stems 40–60 inches in height, bearing green flowers clustered in spikes first, and fruits enclosed in a woody involucre later. It has a biennial life cycle; the roots, used for extraction and separation of crystalline sucrose, are harvested during the summer or fall of the first year of growth.

p. 224 The **Potato** (*Solanum tuberosum*) is one of the best known and most used food plants (its total world production in 1970 was about 300 million tons; wheat approximately 315; rice, 300 and corn, 240). The part of the potato used as food is botanically known as a "tuber", a portion of the underground fleshy stem. This is not, as is commonly believed, either the fruit or the root of the potato plant. If the fundamental parts of the potato plant are examined carefully, it is apparent that the fruit, derived from a violaceous-white flower, is a globose berry, yellow when ripe; the roots are long and narrow, as are those of many other plants, and at a level slightly above the roots, there are swellings on the subterranean part of the stem, which are the tubers commonly known as potatoes. *S. tuberosum* originated in America and came to Europe during the second half of the sixteenth century, since when it has been widely cultivated. Its area of diffusion is very large, extending from 70° latitude North (Greenland) to the equatorial regions, and is also found at relatively high altitudes; in the Italian Alps it is found at altitudes of about 5,500 feet. It is not demanding in relation to the nature of its soil, and can do well in very acid soils rich in organic matter, or in sandy soils, or on almost any soil which is not excessively alkaline. The cultivation of the potato in Europe and throughout the world, has become increasingly specialized; many varieties have been obtained with different shapes, textures, and colors of the tuber, with varying times, late or early, for the maturation of the product, and with different characteristics of resistance to disease and adverse environmental conditions. This large number of varieties includes: the Canadian Kennebeck, white pulp, very good for fried potato chips; the English Majestic 50, (fig. 5), tuber elongated, pulp white and floury; the Italian Como White, round, very white pulp; Chioggia 40 (fig. 1) and Claudia (fig. 4), yellow pulp; Naples Round, white pulp (fig. 7); primula (fig. 2); Bea (fig. 6); and the small farfalletta (fig. 3).

p. 226 The **Sweet potato** (*Ipomea batatas* of the *Convolvulaceae* or morning-glory family) is an herbaceous plant, widely cultivated in the tropical and subtropical regions of Asia, Africa and America. This species has large tuberized roots (figs. 1. var. *alba*, and 2. var. *rosa*), heart-shaped leaves, and campanulate flowers with a purple corolla. The sweet potato grows well on fresh, loose, rich soils, and in mild climates, tempered by the influence of the sea. The food part of the plant is the fleshy swollen roots. Sweet potatoes are used in the kitchen, sometimes as a substitute for the common potatoes, in the pastry industry for their sweet flour, and in distilling.

The **Jerusalem artichoke** (*Heliantus tuberosus* of the *Compositae* or thistle family) originated in North America. It is a perennial plant with a thickened tuberous root (fig. 3), stiff stems, about 6 feet in height, ovate heart-shaped, or lanceolate leaves and with flowers clustered in rather large yellow heads (the head is a dense round cluster of sessile or nearly sessile flowers). The tubers, used in the kitchen or for livestock feed, are irregular in shape, with a reddish skin; their pulp is white, fleshy, sweet and tastes similar to the artichoke.

p.228 The **Water chestnut** (*Trapa natans* of the *Onagraceae* or evening-primrose family) is a small, annual, aquatic plant, with a submerged, simple stem, rather swollen in its upper portion (a), and paired roots with many small barbs. The leaves are of two types: submerged, falling off early, linear-lanceolate, almost root-like; and floating, crowded in a spiral rosette, rhombic, toothed in the upper half (b). During the period following the formation of the flowers, the petioles of the floating leaves become swollen and club-like, in the upper part (c). The flowers are small and solitary; the calyx is 4-lobed and the lobes are persistent, sometimes spinescent; the corolla is formed by 4 white petals. The fruit is relatively large, about $\frac{3}{4}$ inch, coriaceous, from a conical to a flattened triangular shape, with 4 spinescent horns (d). The name of this plant was partly derived from its slight resemblance to the fruits of the common chestnut, but chiefly because the domestic use of both fruits is the same. The edible properties of the water chestnut are good: they are rich in starch, nitrogen compounds and mineral salts. The water chestnut grows sparsely in Europe in lakes and swamps and is diffused in both Asia and Africa and naturalized in America.

p.230 The **Coconut** palm (*Cocos nucifera*) is a handsome plant, probably native to the Malay Archipelago. Today it is widely cultivated in most tropical regions, especially near the sea, and has become one of the most characteristic elements of the landscape of the Pacific Islands and Indian Ocean. The trunk of the coconut palm is rather cylindrical, almost smooth and 60–75 feet high. The pinnate leaves, 9–18 feet long, form a crown near the top of the trunk, where the large fruits are also found. The coconuts take about six months to ripen, and have a variety of uses.

p.232 Fats play an important part in human nutrition, providing the organisms with calories, certain essential fatty acids and fat-soluble vitamins. They can be extracted from plants and animals, and can be solid or liquid. Among liquid fats, olive oil is most prominent, certainly in many European and Mediterranean countries. It is extracted from the fruits of the **Olive** tree (*Olea europea*), which is an evergreen tree, 12–36 feet high, with twisted trunk and branches, that grows very slowly; the leaves are opposite, rather coriaceous, dark-brown above and silvery underneath from the presence of small hairs. The flowers are white and the fruits are fleshy drupes rich in oil. The cultivated olive is O. *europea* var. *sativa*; many forms of this variety have been obtained through culture; they differ in rusticity, oil content of the fruit, shape of the trees, time of flowering and fructification. The classification of so many different forms is difficult, and requires numerous data, covering all the characteristics of the tree. Olive oil is greenish-yellow to yellow; the specific density is lower than that of water; it solidifies at 0° C. and is easily spoiled by light that hastens rancidity. Only about 25% of the oil content of the olives is obtained by pressing; the rest remains in the pressed pulp from which more oil can be extracted using solvents.

293

p. 234 The **Peanut** (*Arachis hypogea*) (fig. 1) belongs to the *Leguminosae* or pea family. This plant probably originated in Brazil and is characterized by the fruits that ripen underground. These fruits are formed by a shell, $\frac{3}{4}$–$1\frac{1}{4}$ inches long, yellowish, creased, narrower between the seeds. The seeds, 1 to 7 per pod, are ovoidal, covered by a membranaceous reddish pellicle and contain about 50% of their weight in oil, which is of excellent quality; one of the best among those extracted from various seeds. Peanut oil is used in the kitchen for cooking and frying, in the sardine-canning industry, in the preparation of margarine and in soap-manufacture, and sometimes as a lubricant. The largest producers of peanuts are Asia and Africa (about 57% and 29% respectively of the total world production of 18 million tons per year). The peanut thrives on loose, sandy soils; does not like cold climates and, during its life cycle, temperatures should be no lower than 60° F. and rains should add up to about 40 inches.

Another oilseed plant of great importance is the **Soybean** (*Soja hispida*), also of the *Leguminosae*, cultivated since prehistoric times in East Asia, especially in China and Japan. Today the largest producer is the United States. The soybean is an erect, branching plant, with trifoliate, pubescent leaves, and with velvety pods containing 2 or 3 oblong seeds. The seeds are rich in protein and fats and are used as foods, especially in countries where protein and fats of animal origin are scarce and insufficient. The seeds are used for the extraction of soybean oil used in cooking; the residue left after the extraction of the oil is milled to produce soybean meal, a flour rich in protein, used either in human nutrition or as livestock feed. The soybean's cultivation requires a temperate climate, warm and humid, but not too rainy.

p. 236 **Colza** and **Rapeseed** are very similar plants; both belong to the *Cruciferae* (mustard family); the flowers of plants of this family have a cruciform corolla formed by 4 petals; both plants belong to the same genus, *Brassica*; the *B. napus*, var. *oleifera* is the colza; *B. rapa*, var. *oleifera* is the rapeseed and also the turnip, and *B. napus* is the rape.

Colza (fig. 1) has leaves that are smooth and glaucous; the anthers of the flowering buds show a small dark spot at the apex, and the fruits are borne almost horizontally. In the rapeseed (fig. 3) the leaves are green, rough, and somewhat bristly, the anthers do not have the dark spots, the fruits are erect and the roundish seeds are redder and smaller than those of the colza. Both plants are cultivated for the oil-rich seeds. After extraction and purification the oil can be used for nutritional purposes. Rapeseed is 10% less productive than colza, and its cultivation is declining compared to other oilseed plants.

Sesame (*Sesamum indicum*) belongs to the small family of the *Pedaliaceae*, of which it is the most characteristic representative and the only plant of some importance. It is an annual plant with erect angular, and branched stem, about 3 feet high, opposite, toothed leaves, solitary rosy flowers, and fruits containing several flattened, oval seeds, ranging in color from white, to yellowish, to pink, to brown, depending upon the variety. Sesame is native to tropical Asia and has been known and cultivated for at least five thousand years. Its seeds are rich in oil and protein. Sesame oil is used as a cooking or salad oil, as bread seasoning (together with the whole seeds), in the production of shortening and margarine, in the soap and perfume industry, as a carrier of fat-soluble pharmaceutical products, and as a lubricant. It is also noted for its stability, that is, resistance to oxidative rancidity.

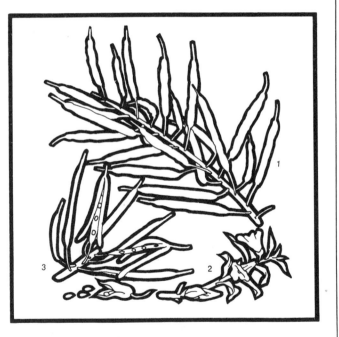

p.238 Although **Cotton** seeds are rich in oil and are used for its extraction, the cotton plant (fig. 1) is much more important as a textile plant. Cotton belongs to the *Malvaceae* (mallow family) and has been placed in the genus *Gossypium*. It is an herbaceous or shrubby plant with an erect and branched stem, large, palmately-veined leaves, variously colored flowers, and fruits containing many oval seeds. Cotton fibers are single plant cells which develop as elongation of the outer layer of cells of the cotton seeds, and all together form the boll. After removal of the fibers, the seeds are used for the extraction of oil that, after purification can be used for human food. Other products obtained from cotton seeds are cottonseed cake and meal, hulls and linters.

The **Sunflower** (*Helianthus annuus*) (fig. 2) belongs to the *Compositae* (thistle family). The name derives from the fact that the heads or inflorescences, through a phototropic stimulus, localized in the terminal part of the stem, tend always to face the sun. The sunflower is an annual herb with a strong, rough, channeled, hairy stem, 3–9 feet high, heart-shaped petioled leaves and flower heads often 1 foot or more wide in cultivated plants. The plant is grown for its oil-rich seeds. Sunflower oil, if extracted with "cold" processes can be directly used for human food since it is almost odorless and tasteless and of a beautiful yellow color; if obtained through "hot" processes, it requires further purification. The oil is also used to make margarine.

Another oilseed plant belonging to the thistle family is *Guizotia abissinica* (**Ramtil** is its common name in Nigeria and Ethiopia). The ramtil is an annual herb, almost glabrous, with opposite, lanceolate, rough leaves, and numerous heads of yellow flowers, appearing only during the summer. Ramtil oil is not highly valued for human nutrition; it is more suitable for paints and dyes and it is sometimes used in the adulteration of sesame oil.

There are many other plants that are cultivated for their oil-rich seeds, but their importance is quite limited and often localized to particular areas, such as *Madia sativa*, a species of the genus *Madia* that grows on the western slopes of the American continent, from California to Chile. This is the madia oil plant or **Tar weed** of the thistle family (not illustrated), with yellow flowers and achenes that in shape, color and size resemble those of the ramtil; tar weed and ramtil also show many similarities in their agricultural and industrial uses. *Lepidium sativum* (not illustrated) or **English** or **Garden cress** of the mustard family is cultivated as a leaf vegetable and for seasoning in Ethiopia, India, Egypt, Arabian countries and Europe. The oil extracted from the seeds smells of garlic, but this is eliminated through purification, as in the case of the colza and rapeseed oils.

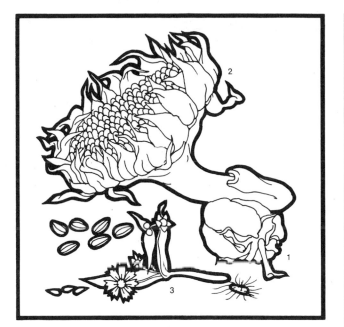

Bibliography

H. E. Jaques, *How to Know the Plant Families*. 178 pp. 528 illustrations. Wm. C. Brown Co. Pub.

H. E. Jaques. *How to Know the Economic Plants*. 176 pp. 341 illustrations. Wm. C. Brown Co. Pub.

B. Brouk. *Plants Consumed by Man*. Academic Press, 1975

J. Janick, R. W. Schery, F. W. Woods and V. W. Ruttan. *Plant Science* (an introduction to world crops). W. H. Freeman & Co., 1974

E. L. Palmer & H. S. Fowler. *Fieldbook of Natural History*. McGraw-Hill Book Co., 1975

A. H. Smith. *The Mushroom Hunters Field Guide*. University of Michigan Press. Ann Arbor, 1958

G. W. Ware and J. P. McCollum. *Producing Vegetable Crops*. Interstate Pub., Danville, Ill., 1968

R. B. Duckworth. *Fruits and Vegetables*. Pergamon Press. Elmsford, N.Y., 1966

F. Rosengarten. *The Book of Spices*. Livingston Pub. Co. Wynnewood, Penn., 1969

The Botany of the Citrus—Chapter in *The Citrus Industry*. W. T. Swingle, 1943

Hill, Albert. 1952. *Economic Botany*. 5th ed. The McGraw-Hill Co. N.Y.

Schery, Robt. 1972. *Plants for Man*. 2nd ed. Prentice Hall, Englewood Cliffs, N.J.

A. Rinaldi and Vassili Tyndalo. *The Complete Book of Mushrooms*. Crown Publishers, Inc. N.Y., 1974. (Originally published in Italy under the title *L'Atlante dei Fungi*, Mondadori, Milan, 1972.)

Index of Latin names

Index of common names

actinidia (Chinese gooseberry), 174, 175, 279
alkekengi (strawberry tomato), 180 181, 280
almond, 194, 195, 284
anise, star *or* Chinese, 102, 103, 260
apple, 126, 128, 266
    Abundance, 129
    Calvilla, 129
    Delicious, 127
    Golden Delicious, 127, 129
    Granny Smith, 128, 129
    Jonathan, 128, 129
    Rennet, 128, 129
    Rose of Caldaro, 127
    Starkcrimson Delicious, 127, 128
    Stayman, 128, 129
apricot, 152, 272
    Caninos, 153
    Imola Royal, 153
    Nugget, 153
arbutus: *see* strawberry tree
ariddari: *see* Indian fig
arrowroot, 220
artichoke, 60, 252
    Roman, 61, 62, 252
    Thick, 63, 252
    Thorny, 62, 63, 252
    Tuscany Violet, 61, 62, 252
artichoke, Jerusalem, 226, 227, 292
asparagus, 88, 257
asparagus acutifolius, 88, 89, 257
aubergine: *see* eggplant
avocado, 172, 173, 278
azarole, 136, 137, 268

balm mint, 204, 205, 287
banana, 176, 177, 279
barley, 20, 21, 242
basil, 204, 205, 287
bay (laurel), 206, 207, 287
beans, 30, 34, 36, 38, 245, 246
    Asparagus (Yard-long), 36, 37, 246
    Blackeyed, 36, 37, 246
    broad, 38, 39, 246
    butter, 34
    Cannellino, 31, 245
    French *or* dwarf, 30, 33, 245
    green, 32
    kidney, 30, 31, 34
    Lima, 34, 35, 245
    lupine, 38, 39, 246
    Madagascar, 34
    Scarlet runner, 34, 35, 245
    Scotch, 31, 245
    shell, 30, 245, 246
    Sieva, 34
    string, 30
    Venetian Wonder, 33, 245
    Yellow ring *or* little hook, 33, 245
beet *or* beetroot, 80, 81, 256
bergamot, 182
bilberry: *see* whortleberry
bitter chicory root, 48, 49, 249
bitter cress, 52, 53, 249
blackberry, 154, 155, 273
borage, 58, 59, 251
Brazilian cherry (pitanga), 168 (not illustrated)

Brazil nut, 194, 195, 284
broccoli, 64, 66, 253
Brussels sprouts, 64, 66, 253
buckwheat, 28, 29, 244
burnet (garden), 56, 57, 250
butcher's broom, 88, 89, 257

cabbage, 64, 252
    black, 64, 69, 253
    common, 64, 65, 252
    red, 65, 66, 252
    Savoy, 64, 65, 252
calamint, 202, 203, 286
caper, 208, 209, 288
caraway, 100, 101, 260
cardoon, 60, 61, 252
carob, 198, 199, 285
carrot, 104, 105, 261
cashew, 198, 199, 285
cassava: *see* manioc
cauliflower, 64, 71, 253
celeriac, 98, 99, 259
celery, 98, 99, 259
ceps: *see* boletus
chanterelle, 122, 124, 265
chard, Swiss, 76, 77, 255
chayote, 106, 107, 261
cherimoya, 176, 177, 279
cherry, 146, 271
    Early Bourlat, 147, 271
    Japanese yellow, 147, 271
    Marchiana, 147, 271
    Morello, 148, 149, 271
    Rainbow Stripe, 147, 271
    Starking Hardy Giant, 147, 271
    Vignolia I, 147, 271
    Vignolia black, 147, 271
    wild, 149, 271
chestnut, 190, 191, 283
chickpea, 40, 41, 247
chicory (endive), 42, 247
    Asparagus, 42, 43
    Brussels, 43, 247
    Castelfranco variegated, 44, 45, 248
    Catalonia, 42, 43
    Grumolo *or* broad-leaved, 46, 47, 248
    radicchio, 44, 45, 248
    root, bitter, 48, 49, 249
    red Treviso, 44, 45, 248
    red Verona, 44, 45, 248
    wild, 48, 49, 249
    Witloof, 42, 43, 247
Chinese gooseberry: *see* actinidia
cinnamon, 210, 211, 288
citron, 184, 185, 281
citrus fruits, 180, 281
clove, 214, 215, 289
cocoa, 216, 218, 290
coconut, 230, 231, 293
coffee, 216, 217, 290
colocasia: *see* taro
colza, 236, 237, 294
coriander, 100, 101, 260
corn (maize), 22, 23, 24, 25, 243
cornel, 164, 165, 276
corn rocket, 72, 73, 254
corn salad (lamb's lettuce), 52, 53, 249

cotton, 238, 239, 295
courgette: *see* zucchini
cowpea, 36, 37, 246
cress, English *or* garden, 295 (not illustrated)
cress, Indian: *see* nasturtium
cucumber, 116, 117, 263
cumin, 100, 101, 260
currant, 156, 157, 273

dandelion, 56, 57, 250
date, 196, 197, 284
dill, 100, 101, 260

eggplant (aubergine), 92, 93, 258
    Neapolitan long, 93, 258
    purple long, 93, 258
    purple thick, 93, 258
    white short, 93, 258
elm, English, 54, 55, 250
endive: *see* chicory
escarole, 46, 47, 248

fennel, 102, 103, 261
fig, 166, 167, 276
    breba, 167, 276
filbert: *see* hazelnut

garden burnet: *see* burnet
garlic, 84, 85, 256
ginger, 212, 213, 289
ginkgo, 188, 189, 282
Good King Henry: *see* goosefoot
gooseberry, 156, 157, 273
goosefoot (Good King Henry), 78, 79, 255
gourd, 108, 262
    club-shaped *or* bottle, 108, 109, 262
    scallop *or* custard, 108, 109, 262
granadilla (grenadilla), 168, 169, 277
grape, 160, 275
    American, 161, 275
    Cornicella, 161, 275
    dessert *or* table, 161, 162, 275
    Lambrusco, 163, 275
    muscatel, 161, 275
    Sangiovese, 163, 275
    Trebbiano d'Empoli, 163, 275
grapefruit, 186, 187, 281
grape hyacinth, 86, 87, 257
ground nut (Dakota potato), 220, 221, 291
grumolo: *see* chicory

hairy bitter cress, 72, 73, 254
hazelnut (filbert), 192, 193, 283
hop, 88, 89, 214, 215, 257, 289
horseradish, 72, 73, 254

Indian fig (prickly pear), 180, 181, 280
Italian stone pine, 188, 189, 282

jambul, 168 (not illustrated)

301